Everything

Need to Know
to Feel

ALSO BY CANDACE B. PERT, PH.D.

Book

Molecules of Emotion: The Science Behind Mind-Body Medicine

CD

Psychosomatic Wellness: Healing Your Bodymind

———◆◆◆———

HAY HOUSE TITLES OF RELATED INTEREST

COUNT YOUR BLESSINGS: The Healing Power of Gratitude and Love,
by Dr. John F. Demartini

*THE DETOX KIT: The Essential Home System to Cleanse Your Body, Clear
Your Mind, and Free Your Spirit,* by Jane Alexander

THE DIVINE MATRIX: Awakening the Power of Spiritual Technology, by Gregg Braden

FLOWDREAMING: A Radical New Technique for Manifesting Anything You Want,
by Summer McStravick

THE GOD CODE: The Secret of Our Past, the Promise of Our Future, by Gregg Braden

INSPIRATION: Your Ultimate Calling, by Dr. Wayne W. Dyer

THE POWER OF THE MIND TO HEAL, by Joan Z. Borysenko, Ph.D.,
and Miroslav Borysenko, Ph.D.

QUANTUM SUCCESS: The Astounding Science of Wealth and Happiness,
by Sandra Anne Taylor

*SPIRALING THROUGH THE SCHOOL OF LIFE: A Mental, Physical,
and Spiritual Discovery,* by Diane Ladd

*THERE'S ALWAYS HELP; THERE'S ALWAYS HOPE: An Award-Winning Psychiatrist
Shows You How to Heal Your Body, Mind, and Spirit,* by Eve A. Wood, M.D.

TRANSFORMATION: How to Change EVERYTHING, by Bill Phillips

———◆◆◆———

Please visit:
Hay House USA: **www.hayhouse.com**®
Hay House Australia: **www.hayhouse.com.au**
Hay House UK: **www.hayhouse.co.uk**
Hay House South Africa: **orders@psdprom.co.za**
Hay House India: **www.hayhouseindia.co.in**

Everything

Need to Know
to Feel
Go(o)d

Candace B. Pert, Ph.D.

with Nancy Marriott

Hay House, Inc.
Carlsbad, California
London • Sydney • Johannesburg
Vancouver • Hong Kong • New Delhi

Published and distributed in the United States by: Hay House, Inc.: www.hayhouse.
com • *Published and distributed in Australia by:* Hay House Australia Pty. Ltd.:
www.hayhouse.com.au • *Published and distributed in the United Kingdom by:*
Hay House UK, Ltd.: www.hayhouse.co.uk • *Published and distributed in the
Republic of South Africa by:* Hay House SA (Pty), Ltd.: orders@psdprom.co.za
• *Distributed in Canada by:* Raincoast: www.raincoast.com • *Published in
India by:* Hay House Publications (India) Pvt. Ltd.: www.hayhouseindia.co.in •
Distributed in India by: Media Star: booksdivision@mediastar.co.in

Design: Bryn Starr Best • *Editorial supervision:* Jill Kramer

Lyrics to "Hold the World in Light" by John Astin used with permission.

Library of Congress Cataloging-in-Publication Data

Pert, Candace B.
  Everything you need to know to feel go(o)d / Candace B. Pert ; with Nancy
Marriott.
     p. cm.
  Includes bibliographical references.
  ISBN-13: 978-1-4019-1059-4 (hardcover)
  ISBN-10: 1-4019-1059-9 (hardcover)
  ISBN-13: 978-1-4019-1060-0 (tradepaper)
  ISBN-10: 1-4019-1060-2 (tradepaper)
  1. Medicine, Psychosomatic. 2. Mind and body. 3. Consciousness. 4. Self-care,
Health. I. Title.
  RC49.P443 2006
  616.08--dc22   2006009763

Hardcover: ISBN 13: 978-1-4019-1059-4 • ISBN 10: 1-4019-1059-9
Tradepaper: ISBN 13: 978-1-4019-1060-0 • ISBN 10: 1-4019-1060-2

09 08 07 06   4 3 2 1
1st printing, October 2006

Printed in the United States of America

This book is dedicated to my husband, Michael Roland Ruff,
who is the co-creator of my dreams and parent of my children.

As a child Michael saw an angel who told him that
he would do something important for the world.
I am grateful to God for bringing him into my life.

Contents

Foreword

by Naomi Judd

First impressions are lasting. I'll never forget finally meeting this brilliant woman scientist who was responsible for putting mind-body medicine on the map, at a wellness conference in 1996. For several years, we'd traveled in the same circles. I'd originally contacted her when I was diagnosed with hepatitis C in 1990 and sought holistic or mind-body-spirit treatment for a disease that traditional medicine had little to offer by way of a cure.

I'd been intrigued by seeing her work on Bill Moyers's PBS miniseries *Healing and the Mind,* so I invited Candace to join me at the University of Wisconsin, where I was moderating a panel of experts speaking on spirituality and health. I stopped by her hotel room to get acquainted in person and talk about the program for the opening day. I was an initiate in this brand-new world of medical science. Just as Dolly Parton, Tammy Wynette, and Loretta Lynn had inspired me in music, Candace was my female mentor in psychoneuroimmunology.

When Candace opened the hotel door, I was blasted with a gust of exuberance. She had none of the stiff, dour personality qualities that I expected of a highly trained, world-class neuroscientist. Three hours later, after laughing most of the time, we had bonded.

Bottom line: Candace Pert is a scientist with heart, a woman who cares and who knows God is her source, even in the laboratory. She's down-to-earth and not afraid to tell it like it is, to walk her talk. She's a living example of what it means to get out of black and white and start living in Technicolor. In this book, she shows you how to get out of your comfort zone and take risks—which is the only way your life is going to be what you've always wanted it to be.

What she found under her microscope is that your feelings are really chemicals that can help or hurt you. Neuropeptides are biological messengers released by the brain; sent all throughout the body; and accepted by receptor sites located on the cells of every tissue, organ, and body part you have. This means that your physical self is constantly registering every word that you believe and say.

In this book, Candace demonstrates how your consciousness changes your body, your health, and even your environment. When you bring real awareness into your everyday life, you begin to heal yourself first and then your world. As you expand and get better on a personal level, the positive changes will be reflected onto those around you. Like the ripple effect when a pebble is dropped into a still pond, as you grow in consciousness, the mass state of mind shifts accordingly.

I've always known this (as so many have), but now, thanks to Candace, we've got the science in place to prove that it's real. And what's really thrilling is that she lives this truth—her life is an example of what it means to feel good *and* God. What she has to say may not be what you expect from an expert, but instead is a candid, intimate disclosure of her emotional, physical, and spiritual life. It's simple: You change everything when you change your mind. You become the architect of your own life; and the way you do so is to love, love, love . . . which starts with loving yourself.

Candace's message about self-esteem is right up my own philosophical alley: You're attracting what you feel worthy of having right now in all parts of your life. Your number one indicator for how healthy you'll be and how long you'll live is your level of self-esteem and self-worth. You'll never allow yourself to have more than you feel you deserve, and nobody does it to you—

you're doing it to yourself *through* others. So start giving yourself the life that you've always wanted!

That's the key to feeling good *and* God, to truly and scientifically experience yourself as first and foremost a spiritual being in a physical body. Once you start doing so, you realize that your purpose is to grow in love and wisdom and to reach out to others—something that even a hardcore, mainstream medical researcher demonstrates is possible to do . . . making it possible for everyone, even you.

Candace is a role model for women, a high-priestess of the mind-body movement, and a human being with human frailty, finding her self-worth and self-esteem through forgiveness and self-acceptance. You're about to take a journey with her that will move, inspire, educate, inform, entertain, and enlighten you—and if you're like me, once you begin reading, you won't be able to put this book down for a second!

PART I

NEW-PARADIGM
PHYSIOLOGY

Chapter 1

Science and Spirit

As the plane began to taxi down the runway, I lay back and closed my eyes. For almost a decade, since my book *Molecules of Emotion* had been published in 1997, I've been on what I call "the book tour that never ends." Frequent invitations to bring the science of the mind-body connection to lay and professional audiences have had me shuttle from coast to coast, the many places in between, and beyond our country's borders.

Actually, I'd been a frequent flyer even before the book was published. In the early '80s, as a full-time, mainstream biomedical researcher at the U.S. government's National Institute of Mental Health (NIMH) in Washington, D.C., I was invited to lecture at scientific symposia all over the world. When my work in the lab permitted, I occasionally traveled to address holistic-health conferences, crossing over from my East Coast–establishment roots into leading-edge, new-paradigm audiences in California. People who attended these talks were interested, even excited, to hear from a bona fide scientist who could corroborate some of their far-out ideas.

But for all the hours I've logged in the sky, I still find flying to be a magical experience. It's exhilarating to enter a world not bound by the daily constraints of time and place, where people come and go so quickly and the usual linearity of life is suspended. Airports always evoke for me a special *in between* state of consciousness, one where the flickering reality of the quantum dimension is almost perceptible. Synchronicity abounds! Pure potential is manifesting—I can sometimes even feel it.

From Scientist to Science Diva

It all began back in the early '70s at Johns Hopkins University, where I was earning my Ph.D. in Dr. Sol Snyder's laboratory. My field was pharmacology, the study of drugs, with a special interest in neuropharmacology, the study of how drugs affect the brain. As a young graduate student, I made one of the most influential discoveries of the 20th century in my field and in the emerging studies of neuroscience by proving that there was such a thing as an opiate receptor. This tiny structure on the surface of the cell is where opiate drugs—such as morphine, heroin, opium—act to produce an effect. For years, scientists had theorized about the receptor, but no one had ever shown that it did, indeed, exist.

Because my discovery held promise for a nonaddictive solution to drug abuse, reports from our lab were suddenly in high demand. Sol preferred not to travel, so he frequently sent me on the road to present our findings to scientific meetings. I was a young woman, not yet confident in my own expertise, thrown into the mix with the biggest and the brightest scientific luminaries of the day. But I got used to being a scientist who communicated with others in my field at universities and drug companies, and I grew to enjoy being a star.

After graduate school, I had many offers to do research at top universities, but chose a juicy staff position at the National Institute of Mental Health in Washington, D.C. There, I rose in the ranks to become chief of brain biochemistry, enjoying the thrill of doing hot science over a span of 17 years with my husbands Agu Pert and then Michael Ruff. During my stay at the NIMH, I evolved my theory of emotions and began to understand the mind-body connection as a widely distributed psychosomatic network of communicating molecules.

When I left the NIMH to develop a drug that Mike and I had invented there, and to head up our own private laboratory, my invitations to lecture grew. After having a leading role in Bill Moyers's *Healing and the Mind* television series, I was in demand with lay audiences who were fascinated with the psychological aspects of disease. My early stumping in the neuroscience-meeting world served me well, and I became a regular on the "body-and-soul" lecture circuit as a hybrid—both scientist and entertainer at the same time. (I definitely am a performer, having danced as a tiny tot in the front window of my grandfather's candy store.) Organizations knew that I would reliably draw a crowd, and I became a professional keynote speaker.

When *Molecules of Emotion* was published, the book's success boosted my popularity, and after my appearance in the film *What the Bleep Do We Know!?* in 2004, I found myself even more in demand. At that point, I was booking as many as three lectures in a single month, a stressful schedule that was taking its toll on my time in the lab, to say nothing of my health and well-being. But I'm a people-loving scientist, and the perk for traveling so much has been the opportunity to connect with the public, to stay in touch with the human side of science. It's a world very different from the isolated existence of a laboratory researcher.

In the Air

The airplane's wheels lifted off the ground, and I watched out the window as the earth grew smaller below me. A window, yes, that's what my travels have afforded me: a window into the lives and experiences of real people, those who have attended my talks and whom I've met and listened to over the years.

In addition to collecting some much-needed honoraria during lean times, I've been getting exposed to new ideas as I've continued to educate lay audiences about the scientific basis for emotions and consciousness, helping them understand why they feel the way they do. The people who attend my talks love the science and want to understand it, but they also want it translated into their everyday lives.

On this jaunt, I was headed to Tucson to deliver a talk sponsored by a local Unity church, one of the many New Thought churches that sprang up at the turn of the 20th century from Christian roots. Originally inspired by leaders such as Ernest Holmes and Mary Baker Eddy, these institutions are growing in popularity today, as people seek a more inclusive brand of communal spiritual practice.

Minutes after takeoff, my laptop was open and my PowerPoint slide show was up on the screen for inspection. I've made some new slides for my lectures since traveling the book-signing circuit, evolving my collection from hardcore-science diagrams to more provocative—even fanciful—visuals to underscore my paradigm-jolting points.

Yes, I've become somewhat bold and daring, willing to explain my theory of emotions as the mind-body bridge. People who attended my lecture in Santa Monica in February of 2005, a gathering that featured the talking heads from the film *What the Bleep . . . !?,* saw me as an icon in the New Age movement, and actually swarmed and crushed me up against a wall, as if I were Brad Pitt without a bodyguard! The whole affair ruffled my scientist feathers, and on this trip, a month later, I wanted to regain my sense of myself as a serious researcher, not a movie star.

A Familiar Insecurity

Lost in thought, I was barely aware that the passenger sitting next to me was glancing sideways, snatching peeks at my laptop screen. I'd noticed her when she first sat down, and we exchanged smiles during the usual juggling of belongings before takeoff. She was an impeccably groomed lady with a beautiful and intelligent face, her shiny, gray-streaked hair attractively swept up and secured. She wore a well-cut tweed suit, stockings, and low heels.

I admired her look, aware of the contrast to my own, which consisted of a sporty T-shirt, jeans, and sneakers. I travel so much that I'm in the habit of wearing clothes that allow me to sit comfortably, stretch, or meditate during long flights, or even race between terminals if necessary. I rarely dress up to fly, even when I'm presenting at prestigious conferences, sometimes as the keynote speaker.

But in spite of this contrast, I felt some kind of link with my seatmate. I do believe that we attract the people we need to meet for whatever reason, and there are no accidents, which was exactly the situation on this plane ride to Tucson. The lady sitting next to me, as it turned out, would inspire me to strike just the right tone of "serious" science for my lecture that evening, helping me restore my integrity without backing down on my wilder theories and speculations.

Unable to contain her curiosity about the colorful slides I was sorting on my laptop, my seatmate finally cleared her throat and, now staring openly at my laptop screen, asked, "Excuse me, but what exactly do you do?"

I responded, ignoring the tiny ripple of disdain that accompanied her words, "I'm interested in consciousness and how the body and mind are one."

"Oh, that mind-over-matter stuff?" She almost huffed at me, no longer attempting to hide a critical attitude, and a part of me cringed inside.

"No," I said, overcoming my reluctance and rising to the challenge. I decided to tell her the whole, frightening truth. "It's worse than that. I actually have come to believe that mind *becomes* matter."

She looked stunned and then paused for quite a bit before asking, "It's not very rigorous, is it? I mean, there's no real science behind it, is there?"

I was appreciating her professorial air—the slightly aloof attitude indicating that she settled for nothing less than proven facts and wasn't easily impressed by radical or far-out ideas. Respectfully, I explained that there was an entire field of science devoted to the study of how the mind communicates with the body, called psychoneuroimmunology. In fact, I told her, I was a Georgetown University professor on my way to deliver a lecture on emotions, consciousness, and healing in Tucson that evening.

"Really? I'm a Princeton professor on my way to Tucson to present a lecture as well!" Looking ten years younger as her face lit up and flushed with color, she giggled merrily at the odds of two lady professors, both on their way to present lectures, being seated together, especially since there were only a handful of women on the plane that evening.

Once our common ground had been established, the conversation opened up, and we enjoyed a friendly exchange for the duration of the flight. I learned that she studied ancient languages, a field not exactly expanding at the rate of mine. She showed me her perfectly prepared lecture with every sentence meticulously written out, the kind of planning that I'd never done. I couldn't help but admire her polished, well-organized simplicity and the quiet dignity she expressed.

As I turned back to the task of organizing my own talk in the short time before our arrival in Tucson, my companion commented, "Well, good luck. I hope that you'll be able to convert your audience!"

Clearly, I had *not* converted her. And as far as convincing my Tucson listeners, well, addressing them would be more like preaching to the choir. The people who attend my talks these days are steeped more deeply than I am in the "new paradigm," a view that gives primacy to consciousness. It is *they* (along with my own laboratory findings) who have converted *me* to the understanding that thoughts and emotions can heal us or make us sick, and that our consciousness determines the reality we experience.

But my traveling companion's parting comment left me

tingling with a familiar insecurity. *Rigorous*, I thought. *I'll show her and all the other doubting Thomases how rigorous the field of consciousness can be!* Right then and there, I determined to accept the lady professor's challenge, to give a talk fully grounded in the science of how our brains and bodies are designed to fully create the reality that we experience.

Straddling Two Paradigms

The woman on the plane had actually done me a service, confronting me with how wide the gap was between old and new paradigms, and how uncomfortable my position was in the middle. She also reminded me of how quickly some scientific colleagues might try to discredit me, being unaware themselves of what I'd learned from my frequent exposure to ideas they called fuzzy, "Californoid" thinking.

How wide this rift actually is—the materialistic versus the consciousness-first viewpoint—was driven home when I visited the NIMH recently to do some business. Finding myself in the building where I'd spent much of my earlier career, I decided to stop a few scurrying researchers and postdocs to ask them the following question: "Who is Deepak Chopra?" Nine out of ten had never heard of the Harvard-trained endocrinologist, who for the past 20 years has been presenting the Eastern view that consciousness precedes physical reality. I was surprised to find that in the nation's bastion of scientific truth, few had ever heard of Dr. Chopra; fewer still were aware of the implications of his radical ideas for their own work.

In my world, a journey of personal and professional trans-formation has led me to embrace the new paradigm that Chopra and so many others have brought to the general public over the last two decades. My scientific work and my private life have gradually come together, no longer running on parallel tracks that never touch. Synchronicity, quantum reality, and energy healing—all elements of a new way to view reality—are part of my life, as I grapple with the scientific explanations of what I experience as real.

At the same time, I strive to stay loyal to my roots, carefully drawing the line at pseudoscience—the "woo-woo" factor—those ideas so ungrounded in any real data that no serious researcher would give them credence. This has me straddling two worlds, with one foot in the new paradigm where the observer's consciousness is valid, and the other foot securely planted in the established, objective method of the old, reigning belief system. From this vantage point, science becomes the lens through which I interpret the mysteries that I experience on my life's journey. I believe that the best of science can provide an understanding, can take us home and give us the truth.

It's been a challenge to stay balanced on the edge of a fresh way of looking at things, where I'm not only bringing in a new consciousness for the public, but for myself as well. I must continually expand my personal integrity, keep growing and exploring unfamiliar ideas and experiences. At times, this can be exhausting.

But what I do know with certainty and apply every day in my life is that the mind and body are one. The basis for this unity is that all systems of our physiology are connected and coordinated by emotion-laden, information-carrying molecules, engaged in constant cross talk, for example, between the nervous and immune systems. This network of communication that takes place throughout the body and brain involves intelligence and emotion to create one entity, which I call the "bodymind."

In fact, the application of what I've found under the microscope is being used everywhere as a rationale in current, alternative modalities. I like to call these the "new-paradigm medicine," instead of "alternative" or "integrative," terms that I believe are inadequate and reflect separation or even a hostile division that must be resolved. The truth is that the centrality of mind and emotions is a new paradigm that sweeps everything away (thus, all the angst!), much like the realization that the Earth revolves around the sun did five centuries ago.

But the key that explains how energy heals, how mind becomes matter, and how we can create our own reality is the emotions. As a trained scientist, I'm an expert on the biochemistry of how we feel, which I believe is the physical demonstration of consciousness in the material world. It's the emotions, I believe, that link us as physical entities to the divine, making it possible for us to both *feel good* and *feel God* at the same time.

The story of my own growth and healing is the most vivid way that I can speak about the convergence of God, or spirit, and the emotional reality of our physical bodies. And my discoveries in the laboratory, as well as in the greater public arena that I enter when I speak at conferences or symposia, always bear me out.

Wounded Healer

In my recent travels to speak about my science and discoveries, two things happened that shaped my current views. First, I became aware that people looked to me for answers. More than that, they revered me, a humble bench scientist, as some sort of scientific goddess. This has been difficult for me, because Candace the person, under the mantle so generously bestowed by an admiring public, is a human being on the steep learning curve of a major transformation. Especially in recent years, there have been struggles, shocks, and disappointments that have left me quite flawed and stricken—talk about the wounded healer!

They say you teach what you need to learn, and that was certainly the case with me. Here I was traveling the world to deliver the latest in scientific advancements to help others, when I was the one who needed a hand! Gradually, I became more and more aware of just how much help I needed, and I sought it out.

And that's the second thing that happened to change my view. It was through my appearances on the lecture circuit that I was exposed to a wide variety of amazing healers, the crème de la crème of practitioners in bodywork, acupuncture, energy psychology, chiropractic, and the many forms of hands-on healing. I've had opportunities to be treated through every known modality, and I've tried them all. The funny thing about being a scientific diva is that people practically fall over backward to treat me, often for free. This has allowed me to experiment and mend my own wounds by following my intuition and using treatments that my research-based theories can often explain.

Even though people see me as something of an expert, as I've said, I'm very much the wounded healer. I may be a "doctor," but I'm not a medical doctor. I'm a researcher with a Ph.D. and a lab scientist whose career has been mostly spent at the bench working closely with test tubes, microscopes, and rats. I may have written over 230 scientific papers, but they were detailed works on how to measure and visualize receptors, or how the brain and the immune system interact, from which I developed a theory of the molecules of emotion. But none of that makes me an expert advisor to others in pain. I only have my own healing experiences to share, and I have plenty of those!

It's clear in my mind that the new-paradigm therapies are the final arena for my own healing, a place where I'm seeing more and more how science and spirituality converge. And this is my current growth curve, taking me, like Amanda in *What the Bleep Do We Know!?*, down the rabbit hole to ultimately discover light-filled realms that are peaceful, joyous, and empowering. And the best news I've discovered so far on my journey is that the science still holds.

Bringing It All Together

In many ways, my life is a microcosmic laboratory of how science and spirituality converge in a new paradigm of reality. For me, God—a holy spirit, higher consciousness, or transcendent self—is found within the nonmaterial, nonlocal world that's the source of our mind, thoughts, and emotions. I've called this the information realm, or "inforealm," but it can also be called the field of infinite possibility, or the nonlocal or zero-point field. In this domain, which is everywhere and nowhere, we're all connected, all one. To me, this provides the spiritual component of our interrelation as humans tied into a larger divinity.

As a bench scientist, looking through my microscope many years ago, I saw the unity of life firsthand. It was mind-blowing to find that simple one-celled creatures have the same biochemical substrates for emotions—the tiny peptide and protein molecules known as endorphins and opiate receptors—as we humans do. These fundamental, biological mechanisms have been conserved over the millennia of evolution, connecting us deeply, human and animal, in our experience of being alive.

As for religion, I prefer to speak about spirituality. I draw much wisdom from the teachings of Christ, and have written in the past about my life-altering experience of forgiveness while singing in a church choir. Over the years, I've revisited my religious roots of both Judaism and Christianity, absorbing the Eastern view along the way to embracing an eclectic brand of spirituality. But the bottom line is that I'm a scientist viewing the realm of the spirit, approaching it with hardcore, observable evidence; and from the data I've seen, I can no longer deny the existence of God.

In the matter of science and God coming together, I'm in good company with another scientist, one much more famous and influential than myself: Albert Einstein. His professional journey brought him to a personal epiphany in which he proclaimed that the more he understood the universe, the more he believed that a Creator was at work.

Spiritual Awakening: Child of the New Paradigm

The turning point in my own spiritual evolution, as well as my development as a scientist, occurred in 1985 at a scientific symposium on AIDS, on the island of Maui, Hawaii. It was there that I heard and followed the voice of God, an inner guidance that set my mission and life's purpose for the next 20 years and continues to inform the thrust of my research today.

In 1997, my first book described how I'd developed my theory of emotions, and how my husband, Dr. Michael Ruff, and I brought forth an interdisciplinary revolution showing the ways that the body and mind are inextricably linked as one entity. But the real reason that I wrote the book was to tell the story of our joint invention—a nontoxic, highly potent drug for use in the treatment of AIDS, called Peptide T.

The actual conception of Peptide T occurred after Michael and I had hiked to the summit of Haleakala Crater on Maui and then spoke at the American College of Neuropsychopharmacology's first world symposium on neuro-AIDS. The year was 1985, and neuro-AIDS was the newly recognized condition in which the HIV virus affects brain functioning.

Coming off the hiking trail and arriving back down at sea level, Michael and I were elated from the strenuous-but-inspiring, endorphin-pumping adventure and eager to attend the conference. We had much good data to present about the brain and immune system sharing a common cellular receptor—a tiny structure on the surface of cells—called the CD4 receptor. At the time, this was thought to be the only entry point into the cell for the infection of HIV, and finding it on brain, as well as immune cells, had all kinds of very exciting implications for finding a treatment.

We sat in the audience, still in an altered state from the 12-mile round-trip, 8,000-foot climb and hike through the crater, and listened carefully to what others were presenting about the new disease known as AIDS. Up until that time, the condition had been somewhat abstract to me. Scientists in the infectious-disease department of our research world, the National Institutes of Health (NIH), were working on it, but AIDS wasn't something that those of us in mental health had paid much attention to.

The last presenter to speak before me, a woman psychologist, showed slides of her patients ravaged from the disease—mostly artists, musicians, and sensitive-looking men from the gay communities of San Francisco; Provincetown, Massachusetts; and New York City. As I watched, I had a chance to study the gaunt, terrified faces of these suffering human beings. I felt my heart open with compassion for their plight, and I was so moved by the intensity of their condition that my eyes filled with tears and I had to choke back sobs. These days, I cry for the women, children, villages, societies, and nations that bear the brunt of the current pandemic.

Finally, it was my turn to lecture. I stood up and walked slowly to the podium to begin my talk. I was alert and emotionally open as I clicked through my slides, describing the hard data. It was toward the end of my presentation, when I was showing a visual of how CD4 receptors are distributed in the brain, that I heard unplanned words coming out of my mouth.

"Here we have what looks like a typical peptide-receptor pattern," I began, pointing to the pattern of receptors where the virus was connecting. But then I shocked myself by saying, "If we could find the natural, bodily peptide that fits into this CD4 receptor and blocks the entry of the virus, we could manufacture this peptide and produce a drug that would be effective and nontoxic to treat AIDS."

I was so surprised to hear my own words that I paused, and in the gap, I heard a voice—one that was loud and booming—coming from inside my head and commanding me: *And you should do that!*

Was it the voice of God that spoke to me? Maybe it was my subconscious mind, or the archetypal unconscious, or a spiritual higher consciousness—I didn't know! I could only be certain that I'd been given my marching orders to find the body's own peptide, one that would fit a receptor to inhibit entry of the virus, and then create a drug from it in the lab. I was immediately electrified by the possibility of a receptor-based treatment for AIDS, one that would be totally natural, an imitation of the body's own internal chemical!

The very next morning, I was on the phone from Hawaii to my lab back in Maryland, setting up a computer-assisted database search for our entry-blocking peptide. At the time, scientists had cracked the complete sequence of over 5,000 amino acids contained in the part of the HIV virus that sticks into the receptor to gain entry. Now all we needed to do was search the sequenced peptides in the body for a match.

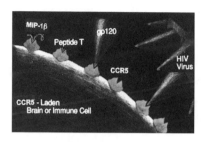

We found it right off. The matching peptide was only eight amino acids long, making it short and easy to manufacture. We did an experiment to show how our lab-made version of the body's own chemical worked; and in 1986, we published our very positive results in *Proceedings of the National Academy of Sciences,* one of the scientific establishment's most prestigious—and difficult to get into—journals. What we'd found was a mimetic (or "imitation") of the body's own neuropeptide hormone, a natural, nontoxic, highly potent, antiviral treatment for AIDS that we named after the amino acid that composed four of the eight in the chain, Threonine, or Peptide T.

On Our Own

I honestly thought that within a few months, the U.S. government would move right in behind Michael and me to support our research and bring Peptide T to clinical trials. But other labs who'd tested the drug were claiming a "failure to replicate," which meant that they couldn't get it to do what we said that it had done in our lab, a finding that almost delivered a death sentence to our venture. The chance for developing Peptide T at the NIMH was over, and we left the best jobs in biomedical research to follow an offer of private funding to do further research on our own.

In retrospect, the failure-to-replicate pronouncement occurred because scientists at the time believed that there was only one receptor, the CD4, used by the HIV virus to enter the cell. But ten years later, in 1995, scientists discovered that other co-receptors were necessary for the virus to enter the cell. One of these was the so-called CCR5 receptor, whose natural fit was a group of peptides called "chemokines." We were able to prove beyond a shadow of a doubt—and ultimately publish several papers proving it—that CCR5 is the receptor for Peptide T, not CD4, as we'd originally thought when that was the only receptor known for HIV.

The weird thing is that CCR5 turned out to be the most important therapeutic target, and today many big pharmaceutical companies are searching for a nontoxic antiviral that blocks this receptor. *Weird* comes from an old Anglo-Saxon word meaning "spiritual" and "related to fate," and everything about Peptide T's discovery fit that description—that is, lucky in an odds-defying way.

Peptide T was discovered almost ten years before the chemokine receptors were found to be used by HIV, and it was first demonstrated as an antiviral in the NIH lab of Frank Ruscetti, the only guy studying his own virus, of a strain which turned out to use CCR5 to infect cells! (You see, when Peptide T was first discovered, virtually every other virologist was working with the laboratory strain that uses the so-called X4 chemokine receptor. Although that type of the virus is relatively rare in people, it was the first one isolated and passed around for test-tube experiments.)

No wonder people "couldn't replicate" our early experiments with Peptide T! Today, we know that they were using the wrong virus, but back then I was crushed and filled with despair and paranoia as government and pharmaceutical resources were poured into testing other, less-promising (to my mind) drugs, despite the early clinical benefits with Peptide T.

I wondered, *Is this happening because I'm an outspoken woman? Not one of the good-old-boy virologists at the NIH, but an outsider from the mental-health institute across the way?* I kept trying to figure out who to blame, but perhaps in my angry petulance, I was only sabotaging my own efforts.

The funding for Peptide T eventually came—albeit slowly and painfully, with Michael and me eventually creating a foundation to raise the funds ourselves. Today, our drug has been tested in several clinical trials with positive results and published data showing that Peptide T is highly promising to effectively treat, and possibly even cure, HIV disease because of the things that it does. Two important effects are lowering the level of the virus in human blood plasma and flushing the cellular reservoirs where the virus hides, waiting to emerge and reinfect new cells.

Premature Discovery

Today, HIV has become a global pandemic, infecting an estimated 40.3 million people, including 5.1 million in India and a record 1 million in the U.S. According to a 2005 report of the UN World Health Organization, some progress with current drugs has been made in Africa, home to more than 60 percent of all people infected with HIV, with women and children being the most common victims. But more aggressive treatment programs are critical as the virus continues to spread and mutate. Only a tiny fraction of people with HIV receive highly active anti-retroviral therapy (HAART), the combination of current treatments. There are 17 million children in the world who have been orphaned by AIDS, and every day, over 1,400 children in sub-Saharan Africa die from this disease.

Michael and I have gone from privately railing against the politics and economics that have prevented our drug from coming to the market, to understanding a concept called "premature discovery." This occurs when a discovery is so radical, so advanced and out of tune with the accepted thinking, that some details aren't entirely accurate or complete. The t's aren't crossed, the i's aren't dotted, and people can't really believe it. Such a discovery may be proven by one set of researchers, but not validated by any others, leading to the failure-to-replicate stigma that Peptide T initially received.

Interestingly, premature discoveries are most often credited to women scientists, whose intuitive thinking may be ahead of their time. Likewise, the idea of the conscious mind healing the body may fall into this category, being dismissed in the wake of denial that occurs when something new rocks the reigning paradigm.

I pondered: *Is it really that our fellow scientists haven't been ready for Peptide T, or is it that I, in some metaphysical way, haven't been who I need to be in order to own our extraordinary discovery and bring it into final manifestation?* In either case, the scientific advance remains unformed, a discovery of infinite potential that's not yet in the hands of the people who need it.

Michael and I recently founded a company named RAPID Pharmaceuticals—**R**eceptor **A**ctive **P**eptides **I**nto **D**rugs. This organization's purpose is to raise money to develop Peptide T for AIDS. Now, what's left to do is secure the commercial license from the government to give us ownership of our invention, enabling us at last to raise the funding necessary to begin new and conclusive clinical trials.

Consciousness and Reality

The discovery of Peptide T was a turning point for me in embracing the power of consciousness to manifest miracles and bring about unpredictable futures, and it has been a humbling journey. It wasn't my idea to go looking for this premature discovery—I was simply following directions!

But I did allow myself to be moved by compassion for people

suffering from AIDS, and that was the key to me hearing my own inner voice. I've said that emotions are a bridge that links the spiritual to the material world, and the discovery of Peptide T clearly demonstrates the truth of that statement. When our hearts are open and our feelings are flowing as they're designed to do, we're all vulnerable to the divine. In the case of my discovery, compassion opened the door for me to literally see and hear the way to bring an end to the disease.

In other words, when we feel, we heal. The word *heal* has a common origin with the words *whole* and *holy,* pointing to a relationship of body to spirit. All emotions bring us closer to our true nature and powerful creative capacity, whether we call it "consciousness" or "God." How our biochemicals of emotion make this possible, the very physiology of the bodymind, is the science that underlies feeling good and feeling God.

Landing in Tucson

As the flight attendant asked me to stow my laptop for landing, I rushed to arrange the last few slides for my talk. I looked at my watch with growing panic and realized that it was going to be tight—again. The plane was more than an hour behind schedule, leaving me a only few moments to close my eyes and go over what needed to be done before showtime, which was less than an hour and a half away.

The lady professor and I said our final good-byes, wishing each other the best in our lectures. I envied her poise—and the fact that her event was tomorrow. *Why do I punish myself like this, scheduling myself so tight?* I wondered for the hundredth time, as I skillfully grabbed my bag and maneuvered my way to the front of the plane. Once on the ground, I met my hosts, Joan and Nick, who took me in their car and graciously dropped me off at the hotel where I would prepare for my talk.

As I hurriedly showered and dressed, my thoughts turned to seeing Nancy Marriott, my oldest friend and writing collaborator on my first book, who was flying in from Santa Barbara. We'd met up a month earlier in February, when I was presenting at a conference in Santa Monica for the *What the Bleep . . . !?* crowd. Nancy had adored the movie and made a big deal about my new fame, while I was uncomfortable with the excessive credit given to me for simply allowing myself to be filmed as a talking head for what turned out to be a few minutes on-screen.

Our meeting in Santa Monica, however, had been propitious. Together, Nancy and I had hatched the idea to write another book, agreeing to rendezvous in Tucson and put a proposal together for submission to a publisher. As I centered myself and reviewed my last-minute notes and slides, my thoughts turned to that conversation, an event I didn't know at the time would lead us, over the period of the next year, on an adventure in growth, consciousness, and manifestation beyond our wildest imaginings.

Chapter 2

New-Paradigm Physiology

"There she is!" I heard my daughter Vanessa cry out as we looked for Nancy, who was making her way through the milling crowds in the Santa Monica hotel lobby. She was browsing at the jewelry and clothing booths when Vanessa spotted her and waved her down. I was glad that Vanessa had come along with me on my speaking engagement, not just for the mother-daughter opportunity, but because she was an excellent assistant and master planner. As usual, her calm demeanor was an excellent balance for my more spontaneous mode of expression.

Nancy and I embraced warmly, and then all three of us quickly made our way toward the hotel restaurant, past the people who were on a break from the talks. Nancy hadn't seen Vanessa since she was a small child, although the two had talked when my daughter helped in the writing of my first book. Now they had only a short moment to get reacquainted.

"Vanessa had to smuggle me down a service elevator to escape after my talk," I told my friend as we rushed along. "Let's get some lunch before I have to go back on again for the 2 P.M. panel."

The last time I saw Nancy was on the East Coast two years earlier, when we were each visiting our families in New England during the summer. My sister and her brother both had homes in the Lyme, Connecticut, area, making it easy for us to meet and keep up our friendship despite living on two different coasts. That year, we included a drive up to Vermont to stay at the lakeside home of Nancy's daughter, enjoying a chance to catch up, relax, and play with my friend's new grandbaby.

But all of that was before I appeared in *What the Bleep . . .!?*, which hit the theaters in late 2004 and turned out to have a huge, almost cultlike following. Now, several thousand excited movie fans from all over the country jammed the Santa Monica hotel hallways and elevators, comparing notes on how many times they'd seen the film. Some had watched it as many as 30 or 40 times, typically joining groups of friends at theaters for a viewing and social event. Nancy told me that she'd seen it a few months earlier with people who were part of her consciousness community in Santa Barbara.

Whenever I came to California, Nancy and I would get in touch and arrange to meet, enjoying a chance to renew our lifelong friendship and have some fun together. It had been almost ten years since Nancy had helped me write *Molecules of Emotion,* the book that thrust me into the public eye, leading to my current *Bleep* fame.

Creative Reunion

As we got a table and ordered lunch, the conversation turned to the important things: husbands, children, careers, personal-growth crises, and professional breakthroughs. Vanessa soon left us to handle some PR business, after installing a conference-staff person to stand guard and keep overeager fans from mobbing me while I shared lunch with my friend.

"Isn't this wild?" I said, excitedly sweeping my hand across the restaurant and hotel lobby where the noisy crowd was congregated. "I call them the Bleepers, and they seem to think I have some kind of an answer—"

"I know," Nancy said, interrupting me. "Which is why you want to write another book!" She looked up from her salad and waited for me to reply. This wasn't the first time that she'd brought up the idea of another big publishing project, but I'd always been quick to dismiss it. Here, however—where my popularity was so evident—I was feeling more positive about the possibility, although I wasn't convinced.

"I don't know." I hesitated. "People are definitely longing for something that they believe I can provide. My hunch is that they're yearning for a sense of the spiritual in their lives, and hoping to find some real science behind it." I sighed deeply.

The convergence of spirituality and science was the theme of *What the Bleep Do We Know!?*, even though some viewers thought that higher concerns had been given a backseat to the science. But the film had posed a fascinating proposition: In a quantum world where infinite possibilities exist, we create our own experience of reality. I'd been the only biologist in the movie's lineup of experts and talking heads: quantum physicists; theologians; psychiatrists; chiropractors; and one New Age channeler named J. Z. Knight, who was the only other female talking head in the film.

"But look," I continued, "all I want to do at this point in my life is get my AIDS drug into the marketplace so that it's available to people who need it. Being on the lecture circuit is not my day job! I'm a serious scientist, and my mission is to find cures for disease— specifically, receptor-active peptides to fight many different conditions, not just AIDS. What I want more than anything is to be back in my laboratory, *not* writing another book."

Nancy listened and gave me a wide berth to vent.

"And anyway, it's all J. Z.'s fault," I quipped facetiously. "If I hadn't accepted an invitation to lecture at her School of Enlightenment up in Yelm, Washington, I would never have been asked to be in the film." I looked around to see if J. Z., also speaking at the conference, was anywhere in sight and might overhear me.

Years ago, I'd told Nancy of my adventures with Ramtha, the name given to the multi-thousand-year-old sage who channeled through J. Z. Knight, a brilliant and feminine woman with an excellent business sense. I found it interesting that the voice she uses to deliver Ramtha's teachings is that of a macho warrior, one that overshadows her diminutive size and makes her appear larger than life. Scientists directed by Dr. Stanley Krippner of Saybrook Graduate School and Research Center had shown that she's not a "multiple personality" because "she has access to Ramtha through a voluntary-induced procedure."

On my trip to Yelm, I learned that the New Age teacher had made my book *Molecules of Emotion* required reading for her students, packing the local bookstore with hundreds of copies that were displayed pyramid style in the front window. It turned out that J. Z. owned the bookstore. She'd wanted to absorb quantum physics and the new biology into her own thinking and had fallen in love with the neuroscience behind the notion that you can create your own reality.

Shortly after I arrived at J. Z.'s school, I was ushered into an enormous hall where her students had been assembled for hours. While they were applauding wildly, I noticed sparks of pink light hovering above their heads. Later, I asked my hostess if they had some special effects going on, which she denied.

"What you're seeing is the love they're generating for you," she told me. Even though I was speaking at this New Age gathering, I was still a skeptical scientist and didn't readily believe in sparkly, pink auras. But I knew what I'd seen, and it intrigued me.

Nancy pressed on: "Candace, J. Z. knew it, and so do I. Coming from your scientific background, you have information that can make a huge difference. Based on your discoveries, you can give people a new, more empowering way to think about themselves, their bodies, and their minds. You've got the key for health and wellness, for wholeness—a new paradigm for the future!" Nancy was pitching hard.

"And most important, you're a real scientist, not a self-help guru dispensing advice. You're the real thing, the bona fide item: a highly credentialed, mainstream medical researcher. People listen when you speak, and they want to hear what you have to say."

I pondered my friend's words and then replied, "Look, there

are only two reasons that I'd say yes to writing another book. One is that I need the money!" We laughed, but the truth was that Peptide T's private investor had recently and abruptly withdrawn, leaving Mike and me with no regular salary. Our savings were dwindling, and my speaking engagements were now our sole source of income.

"And the second," I went on, "is because *you* would be the one doing it with me. You know me like no one else does, except maybe Mike and my kids. In some ways, you know me even better, because we grew up together; we're the same generation."

Nancy nodded in agreement, and I continued. "Let's face it: The truth is, we're each other's pasts! And I've come to realize that healing the past is the key to Peptide T breaking through to the marketplace. God knows I've been doing everything to improve myself—bodywork, meditation, and energy healing—for years, and I've come a long way. But there's still a ways to go, and I believe that together, you and I can help each other grow."

Nancy was listening very intently, and in her silence, I kept on talking: "If we were to write another book together," I went on, "it would have to be about growth and healing, as well as the science." I paused. "Not only is that honest, but if I can heal my core issues and stop sabotaging the success of Peptide T, it would be worth it to me. Because then the world would have the first low-cost, nontoxic, antiviral drug to effectively combat the AIDS global pandemic, which is really what my life is about." The gauntlet was now on the table.

"You're playing for some pretty high stakes," Nancy said, taking in the huge possibility of our potential venture together.

And she was right. Here I was suggesting that we not only write a book that would alter people's understanding of the mind and body, but also accomplish some major personal healing and growth in the process. And along the way, I intended to bring forth and market a new drug to eradicate the AIDS virus from the face of the earth!

"Well, I'm up for it, of course," Nancy declared, expressing the confidence and sense of adventure I knew she possessed. "It's big, but I still want to play."

"Good, because I know we can do it together," I affirmed, cinching the deal. "In this book, we'll not only update people on the latest mind-body science, but we'll give them what they really want, which is some direction for how to feel good—physically and spiritually. People want to *feel good* and *feel God,* and the way to get there is through the emotions. They're the link that connects body to soul, and as such, they're the key to transforming anything, everything."

"That all sounds great," Nancy cut in. "But this time, let's make the science simple. I want everyone to be able to understand it." I liked what she was proposing and listened to her idea. "For example, when you say, 'your body is your subconscious mind,' it's simple enough for people to grasp the underlying mechanism, how cells communicate through peptides, manifesting as vibrations, emotions, and behaviors. *What the Bleep . . . !?* attempted to show the biology by having cartoon characters represent different emotions, unleashed on a group of partygoers."

"I agree, and we can do better than that," I replied. "The movie was art, not science, and of course, the producers were allowed to take poetic license." I looked around the restaurant and noticed that the crowds were thinning as people started to make their way back to the main room where the next event was to begin.

"Don't you have to be on that panel now?" Nancy asked.

"I do, but let's step outside into the sun—God, I love the California sun! I'll give you a basic tutorial in what I call the new-paradigm physiology. Don't worry, I'll give you the simple version, what any reader can understand and will need as the basis for the book we're going to write. Did you bring a tape recorder?"

She had, knowing from experience that if we agreed to write a book, the process could start at any moment. I asked our table guardian to convey to Vanessa that I'd be a few minutes late for the panel, and we slipped out onto the veranda to talk the science and bask in the sun.

Receptor-ology 101

"The nuts and bolts of how body and mind are one—the new-paradigm physiology—involves some simple biochemistry," I began after Nancy signaled to me that the tape was running.

"To begin with, virtually every cell in the body is studded with thousands of tiny structures called receptors. Like the sense organs—the eyes, nose, and ears—the job of the receptors is to pick up signals coming at them from the surrounding space. They're so important that a full 40 percent of our DNA is devoted to making sure that they're perfectly reproduced from generation to generation.

"Once the receptors receive a signal, the information is transferred to deep within the cell's interior, where tiny engines roar into action and initiate key processes. Data coming in this way directs cell division and growth, cell migration for attacking enemies and making repairs, and cell metabolism to conserve or spend energy—to name just a few of the receptor-activated activities.

"The signal comes from other cells and is carried by a juice that we call an informational substance. These juices from the brain, sexual organs, gut, and heart—literally everywhere—communicate cell to cell, providing an infrastructure for the 'conversation' going on throughout the bodymind. You know these juices as hormones, neurotransmitters, and peptides, and we scientists refer to all three with one word: *ligand*. This term is from *ligare,* a Latin word meaning "to bind," and is used because of the way that the substances latch on so tightly to the cell's surface receptors.

"Information-carrying ligands are responsible for 98 percent of all data transfer in body and brain. The remaining 2 percent of communication takes place at the synapse, between brain cells firing and releasing neurotransmitters across a gap to hit receptors on the other side. In *What the Bleep . . . !?,* audiences saw an animated electrical storm taking place in the brain to show what this synaptic activity looks like. But what they didn't see is that there are neurons with this same electrical-sparking activity firing throughout the body, not just in the brain.

"My personal favorites among the ligands are the peptides, which consist of a string of amino acids, joined together like beads in a necklace; larger strings of amino acids are called proteins. There are over 200 peptides mapped in the brain and body, each one sounding a complex emotional chord—such as bliss, hunger, anger, relaxation, or satiety—when their signal is received by the cell. I've devoted my 30-plus year career to studying peptides such as endorphins and other substances.

"In addition, everyone should know that most ligands have chemical equivalents found outside the body, such as Valium, marijuana, cocaine, alcohol, and caffeine, to name a few.

"You've now learned about the two components that make up this bodymind communication system—the receptor and the ligand. These are what I have called the 'molecules of emotion.' But how do the two find each other across the vast reaches of intercellular space, hook up—or bind—and then transfer vital information to affect cellular, bodywide activity?

"We used to explain the attraction by a quality called receptor specificity, which is that each receptor is specifically shaped to fit one and only one ligand. A lock-and-key model helped with visualizing this method of connecting, or binding. The 'key' (a peptide) floats by until it finds its perfect 'keyhole' (the receptor). The key inserts into the keyhole, opening the 'lock' of the cell, and cellular activities begin.

"While this is partially accurate, we now understand a more dynamic relationship between ligand and receptor, involving something called 'vibratory attraction.' Sitting on the surface of the cell, the receptor wiggles and shimmies, changing from one configuration to another in a constant state of flux. This dance creates a vibration that resonates with a ligand vibrating at the same frequency, and they begin to resonate together.

"Cellular resonance—it's like when you pluck one string on

two different guitars in the same room—one will resonate with the other, both striking the same note. This creates a force of attraction, the way that peptides resonate with their receptors and come together to strike that emotional chord as they bind. And that's when the music begins!

"I've said that the emotions are the link between the physical body and nonphysical states of consciousness, and the receptors on every cell are where this happens! The attracting vibration is the emotion, and the actual connection—peptide to receptor—is the manifestation of the feeling in the physical world. That's why I call peptides and their receptors the molecules of emotion.

"What's the result of all this activity? On a bodywide scale, the receptors are dynamic molecular targets, modulating our physiology in response to our experience. Emotions influence the molecules, which in turn affect how we feel. One example is that receptors wax and wane in number and sensitivity, depending on how often they're occupied by peptides or other informational substances. In other words, our physical body can be changed by the emotions we experience.

"And one last thing: We used to think that the peptides latched onto a single receptor, but we now know that receptors are often clumped together in tight, multiple complexes. Together, they form the walls of deep channels leading into the interior of the cell; and they open and close with a rhythmic, pumping action. As they move, these channels let substances in and out of the cell, setting up an ionic flux, or electrical current, which can course throughout the bodymind.

"One of the things that this current does is influence the firing 'set point' of neurons in the brain, determining the path of brain-cell activation. So you can see that the molecules of emotion are directly affecting how you think! If we were to show a cartoon version of this whole process—peptides binding, receptors pumping, electric current moving out— we'd see bright, colorful clouds of vibrating, singing energy surrounding each cell; and we'd hear a chorus of resonating voices soaring in the background."

Nancy had been listening very intently, letting me have the floor. Finally, I paused and asked her if she had any questions.

"Are you saying that these peptides and receptors, the molecules of emotion, actually *produce* the emotions?" Nancy asked. "Do *they* come first and then we have the feelings?"

"It's not a cause-and-effect relationship," I replied. "Rather, it's happening simultaneously, all at once. Remember, these molecules *are* the emotions, not their cause. What we experience as a 'feeling' is the actual vibrational dance that goes on when peptides bind to their receptors, whether it happens in your conscious awareness or not. Below what we notice happening, a huge amount of emotionally mediated information is being exchanged throughout the body and brain, much of which never rises up into our consciousness. This is why I say: *Your body is your subconscious mind.*"

I stopped and took a deep breath. "Do you get it now?" I asked, as I could see Vanessa through the sliding-glass doors, signaling me to come back inside.

Creating Reality

"Just one more question," Nancy replied. "Say more about how all this emotion stuff relates to creating reality—that is, if Vanessa will give us a few more moments." I waved to my daughter, letting her know that we'd only be another minute or two.

"Okay," I began. "First, I'm not saying anything new. The ancients—entire civilizations, such as those in Japan, India, and China—have always held that consciousness came first, followed by manifestation in the physical universe. Translated to our terms, they believed that consciousness is real, and the atoms and molecules we call 'reality' follow. First comes spirit and mind, second comes tangible, touchable 'things.'

"We in the West have it the other way around: We relate first to the physical universe as 'real,' and then consider consciousness as some kind of secondary phenomenon—a by-product, perhaps!

"Eastern thinkers have long said that consciousness precedes the material world, and in fact is at the very source of what we can see and touch. This idea has been around for more than 5,000 years, even though our modern-day science seems to be discovering it anew. Today, through quantum physics—the study of smaller and smaller levels of matter—the East and West are beginning to converge and see the plane of physical manifestation as no longer the only 'real' world."

Nancy interjected: "Are you saying that there's no reality—no one and indisputable reality?"

"Yes! More and more I'm coming to believe that there's only what each of us perceives and then interacts with. But here's how this has played out to give us our modern medical paradigm: In the West, we've denied the connection of the mind to the body—consciousness to matter—ever since the 17th century. It all started when the French philosopher and medical doctor René Descartes struck a deal with the pope to use human corpses for his medical research, a practice that hadn't been allowed up until then. In order to obtain the subjects, Descartes had to promise that he would only study the physical body and leave the soul for salvation, a job done only by the church.

"From that transaction some 300 years ago, Western medicine arose, in all its materialistic, reductionist glory. Consciousness—consisting of the emotions, spirit, and thought—was relegated to the realm of the soul, and therefore wasn't studied as part of the physical body. As a result, the basic tenet of the reigning medical paradigm today is: *Mind and body are separate, and the two shall never meet.*

"Even with the development of modern psychology and psychiatry, mind and emotions are still not studied as part of the physical body, but are kept apart from it in a world of their own. In keeping with this split, still deeply entrenched in our mainstream medical practices, the 'head' and 'body' doctors rarely sit down at the same table.

"In recent years, aided by the new positron emission imaging techniques (PETs), neuroscientists have gone looking for the site of consciousness. The brain is a physical organ, so we could say that this is progress, as scientists map different areas that light up when cognitive functions are performed, such as dreaming, meditating, and thinking. But unfortunately, researchers draw a new boundary at the neck, limiting the search for consciousness to the brain alone. Below the head, that vast territory known as the body is off-limits, a bias that continues to perpetuate a mind-body split in scientific research."

I paused to look at my watch, and Nancy took the chance to ask, "Sounds like we're ready for a paradigm shift, don't you think?"

"I agree, but paradigms don't shift easily. Back in the 1500s, they used to imprison and exile scientists for going against the prevailing paradigms of the day. That's what happened to Galileo when he showed the world proof of Copernicus's theory that Earth revolves around the sun, not the other way around. He challenged a belief that Europeans had held ever since they shed their bearskins. Galileo literally turned the known universe inside out, and for that, he was put behind bars.

"The scientific academy of today is as unwilling to accept that consciousness is in the body, as the 16th-century pope was to accept that the sun was the center of the known solar system. But instead of imprisoning scientists, the academy today takes away your lab and your workers, and blackballs you if you find private funding. My point is that there's much resistance to the idea that the mind is in the body, and the brain is not the mind.

"It took a while after Galileo proclaimed his theory for the idea to be accepted, and when it was, it took more time for the details to be worked out in the scientific community. There were orbits to be mapped, spaces to be measured, and all the details of a new paradigm to be filled in. And so it goes in our own era: When new ideas are proposed, it takes time. The mainstream biomedical scientists are just beginning to investigate the mind-body connection, filling in the details and finding the proof for its existence.

A Psychosomatic Network

"But contrary to the reigning-paradigm belief, the body doesn't exist merely to carry the head around! The body isn't an appendage dangling from the almighty brain that rules over all systems. Instead, the brain itself is one of many nodal, or entry, points into a dynamic network of communication that unites all systems—nervous, endocrine, immune, respiratory, and more. This is called the psychosomatic network, and the linking elements to keep it all together are the informational substances—peptides, hormones, and neurotransmitters—known as the molecules of emotion.

"In 1985, Michael and I proposed the existence of a psychosomatic network that is mediated by the emotions, and we published our theory in *The Journal of Immunology*. It was that scientific paper—along with our earlier research on the connection of brain, endocrine, and immune systems—that helped launch a new field known as psychoneuroimmunology (PNI). PNI, although controversial at its inception, is strong and flourishing today, with thousands of scientists participating through their research.

"This psychosomatic network requires a new way of thinking about physiology in order to be understood. In the reigning-paradigm mind-set, the term *psychosomatic* is used pejoratively, as if symptoms that are psychosomatic are false and don't deserve attention or treatment. After all, they can't be 'real,' because they're *all in your mind!*

"But in the new view of medicine and wellness, a psychosomatic state is the basis for a fresh approach to healing disease; for feeling well emotionally; and for creating a different, more desirable reality. Yes, your symptoms are in your body, but they are also *always* in your mind, either consciously or subconsciously. Mind and body are not split in two, so what happens in one occurs in the other, too. This is the fundamental tenet of what I call the new-paradigm physiology.

"Of course, it's controversial because when *psyche* (mind) and *soma* (body) are seen as a single entity—giving us the term *psychosomatic*—we leave Western dualism behind and enter a new, more spontaneous biology, where we can access states of physical, emotional, and even planetary healing. Our bodymind (what I've come to call the "unified being") is designed to perceive, interpret, and alter reality, whether consciously or subconsciously. As individuals, we actually have a huge say in how life goes, a responsibility that's tremendously empowering to open doors and gain access to unlimited possibilities. And there really is some good science to explain it all. . . ."

Vanessa appeared again and slid the door open this time. "They've already begun the panel, and they're asking for you!" she said urgently.

"I've got to run—more later!" I jumped up and took off on Vanessa's heels. Nancy packed up her tape recorder and followed, rushing right behind me to get into the room and find a seat for the afternoon event.

An Ongoing Adventure

Later that day, after Vanessa and I had gotten into a taxi and were riding to the airport for our flight back to D.C., I reached Nancy on her cell phone.

"So, it's set then—we're definitely going to write the new book!" I said. "Will you meet me in Tucson next month to get a proposal started?"

"Yes," Nancy replied, her voice breaking up as she drove up the Pacific Coast Highway toward Santa Barbara. "I'll get there in time to catch your lecture at the Unity church."

"Great," I replied. "I'm staying with my chiropractor friends, Joan and Nicholas, and you can join us. They've got a big house just outside of the city and offered to leave us alone there while we work."

"Sounds like the perfect setup. I'll be there with a tape recorder and my laptop."

"Can't wait. See you then—'bye!" I signed off.

The adventure had begun! Or I should say, *another* exciting chapter in the ongoing saga of friendship and creativity that Nancy and I had shared for many more years than either of us cared to count.

Memories and Reflections

I met my friend when I was in the second grade and her mother was my Brownie troop leader. Nancy was a cute blonde, and I instantly admired her long braids, which were a contrast to my darker coloring and pixie haircut. Later, we attended the same junior high and high school in Levittown, a suburb of New York City on Long Island. Both high achievers, our paths crossed and friendship grew as we became members of the honor society, performers in school plays, and "advanced" students in the academic-tracking system that aimed to prepare the brightest kids for the future.

After high-school graduation, we went off to different colleges, returning home for holidays and breaks, when we'd always try to get together. I married early, but that didn't stop me from completing college and going on to graduate school. While still an undergraduate—I was scarcely 20, almost a teen mom—I gave birth to my first child, Evan, whom Nancy met as a toddler when she visited me and my first husband, Agu Pert, at the coed dorm for which we were "house-parents" at Bryn Mawr College in Pennsylvania. Agu was getting his Ph.D., and I was completing my A.B.

Whenever Nancy and I got together, the sparks of adventure flew. By the time we were young adults, we'd burned our bras for women's liberation, marched against the war in Vietnam, and weathered the fallout of drugs and sex from the Woodstock generation. In the early '70s, Nancy finished graduate school at Columbia University and left the East Coast to experience San Francisco. We lost contact briefly when she embraced the counterculture to meditate with a guru, explore communal life, and give birth to a daughter.

Back east, I was becoming a superstar in the scientific community at Johns Hopkins, and later at the prestigious National Institutes of Health. I connected with Nancy again in 1980, when she came to Washington, D.C., to lead meditation circles for world peace; and over the next couple of decades, we stayed in touch as we traversed similar life paths.

I took est; had natural childbirth with my second child, Vanessa; and learned to meditate with Deepak Chopra. Nancy would catch my act at Esalen or the Institute of Noetic Sciences whenever I came out west to give a talk; and we'd hang out in hot tubs, restaurants, or hotel rooms to talk and play late into the night.

Shortly after I met Michael in the mid-1980s, I visited Nancy in Santa Barbara, where she'd moved to be with her husband, Richard. While I'd stayed closer to the beaten path, Nancy had become more comfortable with the unproven and the unknown—and I was catching up. We compared notes on our many consciousness adventures, such as holotropic breathing, bodywork, Reichian processes, spirituality, hypnosis, and alternative-healing approaches. These modalities were popular on the West Coast, and I'd previously relied on Nancy to tell me about them.

As we grew, our two paths crossed more and more—Nancy becoming more down-to-earth, and me taking off into the far reaches of consciousness-land. My friend had studied *A Course in Miracles* and was reinventing herself through the transformational seminars of Landmark Education, beginning a new career as a college instructor and professional writer. In the early '90s, we got together and pooled our talents to write an article about my scientific discoveries for *Women of Power,* an alternative women's magazine.

The publication went under shortly after our article appeared, but we emerged as a tight team, emboldened to take on a bigger project—namely, writing a book and getting it published. We got together again on Long Island at our 30-year high-school reunion—class of '64—where we danced late into the night with our former classmates. At breakfast the next day, exhausted but happy, we agreed to write a book that would tell the story of the molecules of emotion.

Ten years later, we were ready to do it again, only this time the stakes were higher, with a lot more to bring into manifestation now on the table.

The Show Goes On

The month flew by between our meeting in Santa Monica and the time of my departure for Tucson. The morning of my flight out, I talked with Nancy on the phone.

"I'm not afraid to use 'the G word' anymore," I proclaimed triumphantly, *the G word* referring to *God*. "I tell the truth on all coasts now!" We both laughed at my reference to the late Willis Harman, who'd said to me, "Candace, you're the only person I know who has both an East Coast and a West Coast personality!" Nancy has always encouraged me to "come out" about my spiritual beliefs and was thrilled that I was going public—a serious scientist ready to talk about God.

In my Tucson hotel room before my talk, I changed into an outfit that bolstered my new self-image—a bright-red, shiny silk suit. No tie-dyed blouse or flowing, New Age–goddess garb for me. And no drab, three-piece, boxy suits either. My outfit hit the median point and boldly declared my new stand: *I'm a serious scientist and courageous pioneer, who, by the way, isn't afraid to talk about God!*

Backstage, I heard my name and walked out to the welcoming applause. Standing before the vast and expectant space, a diva who could entertain and also deliver the truth, I connected with my audience for a moment and then began to speak. Within minutes of my first words, we were all laughing—the throng joining me for an exciting romp through the nature of consciousness, the molecules of emotion, and the science of a new paradigm of physiology.

Chapter 3

The Science of
Emotions and Consciousness

I looked out at my audience, said a silent prayer, introduced myself, and then brought up my first slide. On the screen was a gorgeous, sexy woman, dressed in black and reclining in ecstatic abandonment. A hush fell over the audience as they took it in—a magazine ad for the perfume Opium—and I continued speaking, launching into the information they'd come to hear. . . . This chapter is the substance of my lecture.

The Lecture at Tucson

Bliss! That's what I know a lot about; that's what I studied as a graduate student at Johns Hopkins Medical School in 1973. It was there, along with my mentor, Dr. Sol Snyder, that I discovered the opiate receptor, the key to the body's mechanism for pleasure. The breakthrough caused a revolution in brain science and sent reverberations throughout all of the biological disciplines.

For years, scientists had theorized that drugs acted in the body by attaching to receptors to exert their effects. But no one had ever done simple experiments that demonstrated how this worked. No one had proved that receptors even existed at all, until I developed a test-tube method in our lab at Hopkins to measure the opiate receptor and earned my Ph.D.

As an Associated Press news release flew around the world, I found myself at the center of the scientific community's attention. This was the first receptor to be measured by a method that would later be used to measure many more newly discovered receptors. But the burning question that everyone wanted the answer to was: Why was there a natural mechanism, the opiate receptor, that allowed drugs like morphine and heroin to act in the body?

What followed was a mad dash on both sides of the Atlantic for the discovery of the body's own morphine. A British laboratory won the prize, identifying a tiny protein chain of amino acids called endorphin, as the opiate receptor's key. Endorphin, a peptide bound to the opiate receptor, produces a natural high that drug companies everywhere hoped to capitalize on as a natural, nonaddictive analgesic, but it wasn't to be.

In retrospect, the opiate receptor discovery was important not because it led to identifying the body's own morphine, but because it opened a new avenue of exploration for the invention of drug therapies for disease. The fact that we could now demonstrate that there are receptors on the cells where the body's own chemicals attach—and even measure them—meant that we could make new *external* chemicals in the lab, commonly known as drugs, to access the cell in the same way. This avenue eventually led to Peptide T, the AIDS therapeutic that I'm currently developing with my husband, Michael.

A Bodywide, Psychosomatic Network

Over the decade following the discovery of these newly identified substances, my lab and others around the world rushed to map them, finding endorphin and opiate receptors in parts of the brain known to be associated with the emotions. The amygdala and hypothalamus, two structures within the limbic (or old emotional) brain, were found to be loaded with what I came to call the molecules of emotion.

But a surprise was that we also found insulin receptors in the brain, along with ones for virtually every other peptide in the body. Insulin is a large peptide secreted by the pancreas to regulate the level of sugar in the blood. What was it doing in the brain?

For years, neuroscientists had claimed the brain as the seat of emotions, pointing to the fact that when brain structures in or near the limbic system were stimulated during neurosurgery, intense emotional expression of early memories occurred. But we found that these molecules of emotion aren't just in the limbic system, but throughout the body, linked to form a comprehensive system of communication including the endocrine, digestive, and reproductive systems—literally, every system in the organism. We eventually were able to show a network of intercellular communication, humming along under the coordinated efforts of these informational molecules of emotion, which we called the "psychosomatic network."

The brain, we proposed, is just one nodal point of entry into this psychosomatic network that has *many* nodal points, the spinal cord and the sensory organs being among them. The system could be accessed from different places, depending on a person's focus of attention. For example, if you know any teenage boys, you know that their gonads will tend to override any other information entering this system and drive the organism in a predictable behavior.

The old paradigm held that the brain is the seat of consciousness, and the mind is the brain's by-product. But we can no longer say that brain is to mind as kidney is to urine; the mind is not the product of any organ, not even the brain. Awareness is the property of the whole organism; and in the psychosomatic network, we see the conscious and the unconscious mind infusing every aspect of the physical body. This is why I can say: *The body is the subconscious mind.*

Currents of Emotion

Besides receiving and processing information to unify a single bodymind, the peptides and receptors are clumped to form ion channels to pump ions in and out of the cell. This rhythmic, pulsating movement creates an electrical current that meanders through the body, influencing the state of excitability or relaxation of the entire organism.

One of the most studied receptors is the GABA receptor, which is where the drugs Valium and alcohol bind. (The endogenous, or internal, substance is called GABA.) When those two drugs bind simultaneously at the GABA receptor, because someone has just popped a Valium and then poured a drink, the chloride ion leaks into the cell through the receptor-modulated ion channel. The effect of this flow is to become deeply relaxed, as the threshold for neuronal firing gets very high. This is why the combination of alcohol and Valium can kill, which is what happened back in the '60s, we now understand, when famed columnist Dorothy Kilgallen unintentionally overdosed and died.

The set points of brain-cell excitability vary from place to place and from individual to individual, depending on which receptors are occupied by which neurotransmitters, other informational substances, or drugs. The differences in these thresholds can be the cause of much mischief, especially for marital relationships. The high-strung, excitable, talkative wife and the near-comatose husband with his nose in the newspaper are in an electro-chemically incompatible mode that, if not modulated, could easily lead to trouble!

The Matter of Consciousness

I propose that the matter of consciousness—the measurable, material substance—is the vibrating, moving, breathing, pumping molecular complexes of receptors and their ligands, as they bind to every cell of your body. The activity of these molecules creates an electrical charge and continually generates a current throughout your bodymind to keep you awake, alert, and conscious.

This is why I can say that the molecules of emotion are those of consciousness. Emotions span the material and the immaterial realm; they're the bridge linking the two. Just like the simultaneous particle and wave properties of light, the molecules of emotion go both ways. At the same time, they're physical substances that you can see and weigh on a gel in the laboratory, ones that vibrate with an electrical charge in the living animal; and they're a kind of wave between people that conveys information. They're both physical and psychological, linking brain to body in one vast network of communication to coordinate the entire bodymind.

In the Eastern view, consciousness comes first, and molecules are simply a metaphor, an afterthought, to explain consciousness. I'm amazed by how, over the years, I've come to understand and finally embrace this concept. Even more astonishing is that the science I've done supports the closure of the East/West gap, whether we focus on molecules or consciousness, matter or spirit. The two seeming opposites are simply flip sides of the same coin, or end points in a wide spectrum that's completely traversed by emotion.

New Mind, New Thoughts

I want to tell you about some very astounding data that has come out of the National Institutes of Health laboratory of Dr. Eva Mezey that makes all of this easier to understand. Dr. Mezey recently proved irrefutably that mind and body are one by showing that stem cells migrate from the bone marrow into the brain and become neurons. Equally astounding is that her paradigm-jolting work was allowed to surface, given that the initial reaction to her data resulted in her lab nearly being closed.

Stem cells—cells that are undifferentiated and have yet to

become organ cells—are made in the bone marrow, which we already knew. We also knew that stem cells move through the blood to other systems and organs. But the news that they move out of the bone marrow, eventually becoming neurons in the nervous system, was shocking.

Dr. Mezey found this migration happening not only in response to illness, as when stem cells grew into immune cells, but as a matter of course. And even more shocking was that these stem cells weren't just showing up in the spinal cord (which I consider an extension of the brain), but also in the highest part of the brain, a structure known as the "frontal cortex."

The first experiments were done by injecting bone marrow from a male mouse into a female mouse, but were repeated in a clever way with humans. Dr. Mezey used female subjects—some were children, some were older women—who had leukemia and had been treated with bone marrow transplanted from males. None lived more than a few years, and of the 18 cases she was able to study, every one of the females upon autopsy had plenty of neurons with the male Y chromosomes in them. In other words, male stem cells were in the females' brains, irrefutable evidence that brain cells travel from the bone marrow into the brain.

The bones are giving rise to the brain! Ancient Chinese medicine says that *chi,* loosely translated as "the life force," originates in the bone. Now we are showing in our Western model that cells start as baby stem cells born in the bone marrow, become immune-like cells as they pass through the body, and then arrive in the brain as brain cells. This migration, our lab had shown in the '80s, was directed by the molecules of emotion in a process known as chemotaxis.

We used to think that by the age of five, you had all the brain cells you were going to get. Then neuroscientists discovered that your brain keeps growing when you're a teen, and your frontal cortex doesn't stop developing until you're 25. But the new research shows that the growth of brain cells never stops— this replenishment, the influx of new brain cells, is going on throughout your entire life! Neurogenesis, the birth of new cells appearing, moving, and becoming neurons in the brain, used to be controversial; it now is one of the hottest areas of research in biomedical science today.

So what does this all mean? Well, it means that you can learn and change and grow, because you're literally making a new brain every day. Since you sat down in your seat here tonight, you've made thousands of new neurons! You're literally being given the opportunity to think new thoughts, to change your mind, to create the reality you experience, from moment to moment. It's no longer just a truism that thinking positively is a good idea—thank you, Dr. Norman Vincent Peale! If you have uplifting thoughts, you're building a very different brain than if you have negative ones.

Emotion and Memory

Classically, the hippocampus is the structure in the brain associated with memory, because when you remove it surgically, a person will have deficits in memory. But contrary to what many neuroscientists believe, this doesn't necessarily prove that the hippocampus is the seat of memory.

In fact, recent findings support the theory that recall is stored throughout the body, not in the brain alone. Dr. Eric R. Kandel, a neurobiologist at Columbia University College of Physicians and Surgeons, received a Nobel Prize for Medicine in 2000 for showing that memory resides at the level of the receptor.

The activity of cellular binding throughout the body can impact neuronal circuitry, influencing memory and thinking. When a receptor is flooded with a peptide or other ligand, the cell membrane is changed in such a way that the probability of an electrical impulse traveling across the membrane is affected. Remember, wherever there's a receptor, there's also a vibrating electrode or diode where circuits can change. This, in turn, affects the choice of neuronal circuitry that will be used, impacting brain activity.

These recent discoveries are important for appreciating how memories are stored not only in the brain, but in the body as well, where a psychosomatic network extends throughout all systems of the organism. A major storage area is in the receptors distributed near the spinal cord, between nerve and ganglia, and all the way out to the internal organs and the surface of the skin. This means that your memories are in your spinal cord, as well as all throughout your bodymind.

Whether your memories are conscious or not is mediated by the molecules of emotion. They decide what becomes a thought rising to the surface, and what remains buried deeply in your body. What this means is that much of memory is emotion driven, not conscious, although it can sometimes be *made* conscious by intention. The emotions that you're able to experience can bring a recollection to the surface; if your feelings are suppressed, however, they can bury that same memory far below your awareness, where it can affect your perceptions, decisions, behavior, and even health, all unconsciously.

Buried, painful emotions from the past make up what some psychologists and healers call a person's "core emotional trauma." The point of therapy—including bodywork, some kinds of chiropractic, and energy medicine—is to gently bring that wound to gradual awareness, so it can be reexperienced and understood. Only then is choice possible, a faculty of your frontal cortex, allowing you to reintegrate any disowned parts of yourself; let go of old traumatic patterns; and become healed, or *whole*.

Learning and Emotion

Memory is connected to learning, and we learn and remember not only with our brain, but also with our physical selves. This fits with all that I've said about the mind being in the body, making for one *bodymind* and demonstrating how pervasive and far-reaching the mind really is.

I want to draw your attention to very clear studies done by Dr. Donald Overton that show there are *dissociated states* (not connected) of learning and memory. His data demonstrates that what you learn in one drug-induced state, you can't retrieve from your memory at a later time, unless you're in the same condition. If you're smoking cigarettes and drinking coffee to prepare for an exam, unless you're doing those things when you take the test, you won't be able to remember enough information to pass. This is because various substances (such as alcohol, nicotine, and caffeine) create altered states of consciousness with different emotions and memories, and therefore, different modes in which to learn.

In other words, you acquire knowledge with your entire bodymind, not just with your brain. Also, learning is an emotional event, impacted by how you're feeling. There's tons of data showing that you can't grasp new information in a state of fear. I've lectured to educators about how punishment and threats actually inhibit the learning process.

Drugs and the Bodymind

Emotions are like drugs, all of which—Valium, alcohol, methamphetamine, the opiates, and marijuana—work because they use the same receptors as the internal ligands. Drugs, just like the peptides in the body, find their way to the exact keyhole on a cell's surface in order to bind. For marijuana, the chemical cannabinoid fits into the marijuana receptor. And our own internal version, endocannabinoid, is the only substance made in the body that can fit that receptor, too.

External drugs and internal juices—both of these hum in one giant, emotionally vibratory field as they bind to receptors and make things happen. Your emotions follow the same pathways as your peptides and their receptors, and the same routes as the drugs that you're prescribed or take illegally. All three—drugs, natural ligands such as peptides, and emotions—operate through the same mechanism, which is binding at the site of the receptor.

This is important, because how you think and feel—your emotional state at any given moment—can actually impact the movement, the division, and every other activity of your cells in much the same way as your internal juices and pharmaceutical drugs do. This is a central idea of my theory of emotions, that there's a physical substrate for your feelings, just as there is for the action of drugs and their effects in your body.

Scientists have identified many types of receptors on our cells to fit internal juices that have known equivalent, external drugs, but not all of the scores of known receptors have known external matches. For example, if a plant growing in a rain forest in Brazil made people angry when they ingested it, no one would try to smuggle it into the country and sell it for recreational use. The plants that get cultivated are the ones that make us feel good.

Bodymind Identity

Just as drugs do, emotions trigger altered states of consciousness, each with different memories, behaviors, postures, and even physical processes. We can learn a lot from looking at so-called multiple personality disorder (MPD), a condition that exists when a person exhibits many personalities, each with its own identity and often physiology.

MPD is usually considered a pathological condition, but I believe that normal people like you and me have many subpersonalities, with one more dominant than the other, depending on which stimuli are influencing us. A CEO is a very different person in the boardroom than she is when she's at home playing with her toddler. But is it just the behavior that's different? It may appear so, but in the new paradigm of physiology, we see that much more is actually going on.

Psychologists and authors Drs. Hal and Sidra Stone have utilized this concept in their approach to consciousness and transformation, which they call Voice Dialogue, used to access hidden or deep parts of the personality and integrate all of them into the whole. If you've ever had the experience of speaking to your spouse or child one morning, and the next day you feel as if you're dealing with someone who seems to be a completely different person, then you know what I'm talking about.

But my point is that the accessing of different personalities is a natural expression of how the molecules of emotion are constantly coordinating our memories at the level of our physiology. To expect everyone to be the same all the time is to buy in to the myth that emotions don't matter and don't play a powerful role in who we are, affecting our very identity from moment to moment.

One way to understand how we're all multiple personalities (and that this is normal) is to think of "white" light, which is the sum of all of its visible frequencies. Light may appear white or colorless, but if you filter it through a prism, you see a rainbow of different colors. People are like that, too: We may appear to be a solid, single identity, but we're actually made up of many different states and personalities, each one coordinated by our molecules of emotion. These chemicals in our body are continually orchestrating the movement within us of different states of consciousness, moods, and memories—and even physical conditions and alterations.

Pain and Arousal

We've seen how our molecules of emotion impact memory, learning, and identity. Now let's look at how they impact our perception of pain and the state of arousal or alertness you experience. There's a structure in your brain that sets your threshold of pain—that is, how much you can tolerate a harmful stimulus—called the peri-aqueductal gray (PAG). This is loaded with endorphins, opiate receptors, and many other informational substances that are emotion modulated. Your perception of whether something hurts a lot or a little passes through this gateway and is strongly informed by your emotions.

The PAG isn't near your frontal cortex, but there *are* neurons in your frontal cortex that project down into the PAG, making it possible to have conscious control over the degree of pain or alertness that you experience. This means that you can choose how to interpret the stimuli around you. You're doing this unconsciously all the time, but you can train yourself to interpret stimuli consciously at the threshold that you choose. One way to do so is with repeated affirmations that can help you reframe certain sensations in your body and promote healing.

For example, if I worry about a little buzzing sensation in my knee, and I think, *Oh no, there's that bum knee again. It's going to give out on me someday!* then I'm projecting a negative belief on that experience. I become emotionally involved in a story about my knee, which then influences my molecules to follow my message.

On the other hand, I can respond with interest rather than fear, choosing to feel the buzzing in my knee as a sign that something is obviously moving around in there—opening, closing, and changing—and my knee wants me to stay tuned! That will send an entirely different message to my physiology through the many emotional informational substances that are communicating with my knee and connected to pain centers in my brain.

Remember, the bodymind is a vast network of communicating molecules, involving every cell, organ, and system of the organism. Pain in the knee is determined by emotions impacting molecules in your brain. In fact, any pain is really felt in the brain, which is the final common pathway.

This is useful, because if you know that your thoughts and feelings can influence your physiology for pain, you realize it is possible to decrease chronic-pain conditions, such as fibromyalgia, without drugs by using various methods that access your conscious and subconscious input. Similarly, natural-childbirth training, which can be mastered by just about any woman, transforms pain and fear into pride of accomplishment and satisfaction.

Once again, not only do different emotional states have varied capacities for learning and memory, but they also have different set points of pain and arousal, whether triggered by drugs or by our internal informational substances. The ways that you can change your pain threshold resemble the memory or learning variations that I described earlier, in that your state of mind can affect your experience of reality. Your state of healing and well-being (that is, living pain free), as well as the ability to stay asleep or be alert, will change depending on your emotional state. "Change your mind and change your pain" would be a more helpful aphorism to have in the vernacular than "No pain, no gain."

All of this demonstrates again how emotions are the key to consciousness, determining from minute to minute what you experience, what you feel, and even who you are.

You Create Your Own Reality

Back in the '70s and '80s, whenever our laboratory at the NIMH mapped endorphin receptors, we always found them rich in areas that process *incoming* sensory information, such as sight, sound, smell, taste, or touch, We saw this clearly in the so-called dorsal horn on the back of the spinal cord, where "touchy-feely" kinds of information enter the nervous system from the body. Receptors for endorphins and other neuropeptides (such as bombesin, VIP, insulin, and others) are all confined to a stunning narrow stripe on visualization.

These neuropeptide receptors are never found in the ventral horn, which is the motor part of the spinal cord that directs movement. This is the same in other sensory pathways to the brain, not just for the sense of touch carried in the cord. Wherever the nerves first enter the brain, carrying sensory information about sight, sound, and the like, are sites that are always heavily encrusted with the receptor molecules of emotion.

Different senses have pathways with varying degrees of filtering of information. Vision is very highly refined, traveling six synapses from the time light first strikes your retina, travels to the occipital lobe at back of your brain, and then hits four more way stations before reaching consciousness in the frontal cortex. By contrast, smell only takes one synapse before it hits deep within your amygdala, and then is relayed to your higher brain.

Remember, those molecules along the sensory stopping points are storage sites for memory—but of what? Well, they're recollections of every perception that you've ever had, from your earliest consciousness of bliss at your mother's breast to the emotional upset you had after a fight with your boss the other day. They're all stored at the site of the receptors, which are the most densely populated where information is coming *in,* not going *out.*

In other words, your experience of so-called reality is filtered through your memories, giving your experience a spin, adding meaning, and even making part of each situation go or stay unconscious, as in the case of a core emotional trauma, if the event is too painful to remember.

We're constantly resonating with what we already know to be true. Everything that you feel is filtered along a gradient of past experience and memory that's stored in your receptors—there isn't any absolute or external reality! What you experience as reality is *your* story of what happened.

This has huge implications for healing traumas from the past. Even if you had a perfect childhood, I'm pretty sure that if you went to junior high school, you endured emotional pain. We tend to underestimate and even deny that we're all damaged in some way, just as we refuse to acknowledge that we all have multiple personalities. But experiences in childhood and even adolescence leave scars that affect every aspect of our lives. It's interesting that the word *trauma* refers to both psychic and physical damage. When this anguish is fully processed, constant bliss is a possibility.

Frontal Cortex and Bliss

I want to introduce you to your frontal cortex, the part of your brain that's key in understanding how reality is created. This structure is behind the forehead, and it's what makes us distinct from the apes. Our DNA is 99.4 percent the same as chimpanzees', our closest relatives, but chimps barely have a frontal cortex. That 0.6 percent difference must have a lot to do with frontal-cortex development, and it's this part of the brain that makes us human.

What does the frontal cortex do? Think of it as the "executive level" of consciousness, where you plan for the future and also where you can choose to direct your attention. Just how important these two capacities are is shown by the results of hundreds of neuropsychology experiments conducted on brain-damaged subjects who were asked to sort cards. A normal person can easily change the criteria by which they sort, due to a capacity for *selective attention,* an ability to consciously shift focus to something else at any given moment. But if you have damage in your frontal cortex, you can't pay attention selectively, and you can't truly choose.

I want to revisit those sensory way stations for a moment and show you another aspect of the frontal cortex: how incoming sensory information is filtered along synapses loaded with opiate receptors. In 1981, I published a paper in *Science* magazine with Mort Mishkin and Agu Pert (my husband at the time) entitled: "Opiate Receptor Gradients in Monkey Cerebral Cortex: Correspondence with Sensory Processing Hierarchies." In this paper, we reported how more opiate receptors are found in the frontal cortex than in any other part of the brain or body, and how we found an increasing gradient along the sensory way stations in the cerebral cortex of monkeys. The experiments were done in monkeys who'd already been well studied to determine the information-processing going on at each synapse. In the animals, we were able to carefully map the opiate-receptor density.

Our data showed that as you travel up from the back of the brain (where the occipital cortex first receives sight) to the frontal cortex, you find, as you progress forward and upward, that there are more and more opiate receptors—exponentially more as you move up to the frontal cortex. As I've mentioned, the frontal cortex is the place in the brain where we make choices and plan for the future, and what we saw in the lab was that those pathways are increasingly mediated by the molecules of bliss, the endorphins and their opiate receptors.

This increasing gradient of pleasure and bliss was apparent whether we were looking at hearing or vision. Both sensory pathways increased in opiate receptors as information moved toward the front of the brain. I interpret this finding to mean that pleasure and bliss increasingly influence our criterion of choice as incoming information climbs higher and higher up the sensory way stations. In other words, we make moment-to-moment choices about what to pay attention to and what to plan for in the future, based on the pleasure that we get from our choices. No pleasure? Well, then we aren't very likely to choose it. Without a frontal cortex, we'd be like simpler animals, who have no capacity to choose other than to react to or avoid potential pain and death.

But because we have a frontal cortex—that very important .6 percent of DNA difference from the chimps—and it's loaded with opiate receptors and endorphins, we can experience the higher-consciousness states of bliss and love, what the mystics call "union with the divine." Our biology actually makes this possible!

Unity: This is our spiritual/biological heritage as humans. Animals don't *have* a seventh chakra, no mystical third eye or crown connecting them to something beyond—at least my chocolate Labrador retriever, Tory, hasn't indicated that to me yet!

Humans *do,* and the potential for higher consciousness is built right into our anatomy. Beyond just feeling *good,* we can feel *God,* and from that state of bliss and union, we have the capacity to create a future for ourselves . . . and for our planet.

Manifestation of Your Desires

Attention is important for creating reality, especially when combined with intention. In fact, manifestation, the skill of imagining what you want and making your dreams come true, can be learned. I've understood from mystics and teachings from Eastern sages that such things are possible, and in fact, I've learned to meditate with the intention of removing obstacles to the further manifestation of Peptide T in the world. By focusing attention on a mantra or on breathing, a state of quiet and calm alertness can be achieved. Interestingly, the frontal cortex receives input from neuronal fibers sprouting from a tiny cluster of cells at the base of the brain that make norepinephrine, the brain's own amphetamine.

I've theorized for some time that the frontal cortex strengthens and even enlarges from frequent meditation, just like a muscle in the body gets pumped up from weight training. This has been proven to be true in experiments showing a resulting thickened layer of cells in this part of the brain, performed by Dr. Richard Davidson, director of the Laboratory for Affective Neuroscience at the University of Wisconsin, in collaboration with the Dalai Lama!

The Blame Game

Let's revisit how we create our own reality. You've seen how we filter our incoming sensations and then interpret them along a gradient of pleasure and pain, and how the periacqueductal gray works to set thresholds of pain and arousal. Now I'm going to put it all together to show you the effect on our everyday experience and behavior.

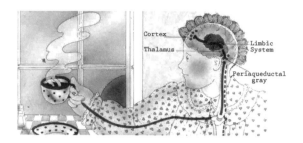

The lady shown in this image has just woken up, and she's groggy, not yet fully awake and alert. She's reaching for a cup of coffee, and within a few seconds, she's going to find out that the cup is hotter than expected, and drop it. At that moment, a sensation enters her bodymind through a sensory pathway connecting her hand to her spinal cord: *Hot!* She reacts on reflex via a local circuit in the spinal cord. But perhaps the sensation travels farther, going up her spinal cord to the area of her brain known as the periacqueductal gray. At that point, our morning-coffee drinker becomes more aroused and wonders what's going on. She's fully awake by the time the painful sensation travels all the way up to her frontal cortex.

It's then, and only then . . . *I pause dramatically until the audience leans forward in suspense, and then continue* . . . that she can blame her husband! *As usual, my audience explodes with laughter, their lesson in neuroanatomy suddenly turning comical!*

Yes, it's funny how we all make up stories to describe so-called reality when incoming information hits our higher brain. And of course, we all get to create our own version of what's going on! But this is so important, this ability to either blame others or take responsibility for our actions, which are both decisions made at the level of the frontal cortex. Perhaps if the groggy lady had splashed her face with cold water before reaching for her morning coffee, she wouldn't have gotten burned!

Blame and responsibility are actually two sides of the same coin, both representing an advanced stage of consciousness that we humans are privileged to experience. I don't see my dog or even other primates complaining about being a victim, nor do I see them apologizing or forgiving others for what they may have somehow played a part in causing.

The Future

If we're so powerful, I also wonder what we want to create for this human existence, this planet of six billion people hurtling through space? It really is the next question to ponder, so I want to conclude my remarks with some speculation about what the future holds, especially the future of medicine.

I think that there will be more and more emphasis on wellness rather than disease. The health that I'm predicting we'll see more of is *psychosomatic* well-being, involving not just the physical body, but the mental, emotional, and spiritual self as expressed in the corporeal.

We can't afford to keep leaving out these aspects of the human experience in treating illness. Energy medicine and psychology, along with forms of chiropractic that treat emotional as well as physical release and alignment, will become more and more popular, as the science explaining the mechanisms of these approaches comes to light. I'm confident that the medicine of the future will include the whole picture: body, mind, and spirit, with a special emphasis on alleviating stress, which is often the result of emotional overload.

Q & A Interaction

My lecture done, I bowed and thanked my audience for their kind attention, and they erupted with a standing ovation, a response that always leaves me feeling uncomfortable. As usual, my mind started to run over what I could have done better. I smiled and invited a few questions, leading into a lively interaction with a handful of people. . . .

Do Drugs Cause More Harm Than Good?

"Let's hear from the woman who's sitting in the very back," I declared. "Yes, you! Please, what's your question?" The woman, who was now standing, didn't smile as she took the microphone.

"You're a pharmacologist—a drug doctor—right?" she began, her tone sounding irritated and belligerent. "Well, I've been reading a book that says that all prescription and nonprescription drugs are toxic and are actually causing illness and disease."

She held up a copy of the book that I was aware had been topping the bestseller charts lately, a work that had been self-promoted by the author to target the growing number of people seeking alternatives to drugs and surgery. "Please tell us if it's true that the drug companies don't mind killing us so that they can make huge profits."

I handled this borderline heckler as best I could. "Thank you for your question. Yes, there certainly is confusion and growing concern about prescription drugs and their side effects. We read almost daily about how drugs are now being pulled off the market because of lethal side effects, or marked with new 'caution' labeling for things that were somehow missed during clinical trials. This is a positive sign that the FDA is finally waking up.

"But as far as the pharmaceutical industry putting profits before safety—hey, you're asking me to talk trash about my colleagues and former students who are working hard to invent new and better drugs." The audience tittered nervously.

I continued, "The problem is that more and more, drugs are used to treat conditions better approached through diet and lifestyle. Pills and potions aren't the *only* answer, and I'm a proponent of the less the better. But when you need a life-saving antibiotic or a titanium implant for a shattered wrist, be thankful that modern medicine has developed them, in spite of all the shenanigans.

"A recently published study in *The New England Journal of Medicine* reports that a new generation of antipsychotic drugs are three to ten times more expensive than the older options, yet they're no more effective in treating schizophrenia. No one would even know about this, except that the NIMH spent more than ten million dollars over seven years to get impartial data on this important subject. Incidentally, before antipsychotic drugs were invented, schizophrenics often spent their lives in quite unpleasant mental institutions; drugs allow them to become functional and return to their lives.

"Make no mistake," I said, "prescription drugs can save and improve lives, so we don't want to throw the baby out with the filthy bathwater. Clinical depression, for example, is a potentially fatal disease because suicide is no joke." My eyes filled with tears as I thought about my little sister, gone these seven years. I regained my composure, glanced at my watch, and decided there was no time to discuss the shortcomings of the new antidepressants. . . .

I thought back to how I'd had a short and unsettling career as an expert witness for a famous trial lawyer who'd focused entirely on the so-called SSRI drugs, the selective serotonin reuptake inhibitors, such as Prozac. This new generation of Prozac-like antidepressants were not only more expensive than the older ones, but also were now being grossly overprescribed for everything from anorexia to shyness for adults—and even children. This came about when the drugs were no longer prescribed only by psychiatrists trained in observing, identifying, and treating mental illness, but were being handed out by any medical doctor.

During my stint as a witness, I'd become convinced by the scientific published papers that I read under the trial lawyer's tutelage that there was compelling—in fact, clear and overwhelming—evidence that the SSRIs could cause violent behavior. I was horrified to read about cases of suicide and even murder, particularly at the beginning of treatment or during a withdrawal phase in a small percentage of patients receiving the drugs.

Something else became clear to me, which is that the old tricyclic antidepressants, while probably more effective at reversing depression than the new ones, were thousands of times more toxic. Thus, if someone tried to commit suicide using their prescribed pills (a common decision among depressed female patients), they'd be much more likely to succeed with the older drugs than with the new ones.

If anything, studies of SSRIs that only looked at "successful" suicides severely underestimated the number of *attempted* suicides, so the problem was even worse than it appeared on paper. After the lawyer lost a big jury trial in which I'd testified, one of a tiny percentage not settled out of court, I was so filled with despair at this nightmarish experience that I exited the "expert-witness" business, pronto.

Can We Protect Ourselves from Cancer?

Refocusing on the task at hand, I scanned the audience and quickly spotted a clean-cut, well-dressed young man sitting in one of the front rows.

"My questions are about cancer," he began. "It seems as if there's so much more lately—what's going on? Is there really scientific evidence that dietary change can protect us? Can negative emotions or wrong thinking really cause cancer? And those stem cells moving out of the bone marrow and spreading to brain really sound like a tumor metastasizing, so—"

"These are all important questions," I interrupted, "because cancer is on everybody's mind. While there are definitely some genetic forms of the disease that are very well studied at the NIH, most types have environmental causes. Cigarette smoking causes lung cancer, for example, although clean-living nonsmokers still do get some forms of this illness. There are lies, damn lies, and statistics, all of which have been used to suggest that cancer rates are decreasing, although it's very clear that we have an epidemic on our hands, and it's *not* because people are living longer.

"Can what you eat protect you? Probably not, unless you also attend to your bodymind's toxic load that comes from chemically tainted foods, industrial pollutants, and even excess prescription drugs in our modern industrialized country today. Can food choices *help?* Yes, you should eat plenty of pesticide-free raw fruits and vegetables brimming with enzymes, antioxidants, vitamins, and minerals, but be aware that the data behind cancer as a disease of *environmental* pollution is overwhelming. Most pollutants are fat soluble, so fatty meats may be unhealthy because of the toxins dissolved in them.

"Did you know that everyone has cancer? Right now, as you're sitting in your chair, tiny cancer cells are running amok in your body, multiplying into minitumors because of errant DNA messages they may have evolved. But because you have a healthy immune system, natural killer cells swarm in to attack and kill those runaway cells, preventing them from forming tumors and traveling throughout your body. However, when there's an overabundance of toxic residue for the immune system to clean up, it may fail to do its job, leaving unpoliced cancer cells to escape under the radar, proliferate, and become full-blown, metastasizing tumors.

"My lab work showed many years ago that peptide molecules of emotion can direct the trafficking of tumor cells. The data shows that tumor progression—or regression—can be highly affected by attitude, but it's absurd New Age fascism to *blame* people's thought patterns for their cancer! And let me close on an upbeat note—the newest, most promising cancer drugs are directed at cell-surface receptors."

How Can I Feel Good?

I asked for one more question. A tired-looking man took the microphone and began cautiously: "This is all very interesting, Dr. Pert, and I'm grateful for the science you've done and brought to us here today," he paused. "But my question is a simple one: What good is it all to just help us *feel good?*"

I looked down in thought, pursing my lips and pondering extra carefully. "I'm glad you asked me that," I finally said, as the silence reached the limits of comfort. "I've been thinking a lot about the answer to that question lately, and I want you to know that I'm working on an answer." We all took a deep breath.

"Feeling good is a subjective and personal state, and having used myself as a human laboratory over the years, my answer will include what I've learned from my own experience, of course. But I also promise that the information is going to be true to the scientific literature where it exists.

"So . . ." Everyone leaned forward expectantly. "I can tell you that . . ." I paused even more dramatically, gave a puckish grin, and continued. "I'll get back to you in my next book!" People laughed at my joke, told at their expense, and wanted to hear more.

"Okay, for the time being, until the book comes out, if you want to feel good, I can tell you this: *Just love.* Love yourself and your family, and seek to create caring bonds in your community. We're all connected, which is our true spiritual heritage. When we're closely connected with each other, we're living as we were designed to do—biologically, psychologically, and spiritually—and that's when we all will truly feel good."

PART II

ADVENTURES IN CONSCIOUSNESS-LAND

Chapter 4

Tucson: Toxicity, Mood, and Food

I both love and loathe the postlecture book-signing ritual. I enjoy meeting my fans, the men and women who come to my talks, because they're exploring and finding solutions from which we can all benefit. But I'm uncomfortable when people expect me to give them the key for eliminating whatever health concerns they have. The truth is that while I may have access to cutting-edge biomedical research, I'm just like them, searching for answers that aren't readily or easily available through conventional, mainstream medicine.

When I'm asked a question that I can't answer, I make a note. And when I get back home, I search the literature—for myself as much as for my audiences—and then mention what I found in my next lecture. Sometimes new information from my public sends me down a trail where I discover material that impacts me personally and helps me transform some aspect of my life. At the book signing following my Tucson lecture, meeting Cori Brackett was one of those pivotal opportunities.

A Transformational Encounter

The book signing began with the usual throng pressing forward, a lineup of people with my first book or my new CD in hand. One woman described her son's battle with drug addiction and thanked me for my research in that area, telling me how it had helped her family. A confident young man pushed his business card toward me, inviting me to deliver a lecture for his organization. Another person wanted me to try a particular kind of food supplement (I don't remember which one).

The line was winding down when I heard a chorus of voices coming from the rear. "Go ahead, Cori, tell Candace! Tell her about your film!" Then a timid young woman approached the table, urged on by a group of friends who stood behind her.

"Thank you so much, Dr. Pert," she began haltingly. "My name is Cori Brackett, and I'm a great fan of yours." Her voice grew soft. "I've made a film . . ." She fumbled in her bag. "It's about a food additive we're all eating that's poisoning millions of people, and I want everyone to know . . ."

Cori told me the story of how she'd gradually lost all mobility in her limbs over a few months' time and had become confined to a wheelchair. Her diagnosis was a fast-moving form of multiple sclerosis, which didn't seem right to her. Acting on instinct, she gave up her habit of two to three cans a day of diet soda and abruptly began to improve. Convinced that she'd been suffering from the side effects of aspartame (an artificial sweetener marketed as Nutrasweet or Equal), Cori and her husband made a film entitled *Sweet Misery,* based on interviews and research they'd done on the toxicity of this substance.

For years, people had been telling me about aspartame's dangerous side effects, but I hadn't believed their claims. Now, someone who said she'd been personally damaged was standing right in front of me, and I was determined to find out the truth. I eagerly took the DVD that Cori handed me and tucked it into my bag, planning to share it with Nancy later when we returned to our hosts' house for the night.

Food and Mood vs. Drugs and Surgery

After the lecture, my hosts, Drs. Joan Norton and Nicholas Tivoli, who are husband and wife and the owners of a highly successful healing and bodywork practice called At-Ease Wellness Center, drove Nancy and me back to their house. We chatted and got the tour of their gorgeous home, located high in the hills above Tucson, before they turned in for the night.

Nancy and I caught our second wind, energized by the prospect of writing the book and brimming with ideas. We agreed to watch the DVD that I'd gotten at the book signing, after the "chiros," as we affectionately called our hosts, pointed us toward their outdoor hot tub and then went off to bed.

It felt good to soak in the hot water, unwinding from the hectic day of travel and work. The city lights twinkled and spread out below the hills, and a gentle wind picked up from the desert floor.

"Didn't that last question say it all?" I asked Nancy, breaking the silence and referring back to the Q & A that ended my lecture. "He wanted to know what use all this science was, if it didn't help people feel good—right?" Nancy nodded.

I continued. "Everyone's so in the dark when it comes to feeling good, whether it involves chronic illness, pain, aging, depression, or just flat-out stress. In fact, *stress* is the new medical word for *feeling lousy,* and reducing it is the new holy grail, what everyone wants. People know that they don't feel good, and they're not getting answers about how to feel better from their conventional medical doctors."

"There's no question that conventional medicine isn't addressing how we feel," Nancy responded. "Fifty million dollars get spent on health care, and yet so many baby boomers I know in California have all but given up on medical doctors. Instead, we go to chiropractors, acupuncturists, naturopaths, and energy healers to help us feel better."

"Yes, but in the rest of the country," I countered, "people are taking their chronic conditions, aches, and pains to their medical doctors, and getting the standard treatments: drugs and surgery. Joints hurt? Get 'em replaced. Back hurts? Take a drug. Then, when the pills fail, you get sent to the surgeon. The traditional physician doesn't talk about the toxic burden that most of us carry in our bodies, the emotional roots of trauma and stress, or how the food we eat can lead to dangerous inflammation. All of these are causes for people not feeling good and getting sick that aren't adequately addressed by the mainstream. Food and mood—these are left out of the equation, replaced by drugs and surgery."

"Sounds like we're writing the book," Nancy interjected.

"You bet we are," I said, starting to get excited. "But don't bring the tape recorder into the hot tub." We both chuckled. "I want to tell people how the paradigm of the bodymind points to new causes of disease, and about how the many alternative therapies work to bring about deeper levels of healing than conventional medicine has come up with so far. God knows, I've experienced enough of those therapies myself, firsthand. When I point the way, people are going to benefit not just from my scientific knowledge, but from my personal experience as well."

"Not exactly what they're going to get from their medical doctor," Nancy quipped. And with that, we both slipped deeper into the soothing hot water and enjoyed the silence of the starry night, relaxing fully and letting our overstimulated minds take a rest.

After we went back inside the house, we put on our pajamas and settled down in front of the TV like two teenagers at a slumber party. I popped in *Sweet Misery: A Poisoned World,* and we began to watch the DVD. Our time in the hot tub had us feeling very cozy and relaxed, open to being entertained and informed in the comfortable home of our hosts . . . but that feeling faded abruptly.

Sweet Poison

For the next hour and a half, we watched in horror and disbelief as Cori's story unfolded, telling how the artificial sweetener aspartame has poisoned millions of people in the 20 years since it's been on the market, crippling many (like Cori herself) and even killing.

One of those people could have been me. I'd always felt good about drinking diet colas, knowing that I was cutting calories by avoiding the sugar in other soft drinks. It was like getting something for free, and while I didn't consume a lot, it had become my favorite social drink—something to hold at cocktail parties, since I rarely chose alcohol. I never imagined that it could literally be pickling my liver, putting me at risk for brain cancer, and possibly giving me wild mood swings.

It turns out that my nonalcoholic drink of choice is highly toxic, filled with substances that turn to alcohol in my body. And not the pleasant kind that gives you a buzz, which is ethyl alcohol, but the kind drunks die or go blind from: methyl alcohol, more commonly known as wood alcohol.

Aspartame, marketed as Nutrasweet, Equal, and Spoonful (in the UK), is a peptide consisting of two amino acids, phenylalanine and aspartic acid, both normally supplied by the protein-rich foods we eat. I'd been mentioning this substance in my talks for years as an example of a very short peptide, without realizing how much data was out there showing how dangerous it is.

Aspartic acid and phenylalanine occur naturally in foods that we eat in small quantities. Both of these amino acids are known excitotoxins, which can cause neurons to become overexcited to the point of burnout and death. Monosodium glutamate (MSG), another legal food additive, also falls into this category.

Another neurological link is that both peptides are involved in neurotransmitter function. Phenylalanine is the building block of norepinephrine, which increases in the brain when you take aspartame into your body. This can throw off the ratio of norepinephrine to serotonin, another neurotransmitter that regulates mood.

The impact of all this unbalancing in neurotransmitter ratios can be panic symptoms; mood disorders; and for some people, altered seizure thresholds, leading to convulsions. Drs. Dick and Judy Wurtman at MIT, whose pioneering scientific work in this area is considered impeccable, have proven convincingly that food has an impact on mood.

As if this weren't enough, attached to the end of the aspartic acid and phenylalanine is a third component, a methyl-ester group that breaks off easily to become methanol in the body.

Methanol is also a naturally occurring substance found in foods that you and I consume. But the key word again is *food*, because when you eat an apple, for example, methanol is carried through your body by the natural apple fiber (known as "pectin") and easily eliminated. Alone, methanol is wood alcohol, a known poison, which causes blindness in those desperate enough to drink it.

And it gets worse: Methanol is broken down in the liver to produce an even more toxic substance, formaldehyde. This is known to most people as the fluid used by undertakers to embalm corpses, and it's definitely not the pickled state that you want to be in. According to the authoritative *Merck Manual,* formaldehyde has been listed as a carcinogen by the EPA, and the reference book clearly states that ingestion of this substance in large doses can cause death.

As a research scientist, I'm familiar with the use of formaldehyde to sacrifice mice and rats in order to get good-quality tissue for viewing under a microscope. Referred to as "fixing," the process involves chemically freezing the tissue as the formaldehyde goes into smaller and smaller blood vessels, making tissue easier to put on a slide.

Sweet Misery went on with astounding but increasingly plausible information about how rashes, terrible headaches, and over 40 other symptoms could be traced to aspartame use. I was in shock, thinking about how the generation of formaldehyde alone could cause all kinds of problems.

Even more alarming, we learned that the National Cancer Institute reported an increase in rates of brain cancer since 1985, very possibly linked to aspartame use. In 1983, the U. S. population began ingesting significant quantities of this artificial sweetener, at that time a substance never before used for human consumption. In 1984, 6.9 million pounds of aspartame were consumed by Americans, an amount that doubled the next year and continued to climb into the 2000s.

Two years after aspartame was introduced, the brain tumor rate jumped 10 percent in the U.S., while incidents of brain lymphoma, an aggressive and unusual type of tumor, jumped 60 percent. This huge increase wasn't due to innovative scanning and diagnostic procedures, as some claimed; other forms of cancer remained the same during that time period.

How in God's name did the FDA, the country's largest watchdog agency for protecting consumers in their food and drug choices, let this slip by?

The story of how aspartame got approval by the FDA has some scary political undertones. For 16 years, the laboratory that produced the food additive, G. D. Searle and Co., had petitioned the FDA for approval, but they failed to show that it was safe, and no FDA commissioner would approve it. Then, just days after President Reagan's inauguration in 1981, a new FDA commissioner was appointed and given the authority to ignore a law that said food additives must test conclusively for safety in order to receive approval.

Politics, economics, and special interests at play? Perhaps. But aspartame was in under the door, and Nutrasweet, the best-known product containing aspartame, came on the market. According to the FDA, aspartame is the most complained-about substance in their history, with over 10,000 official complaints reporting a range of side effects, including neurological ones.

Sweet Misery ended on a poignant and disturbing note with an interview of a woman held in a federal prison. Diane Fleming is serving a 50-year prison sentence in Virginia for poisoning her husband, who died of cardiac arrest after exercising vigorously in hot weather and drinking large quantities of an aspartame-laced sport drink.

In the interview, this tearful, sympathetic woman described how an attending physician suspected poisoning, and upon doing the autopsy, found the body full of formaldehyde that had literally pickled the internal organs. At the trial, the defense incorrectly stated that such a condition could only be explained by someone slipping a methanol-containing product, such as windshield-wiper fluid, into the poor man's drink. The most likely suspect was his wife, whom the jury found guilty, condemning her to a lifetime in prison, where she is today.

The credits rolled and I clicked off the DVD player. Nancy and I sat in front of the darkened screen, stunned and speechless. Finally, I turned to Nancy and said, "Do you think she murdered her husband? My guess is *no way!*"

"I agree!" Nancy exclaimed. "Plus, she had no motive. Her husband had been drinking large quantities of diet soda for years, and on the day he died, he was chugging that diet-drink poison instead of water."

"God . . . if one person can die of an overdose, then all the toxic side effects are plausible," I said. "I hadn't realized that there's a methanol-generating side chain on the end of aspartame!" I mentally vowed to check out the scientific facts as soon as I got back to Washington, already regretting that in my lectures I'd often used aspartame as an example of a simple dipeptide.

Sweet Update

Returning home from Tucson, the book proposal wrapped and ready to go out to the publisher, I went straight to the Georgetown University medical school library where I checked literature, did a thorough Internet search, and also talked with my colleagues.

Cori Brackett had done her homework, and what I found backed her up in spades.

Aspartame is used in over 9,000 commercial food and beverage products, which continue to be on the market. Diet sodas alone are growing in worldwide sales at 6 percent a year—a $1-billion-a-year market—while other soda sales are declining at a rate of 2 percent, according to a 2005 *Los Angeles Times* article.

But I found that it wasn't so easy to teach people about aspartame's dangers, as I took on the task of warning my friends and colleagues. At social occasions, my peers scoffed when I commented on their choice of diet drink and continued to guzzle their poison with complete disregard of the research that's been done, some of it right in their own backyards.

My local drug-store pharmacist, however, was easy to convince. When I saw him sipping a huge bottle of diet soda and told him that the stuff had been linked to intraocular bleeding, he chucked the drink into the wastebasket, vowing to never touch it again. He explained to me that he'd had several episodes of unexplained eye bleeding in the last few years, which is a symptom linked to aspartame use.

As a pharmacologist, I know that the dosage of a drug is a determining factor for toxicity—the higher the dose, the higher the chance of toxic effect. But another factor, the *potency,* contributes to the dosage. Some drugs are so potent that only small doses are needed, such as the opiate etorphine, which is used in tranquilizer guns to stop a 900-pound charging rhinoceros in its tracks.

Nutrasweet, I found out, isn't very potent, so large quantities are required to bring about its sweet effect. One can of soda contains an amount of aspartame that would fill half the center of my cupped hand—that's an awful lot of methanol and formaldehyde for the body to deal with, just to avoid the 17 calories in a teaspoon of sugar. My own review of the literature supports a policy of zero tolerance, regardless of studies claiming to show acceptable levels for daily intake.

Becoming Radical

To say that I was disturbed by what I found in my search is an understatement. If all of this were true—and to the best of my knowledge, it is—then we've all been horribly misled, even damaged by the politics involving the FDA, an agency whose purpose is to protect us consumers. *What other harmful things are out there?* I wondered. *What else has slipped by?*

I was caught in a familiar dilemma: not wanting to knock conventional medicine, but pulled by the sheer weight of so much that's dangerous or just plain wrong to tell all I know. In my first book, I defended many alternative and complementary therapies. I know so much more now, having learned from my audiences and also having checked out what they told me from the viewpoint of a critical scientist. The aspartame fiasco scared the heck out of me and personally impacted me and people I cared for, causing me to rethink my position and take a far more radical stand on the matter. Was it time for me to really come out, to blow the whistle based on what I knew as an insider?

At the same time, I wanted to carefully walk the line, not maligning efforts that have saved lives and afforded us all a better quality of life. Certainly, conventional medicine should not give up doing what it does best. My titanium wrist, reconstructed after a bone-shattering ski accident a few years back, is just one reminder of how I've benefited from conventional medicine; and I'm grateful every day for the full, painless use of my left hand.

Let me be very clear: There's nothing "bad" about conventional medicine, and I'm not attacking it. I am, however, pointing to the narrow range of solutions that it offers, and suggesting that we look outside the box. To do so will require an openness to new possibilities for exploration.

And to give credit where it's due, the mainstream has been coming around (if slowly) to a more holistic view, with some doctors prescribing stress reduction and even delivering acupuncture.

Recently, I bumped into a former colleague, who heads up a prestigious psychiatry department in Boston, a position that to me epitomizes the establishment viewpoint and its limitations. He surprised me when he told me that he'd tried to stop aspartame from coming on the market years ago, testifying and even filing a legal brief. He'd been involved in research showing that aspartame was an excitotoxin that can kill brain cells. He sounded every bit as radicalized about it as I'd become, and quite angry that his testimony had been disregarded.

Mainstream's Answer: Drugs and Surgery

Back in my office at Georgetown, as I prepared talks and worked on my own scientific papers, I continued to think about how mainstream medicine was insufficient to treat so much chronic disease. A full 80 percent of doctor-patient visits today are for conditions that mainstream medicine has no cure for—chronic pain, diabetes, multiple sclerosis (MS), Alzheimer's disease, heart disease, and even cancer. The track record is pretty miserable, showing that for all the time and money that's invested, we've failed to make any significant advances to date.

My sister Deane Beebe, who heads up publicity for a Medicare advocacy organization in New York City, often talks to me about the turmoil in the mainstream medical system today. Recently, she mentioned a family friend, a woman who'd had corrective surgery for her long-term spinal sclerosis. Six years later, the woman experienced discomfort and was advised to have a surgical "tune-up," which she did—and almost died from complications. Why, I wondered, did conventional medicine offer this woman no alternative other than an operation and drugs?

Even in cases where surgery *is* recommended, the evidence leading to the decision isn't always scientific. A Harvard study reported in *The New England Journal of Medicine* showed that in a group of 100 people *without* back pain, almost two-thirds had spinal bulges, protrusions, or extrusions visible on an MRI. These are the same findings that were used to refer people for surgery who came into their doctors' offices *with* back pain. High-tech, very expensive MRIs have all but replaced the common x-ray, but are they causing doctors to rush patients in for surgery who may not even need it?

Chronic-pain complaints comprise 70 percent of doctors' office visits, with back pain being by far the most common. But recent brain-scan studies show that chronic pain is associated with abnormalities of the frontal cortex, the area involved in making interpretations and decisions about incoming sensations.

Agu Pert, my first husband, showed that incoming sensation is filtered heavily by endorphins and other molecules of emotion at the peri-acqueductal grey (PAG), a structure in the brain where pain is first perceived. Moving into higher regions of the brain, discomfort is further filtered; and if it's strong enough, it arrives in the foremost area of the brain, the frontal cortex. There, a decision about the severity of the sensation is made, impacting the degree of suffering that a person experiences. In other words, pain is highly influenced by emotion and interpretation, a fact that points to possible avenues for therapy other than surgery.

But treating the emotional causes of chronic pain is still very much on the outskirts of conventional medicine. An exception is Dr. John Sarno, a New York City physician and author who's had a high rate of success treating patients by addressing emotional conflict as the root of their back pain. And even though it's been shown that an operation on the back is usually not helpful in alleviating suffering in the long term, it remains the method of choice by the mainstream.

Depression and Childhood Trauma

While mainstream's answer to chronic pain is predominantly surgery, the answer for long-term depression is often talk therapy and drugs. But this condition may also have emotional roots, stemming from early-childhood traumas that are forgotten and kept below awareness in the subconscious mind, which I believe to be the body.

Dr. Charles Nemeroff, a psychiatrist at Emory University in Atlanta, worked with severely depressed patients and found that two-thirds of them had experienced traumatic events in their childhood. The top three predictors of depression were: parents who divorced before the child was 15, parents who were substance abusers, and childhood sexual abuse. (I was skeptical when I first heard this. But in reviewing the data, I learned that over half a million children are sexually abused each year, and more often than not, this is related to drugs. I think we've vastly underestimated the effect of substance abuse on our emotional health, and the traumatic impact it has on small children in a family.)

Dr. Nemeroff did an experiment with medical students to prove his point. The subjects filled out a lengthy questionnaire to determine which, if any, of the three conditions of early abuse existed for them. The doctor then took a baseline cortisol sample from their blood.

Cortisol is a stress hormone secreted by the adrenal glands. Its release is stimulated by a peptide called CRF (cortisol-releasing factor) that's made in the hypothalamus, a structure in the brain close to the pituitary gland. Many have called CRF the *real* stress hormone, and it functions not just as a pituitary-releasing factor, but also in neurons throughout the brain—even the frontal cortex—as well as in immune cells and the nerves that connect them.

After blood samples were taken, the subjects were asked to ad-lib a ten minute talk in front of three mean-looking judges, a potentially high-stress task for any medical student. Next, Dr. Nemeroff asked the same individuals to do quick math computations in their heads, telling them that no medical student in the study had ever made an error. Predictably, all of the subjects' cortisol levels shot up, but those with the highest cortisol response were the ones whose biographical information showed one or more of the early-trauma predictors for depression.

This study shows that early trauma predisposes a person to depression, and is supported by biochemistry that produces a long-lasting effect. If serious injury from an early time in a someone's past isn't treated, that person is less likely to recover from depression and must depend on drugs for treatment. A recent study shows that people who are depressed have a ten times greater chance of having a heart attack, underscoring just how important it is for these individuals to seek treatment for unresolved childhood issues.

The trauma-depression relationship is clear, but conventional therapies to heal this root cause don't include approaches that access the subconscious mind in the body. We know from the new-paradigm physiology that emotional memory is stored at the level of the cellular receptor and distributed throughout the physical self, not just the brain. Talk therapy addresses mental aspects of depression but ignores the physical reality of the disease, and therefore treats only half of the picture.

Also, as mind-body researcher and consultant David Lee has pointed out, some severe trauma is stored in old "reptilian" parts of the brain, where stereotyped, repetitive behaviors are mediated. These areas are prespeech and prelogic, and thus require bodywork interventions (such as massage, craniosacral therapy, and chiropractic) in order to be accessed.

When talk therapy fails for depression and other mood disorders, conventional medicine gives antidepressant drugs. Interestingly enough, when chronic-pain patients don't respond to classic pain medications, they're also given antidepressants that may actually be more effective, pointing to a close relationship between pain and depression.

Stress and Depression

Stress is another area that conventional medicine, still clinging to an old paradigm, is struggling to treat. I recently joined a panel of experts on this subject in a roundtable discussion funded and published by Pfizer, a research-based, global pharmaceutical company. Rising rates of stress-related diseases, such as multiple sclerosis, psoriasis, and arthritis, are extremely well documented and reported in the corporation's publications.

The group was convened because drug companies such as Pfizer are aware that Americans are looking for stress-reduction tools other than pills. One panelist, a medical doctor who's an expert on meditation, reported that when he hung a sign in his hospital announcing stress-reduction classes, patients and professionals alike approached him, remarking, "I need that!"

While the relationship of stress to depression has been well documented, one study presented at a recent neuroscience symposium by Dr. Jeremy Coplan dramatically showed the impact of stress over time. A New York University team studied a unique group of monkeys—the bonnet macaques— in which the mother-infant bond is especially strong. Mothers in this primate group are known to suckle infants for six months, gazing into their babies' eyes for extended periods of time.

To test how increased stress on the mothers would affect their offspring, researchers divided the monkeys into three groups and varied their food availability. In one group, the mothers had full food bins kept close by for easy access. In another, the food in the bins was greatly diluted with woodchips, forcing mothers to forage extensively. In a third group, the food supply was changed unpredictably, causing low-to-high foraging conditions. In all three environments, the babies were weighed and measured throughout the study, showing that all of them had the same weight gain regardless of the availability of food and foraging requirements.

Only one of the groups showed abnormality—the one whose food supply was changed unpredictably. In that group, the monkey babies still looked and acted depressed, even years later. Pictures showed them as adolescent and adults sitting slumped over, alone and isolated in their cages. Over time, as they grew, the CRF levels in their blood stayed elevated, a condition that's found in humans who have committed suicide.

Can we apply these findings to human mothers who may be struggling to bring home a second income while scrimping on the cuddling or quality time with the kids? Very possibly. The highly motivated monkey mothers foraged for as much food as they needed in order to continue nursing their babies, as evinced by the similar weight gain of infants in all three groups. It wasn't the lack of time spent emotionally caring for their babies that caused the depressive behavior, but rather that the nurturing was erratic and unpredictable.

My heart goes out to stressed mothers who endure so much guilt due to the demands of their work. Ironically, the study of the bonnet macaques seems to indicate that a regular, predictable routine with *less* one-on-one contact is better for kids than a schedule that fluctuates between high attention and frustrating neglect. When emotional nurturing is unpredictable, it's harder on children than when that affection is available in a short, but predictable, supply. As a working mom for many years myself, I'm convinced that human children evolved naturally to spend hours each day with each other, as well as caretakers other than their moms, and I always felt quite content to leave my kids at well-run day-care centers.

Eating to Feel Good

A bodymind that's overburdened with toxins and also dealing with emotionally rooted chronic pain, stress, and depression can't possibly feel good. A third part of the equation is food and nutrition, because what we eat affects our bodymind. All three factors (toxicity, trauma/stress, and nutrition) can impact the immune system, resulting in health impairment or enhancement—that is, feeling bad or feeling good.

I believe that the whole point of good nutrition is for us to feel good. This may seem blunt, but if you eat crap, you'll feel like crap. That's what I'm calling any food that you buy today that wasn't on the market before World War II, when all farming was organic. During WWII, large chemical companies made munitions for the war, and when the fighting ended, those corporations switched over to making herbicides and pesticides, chemicals needed for mass food production. Commercialization of agriculture since the early 1950s, while fueling the baby-boomer population, has turned much of the food that you and I buy in the supermarket into a collection of chemicals.

An example of a highly processed food is the group known as "trans fats," short for trans-fatty acids, and otherwise known as "partially hydrogenated fats." These substances, which were first used in margarine, don't exist in nature, but result from a chemical treatment of fats and oils to prevent rancidity and extend the shelf life of packaged foods. It works because microbes (bacteria, fungus, and molds), which normally feast on whole, nonchemical food, can't digest trans fats. They have no taste for plastic and leave the altered food alone.

But our human bodies can't digest plastic food either! We don't have the enzymes to break down trans fats for digestion and elimination, so once they're taken in, they can only exit our bodies by clinging to dietary fiber that's excreted in bowel movements. If your diet is low in fiber, and trans fats aren't carried out of your body, they can build up inside your intestinal tract, blood vessels, and brain. A full 70 percent of your brain is composed of fat, so just think about how that buildup could make you feel!

Last Thanksgiving, I ate lightly but had the unfortunate experience of mistakenly eating food containing trans fats, after years of meticulously avoiding the stuff in my diet. I chose a small pastry that came from a gourmet grocery store in an unlabeled box, brought by a guest. I was amazed that it took me several days to recover from the bloated feeling and pain that I experienced around my liver, at the level of my midriff on my right side. However, trans fats not only impact the liver, but many studies with experimental animals suggest that they kick off the inflammatory response throughout the body as well, since they're unnatural.

Having learned my lesson, I now assume that virtually all packaged crackers, baked goods, frozen cakes and pies, and even pancake and cake mixes have trans fats in them. Even though the FDA now requires food manufacturers to list these substances on the nutrition-facts panel, you must be alert enough to eliminate them from your diet altogether. Practice the habit of carefully reading labels on all the foods you buy. It may take a while to get through the fine print, but paying careful attention to this matter is as important as buckling your seat belt to be safe on today's superhighways. And watch out for some foods that are labeled "trans-fats free," as this label is legal permission to slip small amounts into your food—not enough to exceed the allowed limit per serving size—which turns into large amounts by the time you eat the whole bag or box.

It's amazing how much better you can feel simply by eliminating boxed and processed foods that contain many other chemicals from your diet; going for quality, not quantity; and feasting on unlimited amounts of fruits and vegetables, along with freshly prepared meats, eggs, and nuts. Some say that the Roman empire declined because of the use of lead in pottery and as a lining for the aqueducts, which slowly poisoned its citizens. I fear that at some time in the far future, people will look back at our civilization and blame trans-fatty acids and other chemical food additives for its decline!

Arthritis and Inflammation: The Brain-Immune Connection

A major nutritionally related effect not treated by mainstream medicine is inflammation, which shows up in many diseases, most commonly arthritis. This condition is often attributed to the breakdown of the cartilage that cushions bones in joints throughout the body, causing pain and suffering for an estimated 21 million people in the U. S. But we know from the new paradigm of physiology that cartilage in the knees is constantly being renewed, and as a result, you may be able to avoid this illness instead of assuming that it's a normal part of aging.

Arthritis is one of the most highly medicated diseases today, but conventional medicine only treats the pain, not the condition. Recently, several prescription pain relievers used in arthritis were pulled off the market because of cardiac side effects, including Vioxx. Over-the-counter NSAIDs (nonsteroidal anti-inflammatory drugs) such as ibuprofen and Aleve interfere with healthy digestion when used over an extended period of time. We need to think about what else we can do to eliminate not only the symptom, but its source.

What is the root cause of arthritis? The pain occurs when your immune system attacks joints in response to an injury or an antigen, which is any substance that it doesn't recognize. These include chemicals in food such as trans fats, microbes, and toxins produced by microbes.

When immune cells arrive at the scene of this foreign matter, the first part of their job is to ingest it. Redness and swelling follow as waves of additional cells arrive on the scene, secreting the peptides of the so-called inflammatory cascade. The result is hot and painful swelling, or inflammation.

Some of the peptides acting in the early stages of inflammation, such as substance P, also give you a flush in your cheeks when you're embarrassed or cause you to feel hot when you're angry. Substance P is a neuropeptide that's normally found in the nerves around your joints, and is shown to play a role in the development of arthritis in experimental animals. If you cut the substance P nerve, the arthritis goes away, proving that the brain, not the joint, is running the show.

Because the body and mind are one, what you think and say impacts the state of your cells. Your spleen, every lymph node, and all floating immune cells are in close communication with the brain, whether through cellular receptor/peptide–diffusible mechanisms or via autonomic nerves that extend from the brain to the immune system.

As soon as you say, "Oh, I have a bad knee," it's as if you'd pushed the print button on your computer, dooming your mind to produce the painful symptoms over and over again. If you reframe your experience by saying: "My body is capable of healing," you're redirecting those inflammatory immune cells away from the painful joint, and the condition can cease.

If this seems far-fetched, you only need to know that it's easy for a hypnotist to raise penny-shaped welts on the arm of someone with room-temperature coins simply by suggesting that they're red hot! It's been shown in controlled studies on burn victims in emergency rooms that hypnotherapists can drastically reduce the size and degree of the damage by vividly suggesting that the injured skin feels cool, as if covered with snow, especially if the hypnotherapeutic session occurs soon after the burn.

Other mind-body interventions to help arthritis and other inflammatory conditions include stress reduction and meditation. Inflammation is a hyper, souped-up state of the immune system that can be the bodily reflection of chronic, unresolved anger. It's interesting that we speak of "angry" welts, "venting your spleen," and being "inflamed" with anger. Arthritis symptoms are tenfold more common in people with quarrelsome spouses! And forgiveness, studies show, can be helpful for reducing inflammation and healing arthritis.

There are many ways to cultivate this emotional pattern, including participating in religions such as Christianity that emphasize its power. Forgiveness can also come about through regular listening to special CDs before sleep, writing or speaking to a person you may be angry with, or studying programs that focus on the subject (for example, *A Course in Miracles*). Getting bodywork, such as massage and chiropractic, may help you get in touch with painful buried emotions to begin the forgiveness process. Any of these methods can help you release anger so that the emotion is no longer stuck and inflaming your bodymind.

My own experience with arthritis taught me that in addition to mind-body interventions, a dietary approach of raw foods and enzymatic supplements can help. I first encountered arthritis symptoms a few years ago, when my ankle, which had been previously injured years earlier in a fall, began to hurt with a vengeance during a very stressful time in my life. Soon, the ankle flared up so badly that I was using crutches, being diagnosed with arthritis, and being given prescriptions for drugs.

Within days, not able to accept a life of crippling pain and incapacity, I rebelled by hiring a naturopathic practitioner, who moved into my house for a few weeks. His specialty was diet, and he fed me wholesome dishes prepared from scratch, along with raw foods. I took supplements of bromelain on an empty stomach with lots of pure water and moved as much as I could.

Bromelain, derived from pineapple, is a potent enzyme that can eliminate the toxic buildup of food that hasn't been fully digested. In the Ayurvedic tradition, this waste is called "ama," but Western tradition doesn't recognize it, and therefore has no name for it.

After a few weeks, my symptoms disappeared, and I've had only mild recurrences, especially when my diet has veered off the path of whole, natural food.

Ama, I was taught by Western-trained and Ayurvedic physician Nancy Lonsdorf, can also be produced by rushing through a meal; eating while discussing stressful topics; or otherwise impairing digestion by watching TV, driving, or reading while having food. Straight, undigested food from overeating can also contribute to this sludgelike ama. The intestines become bloated and filled with unhealthy microbes thriving on the unprocessed waste (which is antigenic in itself), activating your immune system to continually respond, thus causing inflammation and pain. Shakes prepared from raw fruits and vegetables, I believe, can provide enough enzymes and fiber to start to rid the body of toxic waste and prevent and even reverse arthritis.

Two recently published scientific papers support a dietary approach to treating arthritis. One states that bromelain reduces knee pain and improves well-being in a dose-dependent fashion in an open study of otherwise healthy adults. Another, using a double-blind, random study, found clinically meaningful improvements with enzyme treatments on an unchanged diet. It isn't always easy to find controlled studies in journals on relevant topics like this. Good research is expensive, and frequently only limited government funds are available.

Controlling inflammation is crucial—and doable—in the new-paradigm physiology. It's my belief that what we call "normal" aging is really abnormal inflammation, such as arthritis, and is due to the many foreign substances in our bodies, as well as other forms of physical and emotional stress. Staying youthful means getting to the real sources of inflammation, which is now being cited as a cause in such diseases as Alzheimer's, Parkinson's, multiple sclerosis (MS), and even schizophrenia.

Eating to Feel Good

Arthritis and other inflammatory conditions are completely controllable in the new paradigm of physiology. If you're experiencing arthritis-like symptoms, there are several things you can do to bring down inflammation and protect yourself from debilitating pain, other than rely on medication:

— **Eat simple, nonprocessed food.** Prepare food from scratch with as many organic, whole-food ingredients as you can find. Don't shop primarily at grocery stores, but visit local farmers' markets and health-food stores. Learn how to read labels and understand what you're seeing. An even simpler rule is that if you don't know what it is, don't eat it.

— **Change your diet and/or take supplements to be less predisposed to inflammation.** Include more raw food at meals, and take bromelain supplements when symptoms are active.

— **Eat "good" fats.** The higher the animal fat (that is, cholesterol) in your diet, and the lower the vegetable fats and oils found in fish (omega-3s), the more jazzed up and "angry" your immune system will be. Ecosinoids and prostaglandins are the body's own natural analgesics, and they're made from the omega-3s EHA and DFA, which can be taken as supplements. Thus, we *do* need fats, but the big issue is getting "clean" ones, since many immune system–aggravating environmental toxins are fat soluble and therefore end up in dietary fat.

— **Cleanse your liver and other internal organs.** Put yourself on a cleansing diet, such as the Fat Flush Plan, created by Dr. Ann Louise Gittleman and written about in her book of the same name, or some other regimen. Begin doing this at least once a year, and more often as you age. It's a basic preventive step to take, not a frill or a fad. It's not difficult either, and can be done as you go about your everyday job or other activities. Benefits that you can expect when you detox with liver flushing at the same time are increased energy, antiaging effects, sharpened senses, greater motivation and optimism, increased sense of peace and relaxation, fewer or less severe allergies, more creativity and inspiration, and improved mental and emotional clarity.

— **Stay warm and sweat often.** Remove toxins through heat and perspiration. If you live in a warm climate or have access to a gym, drink lots of water and work up a sweat every single day. If not, just take a walk to get things moving in your body, drink lots of water, and sit in a sauna. Heat makes the condition feel better, since arthritis gets worse when weather changes to cold and dampness. This is because many impurities in your body will precipitate, crystallize, or condense in the elbows and knees, ankles, extremities, and hands, which are cooler than the torso core. So move to stay warm, and ideally, sweat in a hot bath or sauna.

— **Stay mobile.** Get plenty of exercise to keep your joints flexible, and be careful not to sink into inactivity as you age.

— **Practice forgiveness, a powerful healing emotion.** You can bring this about with spiritual or religious support, psychotherapy, new-paradigm bodywork, or one-on-one direct communication with people in your life whom you've been angry at or are still resenting. Most important, forgive yourself! Then watch your arthritis symptoms miraculously disappear.

— **Reduce stress.** Learn to meditate, do yoga, or use relaxation techniques.

— **Practice affirmations.** Talk to your body and say: "I love my knee, which is getting renewed everyday, because I'm treating it well."

— **Lose weight if you need to.** Extra pounds put more stress on joints, so go on a rapid-weight-loss diet, shedding even as few as ten pounds. Again, I recommend *The Fat Flush Plan* by Ann Louise Gittleman, M.S., C.N.S.; and also *The 3-Day Solution Plan* by Laurel Mellin, M.A., R.D. Both of these books address weight loss from the mind-body paradigm and have been helpful to me.

Sugar: An Addictive Drug

If you want to feel good, you must come to terms with your addiction to sugar. You say that you don't have one? Think again. Studies have shown that rats will work as hard to receive a mouthful of sugar water as they will for an injection of cocaine!

Even if you aren't eating straight sugar, your body is making it from the foods you're eating, which may be the way that you're getting your fix. All refined carbohydrates, meaning white-flour products such as bread and pasta, almost instantly turn into sugar in your body, beginning the minute that they come into contact with the saliva in your mouth.

Sugar is a drug in a very real sense, and we're addicted to the "up" feeling we get when our blood-sugar levels soar. This substance directly impacts your molecules of emotion—insulin being the main one. External drugs, internal chemicals, and the emotions—all of these use the exact same pathways and receptors.

The white granules that you buy in the supermarket are actually sucrose, which consists of two sugars: fructose hooked up to glucose. These form a disaccharide that tastes sweet and can be broken down in your body.

Your brain runs on glucose, the only form of sugar that it can use for fuel. For this reason, blood levels of glucose are very carefully monitored by insulin, as well as numerous other neuropeptides, so that they stay within a narrow range. Your pancreas contains many different molecules of emotion to carefully regulate the ebb and flow of glucose to your blood and hence your brain.

Glucose is so central to how you feel that rising levels make you feel almost giddy. Falling amounts can make you feel panicky, hyper, or depressed. The demand for it can override your behavior just as a craving for heroin can, driving you not only to seek more and more sugary foods, but also to engage in behaviors that are associated with blood sugar on the rise.

Unlike heroin, however, sugar is legal, plentiful, and cheap, so you're likely to satisfy that drive from the available supply and become hooked without even being aware of it. Like any drug, the more of the external substance that you take into your body, the less you'll be able to make your own version, just as heroin addicts reduce their ability to make endorphins. Sweets, like heroin, enter the blood (and hence the brain), very rapidly, providing a "sugar rush" that kicks off the release of other neuropeptides to compensate. The higher the glycemic index of a particular food, the faster the sugar is able to leave your stomach and race to your brain. Natural fiber in the diet slows down this high, and also the inevitable crash that follows a few hours later.

Fructose is manufactured from enzymatically digested corn, a cheap sweetener commonly used in many processed drinks and foods. Although fructose fits the sugar receptor on cells and tastes sweet, it can't be used by your brain. It fools your body into thinking that it's getting a dose of brain fuel when it isn't, causing a reaction for some sensitive people.

While I was on a very regimented, sugar-restricted diet, my husband accidentally brought home a protein-isolate breakfast drink that contained fructose, its presence hidden in the fine print. After a long, brisk walk, I had what I thought was a sugarless breakfast drink and became hyper and agitated for the rest of the day. From the taste, my bodymind thought it was getting a dose of glucose, and adjusted accordingly. But it was actually getting a form of sugar to burn that wasn't quickly convertible into glucose for brain-nourishing fuel.

Lactose, found in milk, is a very healthy sugar because it consists of the essential sugar glucose fused with galactose, which is the other vital one. From these two sugars, our bodies can manufacture all the others we need. Although we hear a lot about "lactose intolerance," milk can be very healthy, particularly when boiled to destroy any allergens. With cinnamon, it's a satisfying bedtime drink, since lactose supplies the two essential sugars that you need, and warm milk helps you sleep.

Sugar: Weight, Mood, and Aging

Overeating sugar or foods converted rapidly into it in your body can cause you to gain weight, age prematurely, and undergo disruptive mood alterations. The mechanism for all these effects is the molecule of emotion called insulin, a neuropeptide secreted by the pancreas but also found in the brain.

Insulin's job is to regulate your blood sugar, and when you eat a lot of sweet stuff, it's released into your blood to help cells deal with the excess by storing it. This neuropeptide sends a signal for sugar to be held as fat, a mechanism that comes from a time when our primitive cave-people bodies had to guard against food shortages.

The peptide glucagon, made in the pancreas, is secreted when you have low blood sugar. It stimulates the release of glucose from the liver. The ratio of glucagon to insulin in your bloodstream determines whether sugar will be stored or made. We make our own when we need it by a process called "glucogenesis," in which the amino acid alanine is combined with citric acid, such as that found in grapefruit. But we practically never need to use this healthy, energy-releasing pathway because our typical diet of sugary foods, chips, and white-flour products supplies our bodies with so much of the stuff.

Experiments with lowly worms suggest that eating too much sugar can bring on premature aging. Dr. Cynthia Kenyon's lab at University of California, San Francisco, removed the insulin receptor from *C. elegans* and watched as a worm lived three times longer than its normal one-month life cycle. In addition, the creature actually looked prettier and younger as it aged, staying ten times more active than its peers. The worm probably remained youthful because its insulin circuit was disconnected, a process we can mimic by cutting down on our intake of foods that elevate blood sugar.

There are many studies showing that when we calorie deprive animals, guaranteeing low insulin response, they live longer. So, if you're looking for a fountain of youth, try passing up sweets, as well as those muffins, pastas, bagels, and pancakes.

Sweet Solution

How can you get your body to release less insulin so that you lose weight, stay on an even keel moodwise, and reverse the aging process? Besides cutting down on the refined carbs, try balancing your diet by eating a scientifically proven ratio of 40 percent carbohydrates, 30 percent proteins, and 30 percent good fats (olive or canola oils and omega-6s from fish such as salmon) at each meal to keep the insulin release under control. Both fat and the high fiber from carbohydrates in the form of fruits and vegetables will bring down your glycemic index.

Of course, portion control is paramount. Servings that are too large, no matter how perfectly balanced, will cause weight gain. In addition, only have food when you're truly hungry! Getting to the bottom of emotional eating is an interesting challenge.

Switching to five small meals per day, instead of two or three heavy ones, and treating each of them like a drug dose can be helpful. This boosts your metabolism and helps you burn fat, sending the message to your bodymind that food is abundant. If the message is "Food is scarce," your insulin and other neuropeptides will kick in to store sugar as fat, making you feel and act sluggish in the process. As I mentioned, your body is genetically predisposed to react this way, left over from a time when our primitive ancestors experienced scarcity of nourishment, tribal closeness, and constant exercise. Today, in contrast, we have an abundance of food, social isolation, and too little exercise, confusing our bodyminds and contributing to an epidemic of obesity.

I believe the scientific data is very clear that sugar in the diet causes diabetes, and changes in diet and increases in exercise can reverse it. This disease has doubled in the last eight years, and hospitals are filled with people suffering from the blindness and amputation that often result. It's beyond shocking that children who never used to get what was previously called "adult-onset" (type 2) diabetes are now contracting it in record numbers, as they sit still to watch 70,000 hours per year of TV with commercials advertising sweet, processed foods.

Remember that sugar is a drug, first harvested and refined from fields of green plants in the 1600s. We weren't designed to eat it, and every culture is more or less genetically predisposed to diabetes.

Telling Fact from Fiction

People don't know what to believe anymore, so deluged are they by reports and studies that are hawked daily in newspapers. And given the sheer volume of the information coming out of research institutes, we can't rely on our medical doctors to make accurate interpretations. One day hormone replacement therapy causes cancer, and then the next day it doesn't. The average layperson can't possibly figure it all out, yet everyone is left scrambling to make some sense out of what they read, seeking certainty for conditions that aren't getting cured.

Research scientists, however, are trained to be critical. In graduate-school seminars, we sit together and read papers, trying to find flaws so that we can question the conclusions. A common way to evaluate conflicting information is by a meta-analysis, a survey of many studies that counts up the number of positive and negative ones, basing conclusions on the highest final count. I personally don't believe that meta-analysis is as convincing as two or three positive findings that are flawlessly analyzed.

If you can wade through scientific jargon, a great Website to check out is PubMed **(www.PubMed.gov)**, a service of the National Library of Medicine and the National Institutes of Health that includes over 15 million citations from Medline (an indexing service) and other life-science journals for biomedical articles going back to the 1950s. PubMed includes links to full text articles of peer-reviewed, scientific journal articles. Another resource to help you evaluate new scientific findings is the Website for the National Institutes of Health National Center for Complementary and Alternative Medicine **(http://nccam.nih.gov)**.

Hope on the Way

As I continued doing research at my office in Georgetown and at home, reviewing the literature and checking the data, an article came across my desk that was sent to me by a conference organizer at Kaiser Permanente, the country's largest HMO. The article appeared in the prestigious and authoritative *Journal of the American Medical Association*, and was entitled "Diet, Lifestyle, and Longevity—the Next Steps?" I read it with keen interest, knowing that HMOs can be the true watchdogs of mainstream medicine, keeping an eye out for what works and saves money, even if it's something as simple and low-tech as a clean diet and active lifestyle.

The article reports the findings of a group of European researchers who looked at men and woman in their 70s and 80s who were free of chronic disease. Subjects had followed a "Mediterranean" diet (nothing from a box!), had consumed alcohol moderately, didn't smoke, and walked at least a half-hour daily. Each of these factors was associated with lower mortality rates, and combinations of two or more guidelines were particularly powerful. Coronary disease was reduced by 83 percent, diabetes in women by 91 percent, and colon cancer in men by 71 percent. Compared to drugs and surgery, these lifestyle factors win hands down. If you could get results like those from a pill, the news would be screaming from every headline of every newspaper in the world.

The conclusion of the investigators is worth quoting directly: "As a society, the United States spends billions on chronic disease treatments and interventions for risk factors. Although these are useful and important, a fraction of that investment to promote healthful lifestyles for primary prevention among individuals at all ages would yield greater benefit."

This statement comes out of a journal dear to the heart of the reigning paradigm and shows that *a shift is happening!*

Chapter 5

Washington, D.C.:
Healing and Consciousness

The Fourth-of-July weekend was approaching, a chance for Michael and me to get out of Washington and spend some time on our favorite magical little island in the Chesapeake Bay, where we have a summer cottage. I'd invited Nancy and her husband, Richard, along with our Tucson hosts, the energy chiropractors Joan and Nicholas, to join us for some sun and fun over the extended holiday weekend.

The plan was for Nancy and Richard to stay on the East Coast for an extra week to attend a conference put on by the Institute of Noetic Sciences (IONS), where I'd be speaking. This three-day event would be held in the Washington, D.C., area for the first time in the institute's history—right across the Potomac River in Arlington, Virginia, practically my own backyard. The theme of the conference was billed as "healing and consciousness."

I hadn't seen Nancy since our Tucson meeting, but we talked regularly on the phone, especially since our book proposal had been accepted in June. The start date for our six-month writing adventure was July 1, and it seemed like a good idea to regroup with the original cast of characters for a kickoff gathering of sailing, sunning, and eating crab cakes on the Chesapeake Bay.

Mike and I arrived on the island early to get the house ready and then tool around the quiet streets on our bikes, getting some respite from the tension and stress of our work. *Torment* would be a much more accurate term for how we were experiencing our current situation. Peptide T's long-term investor had recently stopped funding, leaving us high and dry, with our salaries and labs at Georgetown University Medical School unfunded and all research stalled. Over the past six months, surviving on savings, we'd been struggling to get the commercial license to our invention from the NIH so that RAPID could raise funds to launch the pivotal human AIDS trial. We were exhausted.

But here on this lovely island, we let ourselves be transported back to the 1950s. Cars moved slowly, neighbors stopped to chat, and e-mail wasn't available. We were out of cell-phone range and could forget about our fast-paced life back in D.C. When Joan and Nicholas arrived, they brought their chiropractic tables with them and set up in our living room, offering to give us all adjustments as often as we liked over the weekend.

Spiritual Healing, American Style

My experience with chiropractic goes back to the late 1980s, when I met Joe Skinner, the founder of Rappahannock Chiropractic, who tested me through applied kinesiology, a method invented in 1964 by chiropractor George Goodhart. It relies on muscle resistance to access the subconscious and give answers to practitioners for diagnoses and treatment.

A short time later, I was exposed to the brilliant and subtle style of craniosacral therapy, as developed by Dr. John Upledger. Meeting this pioneer at a conference, I sat nearby as he treated a patient and felt a bolt of grief being released from the patient's body. I found his ideas about "somatoemotional cysts" forming in a person's body when strong emotions accompany physical injury to be very compelling.

Later, in the '90s, I explored another branch of chiropractic care known originally as Network Chiropractic and had several adjustments by Dr. Donald Epstein, the branch's founder. Epstein had broken from the more traditional chiropractic training and taught people to focus on energy release rather than structural, or "bone-cracking," release. Clients are often adjusted by light touch in groups, sometimes at a weekend-long marathon called a "Transformational Gate." During treatments, patients experience a somatopsychic wave of energy sweeping the room, triggering emotional and energetic releases that seem to help people feel good.

I was familiar with energy healing from Eastern philosophy, which teaches that consciousness (mind, emotions, and spirit) comes first, and the material universe follows. Chinese medicine, for example, relies on *chi,* a force that travels along meridians— mysterious, energetic pathways—to enliven the body with energy and wellness. Of course, in the biomedical model that I was trained in, the spinal cord is the main energetic conduit, an electrical cable of millions of axons and dendrites extending from neurons throughout the brain and body. No pathways for mysterious "energy" to travel on are acknowledged.

I was surprised to learn of an original form of chiropractic that came into practice at the turn of the 20th century and had a spiritual basis. I like to think of this as our own down-home, American-style spiritual healing—a form taught today in 14 graduate schools across the nation.

The original chiropractic system was "accidentally" discovered in 1895 by D. D. Palmer, a hands-on healer and businessman who'd been exposed to Eastern philosophies when on business trips to Japan. Upon hearing a joke told by a colleague in the hallway of his business building, Palmer laughed and spontaneously slapped the back of a janitor standing nearby. That individual was Harvey Willard, a deaf black man, who felt something in his back pop but said nothing. The following day, Willard returned to Palmer's office to report that as a result of the slap, his hearing was restored!

Palmer attempted to reproduce the "adjustment," but having no appropriate table for the janitor to lie facedown on, treated him with more back slapping and broke Willard's nose, causing blood to gush out onto the floor. (This story was told to me by a chiropractor I met at one of my lectures, a classmate of Willard's great-granddaughter, herself a Palmer-trained chiropractor who had told him this story.)

Eventually, D. D. Palmer evolved his theory that by removing blockages to spinal nerves, the body's own *innate intelligence* could take over and perform whatever healing was necessary. He and his son, B. J. Palmer, along with a faithful group of followers, did time in jail for practicing medicine without a license, but the movement survived and grew, becoming a marginalized but increasingly accepted healing modality. The Palmers were the first to coin the phrase *body, mind, and spirit* as the threefold essence of the human being, and the first to say: "The power that made the body, heals the body."

Today, 14 graduate schools of chiropractic train practitioners in the U.S., the two most famous, perhaps, being Palmer College in Davenport, Iowa, and Life University in Atlanta. Typically, a student does two years of full medical training, similar to that required for an M.D., and then another two years learning the methods of Palmer's chiropractic. After graduation, even though their discipline was spiritual in origin, most chiropractors stick to the more medically acceptable (and reimbursable) method of using x-rays to determine treatment. This more mainstream variety of care is what you're more likely to encounter when looking in the yellow pages, but many variations and styles exist, with more or less emphasis on removing "subluxations," or misalignments of the vertebrae, by hands-on manipulation.

The style that Joan and Nicholas practice, named At-Ease Wellness, was derived from Epstein's Network Chiropractic. It's an energetic approach taught in post-graduate seminars, not a part of the accredited, licensed training required for chiropractors to hang out a shingle. The truth is that there are as many styles of chiropractic as there are practitioners. As a practical matter, friendly recommendations and trial-and-error experiences help most people find the best chiropractor for them. More reliably, academic practitioners like Dr. Joseph Sweere, a professor at Northwestern Health Sciences University in Minneapolis, are at the leading edge of holistic-health advice.

The idea of the body having an innate intelligence, of course, made sense to me from the research I'd done on informational molecules, but the mechanism for the movement of energy throughout the body and from one person to another was a bit vague in my scientific understanding. I realized from Joan's articulate explanation of how Network Chiropractic worked that group adjustments were possible through a resonating web of vibrating energy. Could that be carried through and outside of the body, causing a healing connection from one person to another? And if so, by what verifiable mechanism did it happen?

I questioned this for many years, personally getting the benefits of energy healing in many different modalities, but unable to understand the physical mechanism that correlated to it—that is, until I encountered Dr. James Oschman, whose work enabled me to understand the scientific basis for energy medicine, a field that including chiropractic, hands-on healing, Reiki, kinesiology, acupuncture, shiatsu, and others. But that understanding—so radical, and such a new paradigm—took a while to sink in and become real for me. I'd have to wait another three months, when Oschman himself was scheduled to present in D.C. and would explain the basis of energy medicine to me in person.

Jump-Starting the Core-Trauma Release

"Put that laptop away!" I teased playfully, meeting Nancy in the kitchen of our cottage on the first morning of our stay on the island. The rest of the group was relaxing on the screened-in back porch, sipping morning beverages and enjoying the cool breezes before the day's high humidity set in. I'd been eyeing Nancy's slim white iBook computer on the kitchen counter where it sat unopened, reminding me of our impending book project.

"You promised that we weren't going to work on the book here," I scolded in jest. We'd planned to begin our task when the Fourth-of-July weekend was over, after we'd relaxed and enjoyed some time off. We'd then return together to my house in D.C. to write for the few days before the conference.

"Okay," Nancy replied. "But just in case, I've got my tape recorder with me, and who knows . . ."

I knew she was right, and that at some point we'd want to capture the ongoing saga of our own healing for the book, especially with our private healers in the house. I didn't have to wait long: Shortly after breakfast, I lay facedown on Nicholas's table, breathing deeply, while he did his magical energetic adjustments, networking between himself and whoever else came in to lie on the other table in the room.

Nicholas went back and forth between the two stations, using his hands to lightly touch key points of my back and clearing blockages of stuck energy. From my previous "Gate" experiences, where hundreds of people were treated in the same room, I knew that deeply buried memories could surface during a treatment, releasing a torrent of sudden emotion when triggered by a somatopsychic wave. Sometimes whole scenarios from the past would come up from the subconscious mind where they'd been stored in the body.

That morning, as Nicholas was working on me and no one else was in the room, I began sobbing like a child. Nick stood by, and when I stopped, he asked me, "Candace, something happened when you were about three years old. Do you remember what it was?"

"How do you know? I mean, why that age?" I asked.

"Because your body was contorted like a three-year-old's," he replied.

Then it started to come back to me . . . a traumatic incident from my childhood that seemed to be buried and forgotten, yet I was to learn that it was actually at the core of emotional issues affecting my entire adult life.

The scene was somewhat familiar, having come up occasionally in snippets (although never the whole picture) during my meditations over the years: My small three-year-old self was standing at a doorway, peeking through a crack, curious but afraid to go inside. That morning on the island, I remembered what was on the other side of this door to my parents' bedroom.

After knocking, I heard my father's voice telling me to come in. The door opened fully, and I saw someone else with him—a strange woman, not my dark-haired mother, but a blonde in the bed. She and my father were smoking cigarettes.

Dad motioned me over and introduced me to the woman. I liked getting my father's attention and being included. Both adults were acting normal, not at all disturbed by the presence of a small child, whom I'm sure they figured would never say a word about their tryst.

But they were wrong. Somehow my mother got wind of the incident and pumped me for information, which I reluctantly gave, all the while sensing that something was very wrong. Later she confronted my father, and there were repercussions, with him shouting at my mother, her screaming and crying. And then I was trotted out, the key witness, and made to tell my story of the blonde in the bed.

I don't recall what words were said at that point, or who hit me where. I only remember that I was left sobbing on the floor, my parents were splitting up, and it was all my fault. They reconciled after a short separation, but by then, my small bodymind had absorbed a huge dollop of guilt and a hefty helping of abandonment. How could anyone trust me—and how could I trust myself—when I'd been at the crux of so much anger and pain experienced by the most important people in my life? As a core trauma, this incident had been fueling my lifetime angst: *What can I possibly do to be good enough to deserve love?*

While some of the historical details I filled in later by checking with family members, the central drama—seeing the blonde in the bed and feeling my parents' anger and my own pain—was clearly recalled in our sunny cottage. The traumatic memory was no longer stuck in my body, where it had probably been stored in the cellular receptors of my spinal ganglia, or nerve cells, since the age of three, holding me in an emotional pattern of guilt and "undeservedness"—what I call my low self-esteem today.

Coming Full Circle with IONS

Our Fourth-of-July island adventure came to a close, and Mike and I, joined by Nancy and Richard, made the two-hour trek over the Chesapeake Bay bridge back to our house. For the next few days, Nancy and I taped interviews and began to flush out our outline for the book. We were all looking forward to the three-day IONS conference, with my friend excited to reconnect with an organization she'd been on staff with back in the early '80s in San Francisco.

As far as consciousness-research organizations go, IONS was the crème de la crème, exploring phenomena that don't fit conventional scientific models, while still maintaining a commitment to scientific rigor. And it certainly spoke to IONS's credible status in the public eye that they were holding their conference in D.C., both the capital of the free world and an old-paradigm stronghold. But the city was also my own home turf, the place where I had a visible presence in the mainstream, and I was anxious about what my colleagues might think if they got wind that I was presenting across the river for those fuzzy "Californoid" thinkers.

Founded in 1973, IONS was the inspiration of Edgar Mitchell, former Navy captain and *Apollo 14* astronaut who traveled to the moon and back. On his return trip, from a tiny window in the cramped cabin of his space capsule, Mitchell saw Earth floating freely in the vastness of space and had a spiritual epiphany. In his own words: "The presence of divinity became almost palpable, and I knew that life in the universe was not just an accident based on random processes. . . ." He began the institute with a focus on studying telepathy, clairvoyance, and psychokinesis, but that shifted over time to include mind-body health and science.

Interestingly, my first "coming out" as a new-paradigm thinker was at an event sponsored by IONS and the U.S. government back in 1985. It was then that an aide to Senator Pell knocked on my office door at the NIMH and asked if I would give the keynote lecture to a symposium cosponsored by his office and IONS.

At the time, I was doing my job as a classically trained bench scientist. The theme of the symposium was "Does Consciousness Survive Death?" I'd lectured all over the world, but only as a "straight" scientist, and the idea of delivering a lay lecture, especially one that sounded so unscientific, made me very nervous.

Mostly because the gig was so lucrative, I overcame my fears. But I was so uncomfortable to hear the other presenters that I stayed out of the hall until it was time for me to speak, sitting on the front lawn to arrange my slides before I went in. I answered the questions posed by suggesting that information released at the time of death might survive in some form of consciousness. Sitting next to me on the panel was Dr. Stan Grof, a psychiatrist who would later lead me in "holotropic," mind-expanding breathing with Michael Murphy and a group of Russian scientists at Esalen Institute in California. But back then, I was stunned to see the title of Dr. Grof's book, *Beyond the Brain,* which seemed very far-out to this neuroscientist.

After I delivered my talk, I met with Brendan O'Reagan, who was the organizer of that meeting (and has since passed away). As we walked along a path at Georgetown, he explained to me that the word *noetic,* from the ancient Greek for "inner knowing," was used to mean "pertaining to consciousness." Later I looked up *noetic* in a dictionary, which defined it as "direct and immediate access to knowledge beyond what is available to our normal senses and the power of reason."

Now, in July of 2005, my association with IONS and the consciousness movement was coming full circle, with the opportunity to present my own leading-edge research in my hometown once again. Only this time, I was no longer a scared novice, but a highly sought-after "real" scientist, a star with media presence, and in some eyes, a New Age diva.

I'd come a long way as a scientist and new-paradigm thinker. Even back in 1997, when my first book came out, I wasn't quite ready to say what I now believe and would be boldly presenting, which is this: The challenge for science and our culture is to bring scientific, even mathematical, rigor to our understanding of consciousness and energy, putting them both together in a grand unified theory that includes and even expands Einstein's famous equation, $E=mc^2$. In the days before the IONS conference, I was checking with my son Evan, an electrical engineer/physicist/ patent examiner to find out whether or not such an approach made sense.

At Play in the Field

The first day of the conference dawned, and for the kickoff event, I joined a cadre of speakers addressing the medical aspects of healing and consciousness. I'd been invited by my friend Dr. Marilyn Schlitz, the scientific director of IONS whom I highly respected, to participate in a preconference workshop, "The Emerging Field of Integral Medicine," and eagerly accepted. Marilyn, whose experimental work suggested electrophysiological evidence for precognition and mental telepathy, had scheduled my appearances over the next three days of the conference.

When it was my turn to talk, I introduced myself as I'm accustomed to do at scientific meetings: "I'm a professor at Georgetown University Medical Center in the department of physiology and biophysics," I began, and then went on to describe myself and my work as I've never done before.

"Physiology, as you all know, is the study of the processes and the workings of the human body. But the term *biophysics* is a bit more obscure, a word that isn't used much anymore, and it refers to the electrical nature of the nervous system. I began my career as a pharmacologist, but have also been a biochemist, neuroscientist, and even a psychoneuroimmunologist, due to my interdisciplinary excursions over the years. But today, I believe that I'm in the right department because the new paradigm I'm exploring has everything to do with energy and the electrical nature of the body."

There, it was easy. I'd blended my current reality with my past, and the rest of my talk flowed from the integrity this had established, bringing with me, I hoped, others in the audience who were grappling with the same paradigm crossover. But the next few days would be more of a test, as I'd been asked to give more talks and also to conduct a day-long experiential workshop, something I'd only reluctantly agreed to do.

What kind of serious scientist gives an experiential workshop? I asked myself, annoyed in my rigorous personality, but actually tantalized in my more playful one. In preparation, I'd decided to show a few slides and then have my participants experience my own CD, entitled *Psychosomatic Wellness: Healing Your Bodymind.* I honestly had no idea what else I'd do or how the workshop was going to turn out.

I'd actually made the CD for myself, inspired by a psycho-therapist I saw during a dark period in my life when my mother and sister passed away within a period of three years. The production of the CD was truly a family affair, involving my husband, Michael, and two of my children, Vanessa and Evan Pert. Evan assisted in making mathematical transpositions between musical notes and colors, and Vanessa edited an illustrated booklet that accompanies the CD. The content of the booklet is the nature of physiology, consciousness, and healing, based on my lectures over the years.

Up until that dark time in my life, I'd avoided what I called "talk therapy," believing that it kept people in the rut of replaying their sad old stories. But devastated by my personal loss, I sought out, and was very fortunate to find, a fabulous psychotherapist, a woman who helped me with my grieving and introduced me to the power of music and affirmations in healing.

During one of my therapy sessions, I noticed a CD on a side table with the word *grief* on the cover, and was pleasantly surprised when the therapist told me that she had intended to give it to me. I took home this recording by Belleruth Naparstek and listened to it every day, lying down with my eyes closed, with remarkable results. I processed my grief so efficiently that after two months, with my therapist's blessing, I ended the talk sessions. I decided to create my own wellness CD to allow people to relax and effortlessly reprogram their subconscious minds to forgive, enjoy, and feel good.

When I arrived at the room for my workshop, which was named for my CD, "Psychosomatic Wellness: Healing Your Bodymind," I was glad to see the 75 chairs set up in a circle. I was weary of the more formal setting of neat rows facing the front and liked this new arrangement where I could see everyone, and they could see me and each other. It felt natural and appropriate for the subject, which was a practical application of the new-paradigm physiology, scientifically designed to rest and heal the bodymind.

The conference room filled up quickly. Looking out from where I was sitting, I faced a round of expectant faces, and for a moment I felt strangely vulnerable, seeing the empty space in the center of the circle. But it was time to begin. After a brief overview of the new-paradigm physiology—how peptides communicate with cellular receptors in a bodywide system of information and energy—I dove right in with my favorite slide.

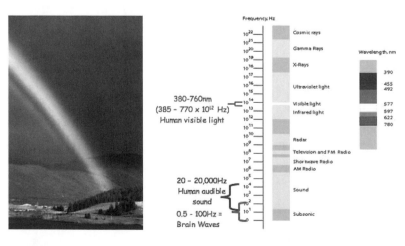

Healing Sound of Music

"Here we have the spectrum of all possible vibrations in the universe," I began. "You can see the full range of frequencies from cosmic rays at the top to subsonic sound at the bottom. We humans can supposedly perceive a very limited portion of these, mainly those that translate to light and sound. Visible light, as you can see, is confined to a very narrow range that's further broken down into the seven colors of the rainbow, each vibrating at its own specific, measurable frequency.

"I'd like you to look at audible sound, which includes everything you can hear—music, spoken words, and sounds from nature. The range of audible sound is 20–20,000 hertz (Hz), which is a measurement of frequency, or the rate of vibration of air. Notice also that the frequency of human brain waves falls within this audible range, overlapping on the low end, the same frequency at which channels in a cell pump ions as they are driven by peptides and other informational substances. Various receptors—such as those for endorphins, endocannabinoids, interleukins, Valium, and alcohol—thus vibrate at these frequencies and higher harmonics.

"Music, which is a patterned vibration, can bypass the ligand and directly resonate those receptors, interacting like a peptide or a drug—or an emotion. The vibrational frequency of the notes turns on the receptor, setting in motion all kinds of cellular activities. That's how music can heal, interacting directly with your molecules of emotion to charge you with energy, get your juices flowing, and make you feel good.

"These molecules are not only vibrating to cause bodywide changes, but they are 'hearing' each other through the psychosomatic network of cellular communication. You can see that we don't just hear with our ears, but we 'hear' with every receptor on every cell in our bodymind. We're literally alive with the sound of music!

"In this same sense, consider that we really do have extra-sensory perception (ESP), given that our receptors, not just our ears, are 'hearing' as they vibrate. Possibly, when the mechanism of ESP is understood scientifically, it will be recognized as the resonance of our molecules of emotion, vibrating across distances from receptor to receptor.

"Your cells resonate with the internal chemicals your body makes, the external drugs that you take both legally and illegally, and with the emotions you feel. They also resonate with the sounds you hear."

How Words Heal

I continued, "Words are equally powerful to heal by the same mechanism as music. I've talked before about how thought patterns—what you think—can be identified as networks of brain cells that fire together. The threshold of a neuron firing, an all-or-nothing event, depends on the state of sensitivity of the many thousands of receptors on its surface, composing the ion channels. Each of these canals has a quantal nature, as it is either open or closed, never in between. Spoken words, just like music, can vibrate these channels to close or open, and thus regulate how often a neural network fires.

"The more often a neuronal network fires together, the stronger the synaptic connections become—and the more the thought pattern is fixed at the cellular level. Networks that fire together, wire together. Not just neurons, but all cells have ion channels and electrical properties, so thought-pattern conditioning extends throughout the psychosomatic network of the bodymind. You're literally thinking with your body and the words you say, because sound is vibrating your receptors, which actually affects the neural networks forming in your brain.

"The movie *What the Bleep Do We Know!?* explains how you can make new patterns in your brain by affirming what you want to create. Literally, you 'create your day,' as suggested by one of the talking heads in the film. Of course, Louise Hay had shown people how to do this several decades earlier, when she introduced affirmations as a way to heal. The movie dramatized that your words and thoughts strengthen synaptic connections in your brain, changing your neural patterns, or networks, giving you a personal experience of reality and potentially bringing about the results you want. Spoken words—either positive or negative—have the power to create a reality you either want or don't.

"This is why I've included music on every track of my CD, including a track with a powerful guided meditation. But before I play it for you, I want to say one more thing about one of the musical scales that the composer used.

"My son Evan Pert made the correct mathematical transformation for the very first time between the frequencies of light of the various colors of the rainbow and those of the musical notes to which they correspond. In other words, he accurately turned color into sound by calculating the trillion-fold lower harmonics.

"This is important because color is traditionally associated with the Hindu system of chakras, which are vortexes of energy visualized along the spinal cord, considered to be important for healing. Yogis and Eastern masters have ascribed different colors to each chakra, red being the base point at the bottom of the spine, moving up through the rainbow to violet at the top of skull.

"Interestingly, the chakras correlate with physical locations along the spine and ganglia on either side of it, where the molecules of emotion are most densely populated. These chakra locations are nodal points where information can enter into the psychosomatic network, so I can speculate that when we play the note that corresponds to the chakra color, we vibrate receptors at that chakra level, and thus access various informational points of the psychosomatic network.

"For example, red is the color corresponding to the base chakra, and also matching the harmonic of the note F. Playing the frequency of F may activate cellular receptors of the red, or base chakra, directly.

"You can imagine that there's a lot to speculate about, especially when you realize that brain waves (which correlate with states of consciousness) still are quite mysterious as to where and how they originate. Brain waves oscillate at the very same frequencies as ion channels and the color harmonics of music, color, and receptor binding. I'll leave the application of this to you bodyworkers and energy-medicine practitioners. For me, it's enough to know that music, spoken words, the colors of the rainbow, human brain waves, and our molecules of emotion can all resonate together. This inspires me to truly believe that my CD, *Psychosomatic Wellness,* thus has very powerful, scientifically designed (although not fully understood) healing properties.

Dance Connection

The lecture portion of the workshop done, we took a short break before starting the second half, which would be more interactive. I intended for participants to experience the guided-meditation section of my CD, exposing them to the words and music designed by Lanny Meyers to replicate atomic relationships, as defined in the physicist Niels Bohr's electron theory. Lanny had explained:

Following the expansion series of the number of electrons orbiting the atomic nucleus in the full outer shell as molecular density increases, values were used as the basis for thematic progression. The scales derived were the source for improvisation, much as classical Hindu musicians improvise on a raga, a set of tones or scale that evokes a mood. The idea was that this audio tapestry would resonate with universal patterns and relationships, and effortlessly and subliminally entrain listeners toward a harmonic balance.

I thought back to how I met Lanny, a Grammy Award–winning composer, arranger, and musician from New York City. He'd come across my first book when it literally fell off a shelf in a bookstore and hit him on the head. The next day, he saw a flyer advertising an Omega Institute workshop to be held at Maho Bay, a resort on the island of St. John in the U.S. Virgin Islands, featuring Mike and me! Piqued by the synchronicity, he felt drawn to attend.

The Omega Institute workshop was held on an open-air circular space, the night sky providing a dome of starlight. I recall sensing some magic afoot as Mike and I paddled in from our day of kayaking, making it just in time for the event. Lanny performed a spontaneous musical improvisation on a keyboard while we led a guided meditation for our participants. It was all pretty magical, and he and his wife, Marian Schiavo, an accomplished graphic artist, became friends with Mike and me. When I had the idea to produce my own CD, I called Lanny and was thrilled when he agreed to create the music, with Marian serving as the art director for the accompanying scientific pamphlet.

Here we go . . . I said to myself as I signaled for the conference room lights to dim and the CD to begin taking us all on a musically guided meditation. Thirty-five minutes later, when that portion of the recording came to an end, there was an almost palpable silence in the room. The center of the circle was now littered with bodies, as most people had taken off their shoes and lain down to get the full relaxation benefits.

The last track of the CD, an uplifting ballad called "Honor

Who You Are," with a positive, self-esteem building message, had finished, and the rhythmic and exuberant musical reprise had just begun when a woman stood up in the very center of the room and began to move and dance to the music. First I, then one by one others, arose to join her, and soon we were all moving together in a spontaneous dance of bodymind harmony.

People were having fun; smiling; and feeling energized, connected, and happy! I felt as though I were at a six-year-old's birthday party, so joyous and unplanned was the activity in the room. I'd lost all traces of being a serious scientist, yet here in this workshop was the presence of all that I'd done scientifically: people feeling, healing, and enjoying. With movement, music, and connection, it was a living demonstration of how we feel good when we experience being plugged into the vibratory reality of the world around us, extending and resonating our psychosomatic networks to interact with others.

After the session, I sought out the woman who'd first begun to dance after the meditation, and was thrilled to find that she was my friend Charmaine Lee. Petite and gorgeous, as well as incredibly youthful-looking, Charmaine is the originator of SynergyDance, an expressive, energy-aware form of movement shaped by the principles of polarity therapy, a healing-arts system that encompasses Eastern and Western philosophies. Her mentor and founder of polarity therapy, Dr. Randolph Stone, believed that the human body is pure energy in motion, and her dance form had evolved from that belief.

In classes and sessions that I'd had with Charmaine over the past few years, I'd learned that her unique hybrid of dance and healing art was designed to involve body, mind, and emotions in something called "deep play." This is an adult, transcendent form of playful activity, characterized by an extraordinarily intense state. An example of this is the experience of swimming with dolphins or, as in SynergyDance, the freeing up of energy through relaxed, unforced movement.

Charmaine herself was a lifelong dancer who had lived in

South Africa and London, studying and practicing educational kinesiology, yoga, qi gong, tai chi, massage, Feldenkrais, Alexander Technique, and craniosacral therapy—all modalities supported by the new-paradigm physiology. She came from this rich and varied tradition into a growing field of dance therapy, a newly licensed form of treatment taught in the degree programs of graduate institutes across the country.

I hugged Charmaine and promised to give her a call about future classes, thrilled to have someone of her caliber and expertise in D.C., able to give me bodywork and help me achieve my own health goals. Music and movement, I knew, were the keys to fun, feeling good, and losing weight—a combination that I knew was effective, and the science was behind it.

Grand Unified Theory

Mike and I left almost immediately after the workshop, saying good-bye to Nancy and Richard, who were staying on at the hotel for another night of conferencing. They were excited to attend a final event that evening featuring Marianne Williamson and other consciousness-movement luminaries. I'd wanted to join them, but was exhausted after a long day and needed to get home to recharge for the next (and final) day's keynote panel, my last presentation for the IONS conference.

Approaching our home after a short drive, Mike and I turned down the road leading to our house, when we were stopped by an emergency road crew. Although there had been no wind or rain that day, a huge tree had strangely fallen across the road, taking down power lines on both sides of the street and stopping all traffic. After explaining that we lived close by, we were carefully directed around the now-carved-up tree and fallen power line. We arrived during the last glints of dusk to a house that was dark and growing darker.

In the eerie twilight, we fumbled around in the kitchen for

candles and matches. We rarely went without the convenience of modern electricity and were disoriented by this sudden interruption of our usual routine: no television, computers, reading lamps, or phones. Supper was cold, and so was our hot tub, forcing us to forego the relaxing soak we'd been looking forward to after our long day.

Instead, we took a few candles out on our back porch, and in the gathering darkness, we sat and talked. It turned out to be the perfect atmosphere for Mike and me to take another stab at formulating what we half-jokingly called our "Grand Unified Theory of Consciousness." We'd been pondering this idea for some time, noting that the formulae for forming a Grand Unified Theory, which Evan had explained would integrate all physical phenomena into one monster equation, are lacking the critical element of consciousness. This last piece is always relative to whoever or whatever is aware of his or her own thoughts, known as the "observer."

Our conversation took us late into the night, as we mulled over such aspects of consciousness as Dr. Karl Pribram's field of local potential, which is the realm that isn't yet "reality"—the world of spirit and mystery, synchronicity, and the transcendent self that permeates everything and holds it all together. Deepak Chopra calls it the "nonlocal" or "spiritual" realm, where energy and information emerge from a sea of infinite possibility, of pure potential. Lynne McTaggart, a journalist, traced its history and linked it to the zero-point field of quantum physics. She called it simply "the field" in her book entitled *The Field: The Quest for the Secret Force of the Universe*.

From our perspective, of course, emotions are the key, since they're part of the physical world of molecules, and simultaneously, the energetic world of spirit. I'd used the term *inforealm* in *Molecules of Emotion* because I'd been impressed with a unique quality of information, which is that it's constantly increasing, making it "Maxwell's demon," a solution to an armchair experiment that seemed to violate the laws of physics. What we were grappling with is a connecting matrix that defies space and time, and organizes the events we experience as reality. Science is our lens for understanding in the West, and I believe that we're rapidly approaching the inclusion of spirituality into science.

Mike and I argued back and forth about a formulation and wanted to take a stab at an actual equation. Putting all these ideas together, we finally came up with this: *Consciousness, the sum of all possible observer states, equals the flux of information in a field of emotion.* We wrote out this formulation in the following way:

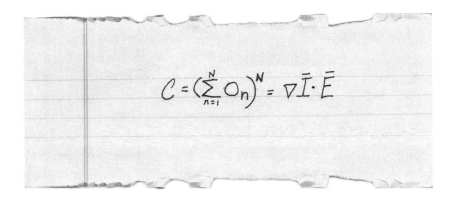

$$C = \left(\sum_{n=1}^{N} O_n\right)^N = \nabla \bar{I} \cdot \bar{E}$$

In this equation, C = consciousness, O = observer (whose strength, Michael pointed out, is a function of attention and intention), I = information, and E = the field of emotion.

Later, we shared this most recent version of our formulation with Evan, whose expertise I'd consulted for earlier versions. This time, after I made his corrections in the notation following his heated discussion with Michael, we were both excited by his encouragement.

———

Healing Leadership

After a panel presentation on the morning of the third day, my job at IONS would be done. During my final chance to talk, I spoke about how Michael and I were in hot pursuit of a new equation, and I shared our progress. This is often how things go in the world of breaking science: Someone sticks his or her neck out with a novel theory or formulation and then waits while everyone else tries to disprove it. In the meantime, new understandings come to light, shifting and changing the initial theory, discovery, or formula, to bring it to its next developmental phase—a very creative process!

We met Nancy and Richard in the hotel lobby and loaded up the car to take them to the airport. Mike drove with Richard in the front seat, while Nancy and I sat in the back. My friend told me excitedly about the event of the evening before, a highlight of which was a keynote talk given by Marianne Williamson. I knew Marianne to be a consciousness luminary and activist and the author of several best-selling books on self-worth, forgiveness, and women's spiritual empowerment; as well as a key transmitter of the *Course in Miracles*.

"What exactly was her message last night?" I asked, as we drove along the Potomac River on our way to the airport.

"On top of being knock-your-socks-off inspiring," Nancy began, "she actually answered a question I've had on my mind ever since the conference began."

"What's that?" I asked. I'd been so busy with my own presentations that I hadn't had much of a chance to take in any other activities going on at the conference.

"I've been wondering these past three days," Nancy said, "after hearing so much about consciousness and healing, what good is all this for the world's problems today? I mean, how does all this consciousness stuff help us solve the problems we're confronted with, such as war, the environment, drug use, and abuse—you know, all those bigger issues."

Nancy paused. "So I was thrilled to hear Marianne talk about government, politics, even Capitol Hill, in the context of consciousness and healing. She was passionate about how the ruling powers need transformation, not just us leading-edge folks. Last night in her keynote, she called for a healing of the hearts of our politicians and announced her own effort to establish a new office in the President's cabinet, which she calls the U.S. Department of Peace."

I nodded, inspired that a woman leader, a woman *spiritual* leader, was standing for a quantum shift for our country and government, and boldly taking the action to make that happen. It was clear that the message of the IONS conference—the convergence of science and spirit—was imperative for much-needed global transformation. I've long thought that my discipline must shift in its viewpoint first, because science as we know it is the bedrock of "reality," the *true* religion of the Western world.

And as the new, scientifically grounded paradigm is accepted by the greater culture, we can then begin to bring about shifts in our institutions, starting with the power structure in Washington, D.C.; and rippling out to include other areas, such as education, the legal and economic system, and the environment.

As we sped toward the airport, and Nancy and Richard's departure, I said, "I'm really glad that this journey in 'consciousness-land' that we've both been on for so long has finally come full circle on so many levels." I paused to look out the window at the brown, turgid waters of the river, full from the recent rain. I knew that some difficult times lay ahead, but for the moment, I was content, at peace.

"I feel like I've finally come home," I said.

——— ———

Chapter 6

Minneapolis: Self-Esteem, Multiple Personalities, and Forgiveness

It was the end of July, and the East Coast summer was at its ripest. Green, lush growth surrounded our Washington-suburb home, carpeting our back lawn, which stretched down to a cool forest glen with shady trails and a rushing creek. In the mornings, I took Tory, our chocolate Labrador retriever, along the creek to get us both some exercise. The days were hot and lazy, the perfect invitation for some serious R & R.

But not for me—I was on the road again. Even though I had "come home," presenting at a consciousness conference here in D.C., I only had a short interlude to prepare for my next tour, a round of talks and panel presentations in Minneapolis. This time, the group I'd be speaking to was the Continuum Center, an organization that had been around since the early '80s and was dedicated to the application of consciousness research for business, medicine, education, and community development.

The bookings were close, five appearances in less than a week, a punishing schedule that I foolishly agreed to in order to create a salary for the month of August. I was exhausted from the accumulation of stressful events that had occurred in recent years, and had reached a point where I just wanted to avoid travel and do my work at home. But our new financial status—*unsalaried*—was causing me added angst, and by accepting this invitation, I hoped to make a funding connection that would allow us to continue our Peptide T research and stay on at the university in our current posts.

The entire Minneapolis gig was cooked up by the director of Continuum Center and long-term friend, Jane Barrash. In the peculiar way that we all seem to attract the energy patterns we need to grow, Jane was a direct reflection of me, never satisfied and always taking on more than was reasonable. Virtually single-handedly (and with minuscule funding), she held up and built up Continuum over the past 20-some years, an effort that I admired. A remarkable, brilliant woman who could have been in my maternal gene pool, Jane had rallied the healing and consciousness community associated with Continuum to provide me with enough work to make my trip financially feasible, and had brought me together once again with the Minneapolis patron and luminary, Horst Rechelbacher.

An Austrian immigrant, Horst was a self-made multimillionaire with a conscience, the epitome of Old-World sensibility combined with New Age panache. He founded the first natural cosmetic and hair-product company, Aveda, and traced his spiritual roots to Swami Rama, whom he met at the University of Minnesota Medical School when the Indian mystic's ability to control his body with his mind was being studied in the States. Horst became a devotee of Swami Rama, and later followed his spiritual teacher to India, where he helped him build a hospital. When the swami died, Horst helped scatter his ashes over the Ganges.

I first met Horst in 1998 when I was invited to speak at an annual Aveda conference held in New York City. Then in 2000, he donated the pivotal seed money to begin a San Francisco trial for Peptide T that was small, but successful in showing our drug to be an effective antiviral—a sure bet to treat AIDS. Now I had a chance to connect with him again, thanks to Jane, and this time I intended to ask him for support to plan the next round of clinical trials to provide conclusive proof of Peptide T's efficacy in treating AIDS.

Post-IONS Soul Searching

Looking back on the IONS conference, I realized that I'd reached a plateau in my adventures in consciousness-land, affiliating myself with an organization and individuals whom I respected greatly. I particularly enjoyed being part of two symposia with Professor Rustom Roy, founding director of Penn State's world-renowned Materials Research.

As a 30-year member of the U.S. National Academy and a foreign member of the National Academies of Science or Engineering of Russia, Japan, Sweden, and India, Rusty (as I call him), is highly respected in the world of mainstream science; and is simultaneously focused on whole-person healing. I asked him what people often ask me: "How solid were Professor Emoto's claims in *What the Bleep . . . !?* that emotions can change the structure of water?"

Rusty authoritatively responded that he thought crystal morphology was some of the most difficult research to establish in the field of variations in water structure. And he felt that for the scientific community, more well-proven examples could have been featured, since the claims presented in the film could take credibility away from the whole field.

Likewise, much of what presenters had offered at the IONS conference was still theoretical, not actually "on the court" the way that mainstream science is. In the consciousness movement, there were no real lives on the line, while in the AIDS arena— the realm of big science where I'd made my mark—there were 40 million people around the globe currently infected with HIV. Aware of the very real need pressing science for an answer, I'd started, to do some deep soul-searching. I began looking deeply into my own heart and mind for what I could heal and transform to open up the possibility of Peptide T coming into the world.

As a result of my healing session with Nicholas over the Fourth-of-July weekend, I'd reexperienced a core emotional trauma that had left my three-year-old self believing I was an undeserving person, one who could never be happy or fulfilled. I saw this early damage as the source of my low self-esteem, a state of bodymind that would sometimes sabotage my success. The pattern was that I'd overcommit my time and energy in a mad rush to do "just one more thing," a desperate kind of overachieving. Then, exhausted by my own unrealistic demands, I would fail.

I can see how the roots of this tendency permeated my childhood, when as a student in school, I would strive to be at the top of every class. "Candy has to be the best in everything she does! She has to win!" I can still hear my mother's voice, commenting sarcastically to my father about my driven, competitive behavior. Today, I miss the way she'd encourage me to relax and take time off to read popular magazines just for fun, like *People* or *Vanity Fair*.

Looking at my father's side of the family, I was descended from John Beebe, who came from England to Connecticut in 1641. The Beebes were a stern and pedantic bunch of highly regarded educators and religious leaders. They were perfectionists who made harsh demands on themselves and those around them. My grandfather Beebe, an accomplished church organist, headed the music department at a leading private school, and his father was the superintendent of schools in Meridien, Connecticut. I had uncles who were church leaders, one a choir director and another the pastor of a Congregational church.

My father rebelled and became an artist and jazz musician, marrying the gorgeous and deep-hearted Jewess, my mother. My parents eventually settled in Levittown on Long Island, where my dad supported our family by running a small ad agency that he started himself. Somehow the overachieving gene had skipped my father and landed in me, manifesting as a harsh and bossy critic, relentlessly seeking perfection and being satisfied with nothing less.

While I was demanding of others, I was much tougher on myself. Few accomplishments left me with an authentic sense of self-worth. It may seem odd that a woman like me, one who's made it to the top of her field and contributed to a revolution in brain science, would have such low self-esteem. After all, to the casual observer, I'm a world-class scientist, a diva who deserves the best. I should feel fulfilled—and travel in style!

But I don't. I carry my luggage on and always fly economy. I'm like the shoemaker's daughter who goes barefoot. Given my accomplishments, I should be inheriting the kingdom, but instead I'm out trying to earn it. This incongruous lack of contentment and fulfillment drove me right into the arms of the consciousness movement, a place where I found people looking deeper into themselves, wanting to understand their true essence and the nature of reality.

"Stop trying so hard!" Deepak Chopra had admonished me, when I asked him what he thought I should do to get my controversial drug out of the gate and into the hands of the millions who were dying of AIDS. He was the first to teach me that consciousness creates reality, and I've been embracing that dictum ever since I learned to meditate under his mentoring in the early '90s. "First comes the nonmaterial, your state of mind, and from that, all material manifestation flows," he'd said. He meant that our inner thoughts and feelings can bring about a transformation of the outer reality.

Well, if that's the case, I figured, *my inner world of inadequacy, self-sabotage, and undeservingness certainly isn't going to manifest the resources I need to get Peptide T out.* What needed to be transformed was *me.*

"Trust the infinite organizing power of the nonlocal field!" Deepak had said, referring to the quantum God-realm that he's written and taught about for the past 20 years. "By trying so hard, you're just putting more obstacles in your own way!"

And I'd been learning my lesson. But especially in the past seven years, I'd been so beaten down from the stress of events and personal tragedies in my life that I'd almost given up. My passion, my mission of curing disease, had faded in the wake of underfunded—hence, *equivocal*—clinical trials, failure to get grants, and my own unforgiving grudges and anger.

Heart of Darkness

Talking with Nancy about our book before I departed for Minneapolis, I discovered that I'd repressed much of that dark seven-year period in my life, even "forgotten" it, because it was so agonizing to think of or talk about. It's interesting how often only the memories and perceptions that make us feel good are allowed to surface, while others stay immobilized in our subconscious and impact our choices, usually for the worst. Now Nancy's probing was bringing up the "heart of darkness," the story of what had gone on with Peptide T during that time. It was very painful to recall how the government's equivocal clinical trial had spun out in a series of events that impacted the tragedy of my sister's suicide, exacerbating and bringing to an end her years of struggle with depression and bipolar disorder.

In 1998, seven months before Wynne's death, the NIH finally published the results of their 210-person, three-site, placebo-controlled clinical trial designed to investigate Peptide T's effectiveness to treat AIDS. The report showed that the drug caused a statistically significant improvement in neuropsychological measures for clinically impaired people with HIV disease, the study's focus, but mentioned nothing about the drug's ability to decrease the viral load in the blood of a controlled group of AIDS patients. The report was published with zero fanfare, which wasn't surprising, given the conflicts and controversy that had played out over the eight years since the study had started.

That NIH trial had been initiated by the demands of AIDS activists who'd seen positive results for Peptide T in an earlier trial in Boston, one funded by Peptide Design, the company that Mike and I founded after we left the NIH. The activists actually descended on the NIH in a wave of protest, frightening and offending a key government official, whom I'll call "Dr. AIDS Trials."

A tribunal of investigators from various departments and agencies was called, and it was determined that previous Peptide

T results were worth the funding necessary to carry out a double-blind, placebo-controlled trial. Four years into the study, in 1994, when investigators opened the sealed envelope revealing who'd taken the placebo and who'd taken Peptide T, Dr. AIDS Trials called a press conference. Claiming that they were unable to replicate the results of the earlier Boston trial, she called the NIH trial a failure and sent a press release out over the Internet announcing that Peptide T had been found ineffective.

We were devastated. Our drug, it seemed, was dead in the water. Our Dutch investor at the time was also devastated and took away from the NIH announcement a clear but inaccurate message: *Peptide T doesn't work for HIV disease.* Our investor shifted his focus and began to look at other possible uses for Peptide T, in particular, as a treatment for the skin disease psoriasis.

The premature press release—before a scientific report of the trial—had reverberations within the group that had been investigating the drug. Doctors who'd been in charge of the three trial sites objected, saying that they'd seen a definite improvement in their subjects' cognitive impairment, not to mention T-cell numbers. Fractious meetings followed as the controversy deepened, with people literally screaming at each other behind closed doors.

Michael and I were banned from these meetings because we were considered too emotionally invested to attend, so we were kept at arm's length while the battle raged on. During this time, we seethed with anger and resentment, blaming Dr. AIDS Trials, the virologists, and anyone else involved in the debacle. Like two parents watching their drowning child, we stood by in horror when we weren't railing against the injustice of it all. It was a very dark time.

Well before all of this began, my sister, Wynne, had moved to D.C. from New York City, where she was a paintings conservator at the Metropolitan Museum of Art. At the museum, she'd worked closely with gay men, many of whom began to die of AIDS, and she wanted to help Mike and me with Peptide T. Unbeknownst to us, Wynne had started a network to distribute the drug on the AIDS underground when our company Peptide Design went under and became "Peptide Demise." She founded the Chesapeake Bay Buyers' Club, billed on the Internet as a clearinghouse for information and access to AIDS therapy. My sister became our heart and our conscience, reminding us through her compassion why we did what we did. She was also a "brain," learning about Peptide T from her experience and later sharing her knowledge of how the drug could be better formulated and stored.

But because Peptide T was stalled and going nowhere, starting in 1990 and staying the same through much of the decade, it was a sad time for us all. Mike and I did our best to keep the drug research alive, but we had few resources other than our small salary. Our persistent but inexperienced attempts to get NIH funding had failed. Most of the experiments we were able to perform happened because I convinced friends and colleagues to join us in collaborative studies. The deck, it seemed, was stacked against us, and we did our best to simply survive.

In 1998, the weekend before Wynne died, I was invited by Horst Rechelbacher to speak at an annual Aveda conference, a lavish show held in New York City at Radio City Music Hall with a panel of bigwigs of the mind-body movement, including Andrew Weil, Deepak Chopra, and me. I'd gotten a glamorous makeover and a new hairdo, all gratis from Horst, himself a former hairstylist. During my solo lecture, in a flagrant display of my unscientific, playful personality, I turned into an unabashed entertainer, dancing on the stage and telling the audience how as a child I loved seeing the Rockettes when I visited Radio City with my grandmother every Christmas season.

Meanwhile, my sister was becoming suicidal, and a few days after I returned to Washington, she took a fatal overdose of her medications. She was found unconscious in her apartment by our visiting mother, lying in the bathtub with the water still running. We'd all been keeping a close eye on Wynne, planning to take her to the hospital on the very morning that we found her, because she'd been so depressed and had become dysfunctional once again. At the age of 48, it was her third and final attempt to end her life.

Three days after Wynne's death, I made an appointment for a therapy session with the world's top expert on suicide, hoping to get help in my grief and quell my gnawing sense of responsibility. I was comforted by what the therapist told me: For every person who commits suicide, there are eight others who blame themselves. I could easily count that many people in this situation, but dealing with my sister's death was still the most difficult emotional challenge I've ever encountered. I continue to work on forgiving myself, learning again and again the lessons of responsibility and courage that it taught me.

Turning Point

It was shortly after the NIH trial results were published in the January 1998 *Archives of Neurology,* showing statistically significant improvement from Peptide T for neuro-AIDS, but no other standard, that I got wind of some amazing news from a medical technician who'd been involved in the trial. Blood samples of the participants had been taken at many points during the trial, carefully labeled to indicate drug or placebo, and then frozen for storage.

I was shocked. Why, in the five-year duration of the trial, had no one analyzed blood from the placebo group compared to blood of participants given the drug? Viral levels could be shown to go up or down this way, the gold standard of whether an antiviral is effective or not. It was as if the trial investigators had gone to the moon and failed to pick up a rock!

After this discovery, we had new fuel for our anger, which continued to fester. We came up with many theories about how the oversight had happened, but all we really knew was that four years into the trial, the offended Dr. AIDS Trials had concluded, based on partial results, that Peptide T held no future promise. From our perspective, she hated us, hated our drug, hated the activists who were calling her and threatening to come to her house with demands that the drug be released to the public. She put the whole thing to bed by issuing a premature release saying that it didn't work, and no one even thought about looking at the blood samples stored in the deep freeze.

Even more riveting was the news that the blood samples—after four years—were still sitting on the shelf of an NIMH-controlled freezer in California, clearly numbered in code to show when and from whom they were taken (either the placebo group or the group that had taken Peptide T). Knowing that measuring the virus was the key to proving the drug's effectiveness, I immediately began a letter-writing campaign to get the blood samples released to be tested for further analysis.

I was on fire once again, determined that Peptide T be given a second look and that my sister's efforts not be in vain. With advice from a lawyer friend, however, I toned down my sharp, demanding verbiage. A few months later, my efforts culminated in the NIMH agreeing to contract with a university laboratory to finally measure the virus in the blood samples of patients who'd been in the original trial.

Deep Throat

We waited, but heard nothing for three more years. Then one Sunday afternoon, I got a call at my home from the university professor who'd been contracted by the NIMH to run the additional tests. In a slightly muffled voice, he asked Mike and me to meet him at a sushi bar in downtown D.C. (not a parking garage, as in the political "Deep-Throat" operation!), which he'd chosen in order to maintain the secrecy of his mission.

"I've got the data," he blurted when we were all seated at the restaurant. "The HIV virus levels went down in blood samples of people who were given Peptide T and went up in the placebo control group." He'd been frustrated with the process that had kept these new findings from coming to light and wanted us to know what he'd found.

Mike and I were ecstatic to hear this news and started to make plans for using the data, when our informant told us he couldn't give it to us, that he'd lose his funding and be toast in the eyes of the U.S. government for any future opportunities. We left the sushi bar more frustrated than ever, gagged and bound from taking any action that might lead to our drug being exonerated. We continued to petition the government for the release of any new data, but our pleas fell on deaf bureaucratic ears.

The only light in those dark times was the results from the trial that Mike and I raised funds for, reported in the journal *Peptides* in 2003. Our trial of 11 AIDS patients showed that Peptide T caused blood cells to stop making the virus, T cells to increase, and cellular reservoirs (where HIV often lurks, awaiting opportunity to reinfect the blood) to be flushed clean—all in the absence of any drug-related toxicity. Unfortunately, the study was too small to create the ripple we needed for more funding, but it did bolster our hopes and indicated that Peptide T had some unique antiviral effects.

Then, in 2004, a miracle happened. Dr. Tom Insel—a colleague, superb neuroscientist, and peptide expert who'd trained briefly in my laboratory years ago—was appointed director of the NIMH. I visited him shortly after his installment and requested that the data from the contracted test be released into my hands. With a sweep of his director's arm, Tom wiped away years of bureaucratic stonewalling, and the data was in our hands to analyze, publish, and post on our Website, **TINM.org**. The promise of Peptide T was restored, and Mike and I began to write an abstract to present to our colleagues at an upcoming scientific gathering.

The Stress Goes On

By the summer of 2005, I was hopeful but exhausted. The stressful events of the last 15 years had culminated in me gaining weight; suffering financial setbacks; and surviving some serious blows to my relationship with Michael. It was all finally catching up with me and hitting hard, perhaps because the breakthrough was in sight and somewhere in my bodymind, I knew that I'd be getting a rest.

So it was no surprise that on the morning of my departure for Minneapolis, I fell and injured my ankle. I was at breakfast, engrossed in reading about the funding that was newly available for avian-flu research, when I jumped up to answer the phone. I put my weight on my foot, which had fallen asleep, and tripped over it to fall hard on my kitchen floor. I was instantly in agony, having twisted and sprained my ankle, which immediately started to swell. Within minutes of icing and elevating my foot, a large purple-and-yellow bruise appeared.

I considered canceling the trip, but Mike reminded me of all the people expecting to attend my lectures. Within an hour, I was hobbling around, throwing clothes into a suitcase and barking orders at my husband to make sure that a wheelchair would meet us at the airport. Mike was stressed, I was stressed, and even the dog was stressed, but the show must go on. . . .

On the plane, I had some time to regroup and make sense of what had happened. On one level, I'd simply tripped, but on another level, where there are no accidents and consciousness gives rise to outward manifestation, I was responsible for my fall. Examining this deeply, I could see how my behavior fit a theory I'd been developing in my new-paradigm physiology that each of us is a collection of different and conflicting multiple personalities.

Quantum Psychology: Multiple Personalities

I've been thinking and lecturing for years about how the disease called multiple personality disorder (MPD) has a great deal to teach us about who we are—our "normal" identity—in the new paradigm of bodymind.

Freud opened the door for an exploration of multiplicity with his descriptions of the id, ego, and superego; and Jung discussed archetypes, taking the notion many steps further. But my own theory isn't about divisions within the mind or psyche, but rather points to a whole range of normal subpersonalities at the level of the bodymind.

As often happens when I come up with a new theory, I discovered that parts of the idea were already out there, in this case as developed by psychologist Richard C. Schwartz, who described a theory of nonpathological multiplicity. The holistic, spiritual approach to normal multiplicity was provided by Drs. Hal and Sidra Stone.

Most people are familiar with MPD from movies such as *The Three Faces of Eve* and *Sybil.* Traumatized horribly and repeatedly as young children, some individuals somehow become shattered or disintegrated into many personalities in order to survive. In extreme cases, where trauma is especially severe, they may have as many as 10 or 20 different "alters," or subpersonalities, that are completely isolated from each other in terms of memory, behavior, and even physiology.

The classic case of MPD is characterized by the wild, nymphomaniac barfly showing a lot of cleavage who wakes up in a strange bed, searches for her glasses and hair band to tie up her tight bun, then buttons her blouse to the very top and rushes off to her library job where she becomes an exacting "Ms. Prim" personality. (Sexy librarians, please forgive the stereotyping!)

Sometimes one personality hides things from the others, or may sabotage and even plot to kill an alter because of the interpersonality warring and hatred that's common in MPD. The physiological differences can be so extreme that one personality might be a cat fancier while another is allergic to felines. When the allergy-prone personality is dominant, all the symptoms are exhibited, but when the cat fancier is in charge, the person is symptom-free.

The fact that subpersonalities such as these have been shown to have different brain scans is less interesting than the fact that they truly look physically distinct. This isn't just because they have different hairstyles and clothes, but because the muscles of their faces are held and shaped differently from one personality to the next. Films of patients taken by psychologists show that these whole-body "state changes" occur instantaneously during transition—truly quantal shifts.

Dr. Frank Putnam, who had made many discoveries about MPD at the NIMH, occupied an office that I inherited shortly after he left. I'd wondered why a window in the office had been bricked up, and when I met Frank at an event and asked him, he told me an amazing story that illustrates the nature of the MPD "shift" between different personalities.

Frank was interviewing and filming an MPD patient in his office when workmen began to brick up the one window from the outside in preparation for building a new wing. (This is typical government-style expansion, as a new building can require an act of Congress, while multimillion-dollar additions can be slipped through bureaucratic cracks.) Becoming aware of the window being sealed off triggered a claustrophobic panic in Frank's patient, who instantly changed from a hunched, shy person into a towering, threatening alter personality, and Frank caught the switch on film. There was nothing gradual about the shift. Rather, it was instantaneous, providing a piece of data suggesting the quantal nature of MPD state change.

After I learned about this story, I decorated the bricked-up window with some artistic graffiti that read: "Reality is for people who can't handle drugs." Not only did this decorative touch improve the appearance of my office, but it also reminded me that what we call "reality" is *already* a drug-induced state, only the "medications" are natural and produced internally, not lab-made and prescribed or bought on the street.

My theory is that there's a normal state of MPD, not just a pathological state. The latter occurs when a person is disintegrated and has no recognition or control from one state to another, with each personality existing completely separate from the others. In the former, we can recall the other subpersonalities, although we may not be able to change from one to the other easily. Think of a time when you've been angry or humiliated and acted in a way that wasn't "you," yet you couldn't change your reaction—even though you wanted to.

In the laboratory of my own self-development, I'd observed my subpersonalities for years, noticing how one would frequently block the intentions and desires of the other, sabotaging efforts that had to do with success, money, and relationships. Without an understanding of new-paradigm physiology, I might have thought I was going insane, as so many different aspects of myself have been in conflict with so many others!

We all have many subpersonalities, or altered states of consciousness, that are happening at the level of the bodymind. To understand this is to give new meaning to psychological growth. Our old-paradigm psychology is highly biased to consider mental health a matter of one stable, integrated personality, causing us to deny that we are multiple selves and believe we must be a single self.

In the old paradigm, where mind and body are two separate entities, we think of change and growth as occurring in the brain. In the new paradigm, psychological change occurs in the bodymind, not just inside the skull. In the bodymind, change is more of a multidimensional "state change," whereas in the older model, shifts are linear, not holistic and involving the entire organism. In the bodymind, what transforms is the whole, which includes and is simultaneous with thoughts, emotions, physical reality, and even the soul or spirit.

Our "Selves-Esteem"

This new view, grounded in the physiology of bodymind, allows us to have compassion for and forgive our many *selves,* leading to a new state of "*selves*-esteem!" We can apply this understanding to many troublesome problems, such as drug addiction and weight control, realizing that some subpersonalities can make decisions counter to other personas. If we can accept that we aren't crazy when this counter decision-making happens, we can start to explore and integrate the many aspects of our multiple selves.

In normal people, emotions are the quantal trigger for changes from one personality to the next. In one we're forgiven; in another we aren't. The link, the bridge between them that transforms one to the other, is the emotions. Like light, which is both a wave and a particle, feelings become matter (receptors, ligands, and sudden expressions of gene programs like that for inflammation) as they vibrate in the quantum field.

If you think about the effects of drugs such as marijuana, alcohol, and heroin, you see that drugs alter behavior and expression much as an emotion can, sometimes changing someone so remarkably that he or she is no longer recognizable as the same person. In other words, feelings are as powerful as drugs, and they work the same way biologically, utilizing cellular peptides and their receptors—our molecules of emotion.

Thinking about who we really are and the role that emotions play, I've come up with a definition of them that's relevant to my theory of normal, nonpathological subpersonalities: *Emotions are the flow of information perceived to be essential for the survival of any particular state of consciousness being observed.* This definition recognizes that our own observations, perceptions, beliefs, and notions of reality can switch around. Because emotions have their hardwired roots in millions of years of our survival and evolution, any given subpersonality observing the world will be pretty darn sure that he or she is the "right" one. This explains why being right sometimes feels like a matter of life or death!

The theory that normals can be MPD-like has many interesting applications in self-development and psychology, but it can also help us understand our spiritual selves. Studies done by Ralph Allison on pathological MPDs who underwent an exorcism shed light on our spiritual identity. From his observations of MPD patients, Allison coined the term *inner self helper* (which his colleagues evolved into *higher self*) to apply to the one personality he observed that not only knew all the other aspects, but was also aware of events that none of the other personalities could possibly know, such as things that had occurred before birth.

Allison also found that true MPDs are in the top 4 percent of people who are able to be hypnotized, indicating their greater suggestibility. I believe that the key to successful psychospiritual therapy and/or feeling good is to train yourself to come from the highest possible "observer"—the subpersonality that's most closely associated with the divine, or the higher self.

How do you get there? For me, the daily practice of meditation is the best way to anchor a "personality" of higher consciousness. In recent years, a number of people have developed electronic brain-biofeedback systems that promise to achieve quickly what years of meditation can do. My experiences with these approaches have been personally positive, but they don't have the quantity or quality of data associated with them. Of course, for many people the altered state of daily prayer works just fine.

A Reception in Minneapolis

While our plane was taxiing to the terminal, I glanced at a copy of *USA Today* and saw that Minneapolis had the nation's highest percentage of households in which both spouses held jobs. I thought about the bonnet macaque monkey mothers from the New York University study, and the toll on human children in families where the mother was constantly concerned about survival, leaving little time for nurturing. Like the monkey babies in the study, my youngest son, Brandon, now 23 and a senior at California Institute of the Arts near Los Angeles, had missed out on mothering because of my angst-driven attempt to develop Peptide T during most of his younger years.

There was a lot in my life that needed forgiveness, whether it was absolving others who had blocked Peptide T or releasing my feelings toward Wynne for leaving such a vacuum in my life. And even more, I needed to forgive myself for all the times that I hadn't been there for the people in my life whom I loved—such as Brandon.

The first night in Minneapolis, Mike and I were honored at a party given for us by Horst, who'd sold Aveda in 1997 and then founded Intelligent Nutrients. The bash was held at his impeccably decorated home, a veritable citadel of Tibetan and Indian art where we'd be staying for the first few days of the tour. Horst often entertained, and held forums with, interesting, leading-edge people interested in eco-holism, which is the idea that we're all connected to the earth, a concept that is Horst's own driving passion. The event was attended by a "who's who" of the Minneapolis consciousness community, everyone feasting at an elaborate Indian buffet set up in the spacious screening room. I felt like royalty, or at least a movie star, while at the same time my low self-esteem dogged me with the familiar sense of undeserving.

Adding to my discomfort, my ankle was still swollen and painful, keeping me on the couch with an elevated leg for most of the evening. While Mike brought me food, I got plenty of attention from the healers and psychics who were attending the party. One woman, who was an ex-nurse and now the director of a mind-body unit at the local hospital, did an energy healing on my foot and assured me that it wasn't broken. As she worked, I could feel the pain leaving and the energy flowing. Another woman offered to read my etheric body (a phrase that she used to describe my energy field) and find a psychic explanation for the injury. She closed her eyes and told me that she could "see" something stuck in my energy field, possibly unfinished business that was literally causing me to trip over myself and prevent any further progress.

As she spoke, I knew exactly what she meant. She was noticing the energetic manifestation of my frustration and self-sabotage related to Peptide T: the years of wrong turns, miscalled judgments, blaming, self-recrimination, lost faith, and failed attempts—the whole catastrophe! The injury was letting me know that the past needed to be healed and forgiven, or I'd continue to stumble over my many selves, taking a step forward and then setting things up to fail, not getting what I deserve, and not fulfilling my mission.

At that moment, the full impact of my own responsibility in the matter hit me—and hard. I could no longer afford to hang on to ways of being that didn't support my raising funds for Peptide T, such as working myself too hard; overcommitting; and being harsh and critical toward others, Michael, and myself. I'd have to get over my low selves-esteem and let the abundance I needed in order to move forward flow to me from the universe. Somehow I had to forgive myself.

The next day, my ankle was still bruised, and I could hobble along with the help of a cane. I was scheduled to talk to a group at Northwestern Health Sciences University, a school of chiropractic and Eastern medicine. After my talk, it was arranged that I would have a session with Dr. Wan, a member of the faculty.

Using his needles skillfully, the doctor placed them in various points on my abdomen to impact the meridian that runs through the ankle, and I experienced immediate relief. The people attending my talk had to wait, but they got over their annoyance when I explained to them how my first husband, Agu Pert, and I had shown through early experiments at the NIH that acupuncture released endorphins in rats, contributing to its mainstream acceptance and more widespread use. I thanked them for being so gracious to allow me to benefit from the fruits of this early discovery.

While we were staying at Horst's, Jane had arranged to have us all be part of a local PBS pilot production called *Deep Dish.* She brought the film crew over early, when we were still at breakfast with Horst, enjoying our organic eggs cooked with Himalayan rock salt and sipping our antioxidant tea in the incredibly high-ceilinged breakfast room of his estate. Jane would be the hostess for the one-hour show, posing provocative questions about the future of the planet to a lineup of six guests, including Horst, Mike, myself, and an inner-city youth who'd benefited from Continuum's community-development programs.

Taking me aside, Jane plotted to make sure that Mike and I had some one-on-one time with Horst. "Stay up here and talk with him while I get the shoot set up down there," she said, referring to a building located alongside the river and below the main house, where the filming would take place. Jane knew that Mike and I wanted to talk to Horst about funding our research, but were awkward in striking the perfect moment and pitch.

"Then, you can leave to get your makeup on for the filming and let the two boys talk alone for a few minutes," she said, covering all the bases as she headed down to the set.

Later, after the filming was over, I asked Mike how it had gone, and in his usual, low-key way of responding to my more pressing inquiries, he said, "I think he's considering it." Further grilling only brought more of the same. But I had faith in Horst and believed he'd help us once again. Horst had the vision, enthusiasm, and confidence in our science to help manifest a cure for AIDS.

On the Marsh

On the last day of our visit, we moved from Horst's house to The Marsh, a premier mind-body hotel and spa where I'd be giving my final talk before heading back to D.C.

The facility had been founded by Ruth Stricker, a holistic pioneer who healed herself of lupus through exercise and mind-body approaches, and then designed an environment to bring together the best of East and West. Our stay at The Marsh, which Jane had arranged with Ruth, was intended to be a relaxing interlude—a "vacation," she'd said. But the pain of being injured and the frantic pace of events all culminated in our healing interlude being anything *but*. We were disoriented by the move and were having some trouble getting our footing in the new environment when disaster struck.

Just hours before my presentation, I was in the shower, thinking about Peptide T and how I planned to present the latest chapter in its development to my audience that night. Lost in a reverie about the many twists and turns in the story of what had been stopping us, I stepped out of the shower, slipped on the wet floor, and landed hard in-between the sink and the bathtub's edge. Michael heard my shriek and rushed to my rescue. It was a painful and humiliating ordeal that left me with a badly bruised sacrum. Now I couldn't walk *or* sit!

But there was another lesson for me in this latest mishap. The sacrum is the base of the spinal column, a structure linked to survival and financial issues in the Hindu chakra system. By falling and bruising this part of my body, I'd brought my full attention to an area where I was still carrying my old, unresolved emotional memories that kept me in a perpetual state of worry and concern about not having enough money. It was the story of how Peptide T had been stalled, almost completely derailed, due to lack of funding over the past two decades.

Raising Money Consciousness

Synchronistically, it was Horst who'd been an early money mentor for me, helping me see the subject in a new way. Back in the '90s, when I'd joined him, Andy Weil, and Deepak Chopra for the panel discussion onstage at Radio City Music Hall, Horst had talked about how currency was a spiritual energy that—once released—could make things happen for the betterment of the planet. "When money flows, transformation is possible," he had said.

I was shocked when I first heard Horst talking about cash as energy, because it conflicted with my own unconscious beliefs that it was dirty, a necessary evil to be endured and then moved on from. As he talked, I saw wealth as a tool for the first time, a power that could be used positively to benefit others and bring about desired results. It was an eye-opening experience, pointing out how my childhood and early family background had colored my view of the matter with distrust, fear, and danger.

My maternal grandfather's family were wealthy Lithuanian Jews who'd emigrated in the mid-19th century. Settling in Pennsylvania, my mother and her sister were reared in the lap of luxury, until my mother's senior year in high school—1929. After the stock-market crash, Grandfather Rosenberg, a generous and compassionate property owner, let tenants stay on who couldn't afford to pay rent, until he lost his property and was forced into bankruptcy.

During the Depression, my grandfather's brothers invested in a small business, a candy store and soda fountain in Atlantic City, New Jersey, which they gave to my grandfather to run, providing him with income and a small apartment behind the store. My grandparents were soon joined by my parents, a young couple with a new baby—me—when the war was over and housing and jobs were hard to find. I spent my earliest years in the cramped and chaotic family-living area behind my grandfather's shop.

Only it wasn't just a candy store. The mob had gradually coerced my grandfather into allowing gambling rackets to operate from there. One of my earliest memories is my grandfather putting slugs in the pinball machine and setting me up on a wooden box, watching happily as I pulled the levers and shrieked in delight at seeing the balls go around. But this extra use of the slugs attracted unwanted attention. After that, my grandfather would no longer give me slugs whenever I wanted to play. I also remember cigar boxes filled with cash, and I developed a subpersonality that connected money with fear, anxiety, and even danger. Cash was anything but positive energy; it was a problem best left to others whenever possible.

My mother's shock at going from riches to rags, the threat and violence of gangsters in the only home I knew, and the post-traumatic stress that my father suffered after returning from the war were emotional events that formed my earliest memories, and they were all related to basic survival and money issues.

Soon after I'd had the consciousness-raising money insight, I bumped into an old girlfriend from high school, Olivia Mellan, at a very sad moment. In the oddest of synchronicities, Mike and I discovered my friend sitting in the seat behind us during the train ride we took to carry Wynne's ashes to our family cemetery in Lyme, Connecticut.

Olivia, who was always brilliant and had graduated second in our high-school class, was now a practicing psychotherapist whose specialty was helping couples with their money issues. She had written a book, *Money Harmony,* and had been on *Oprah.* I called her up when we got back to town and made an appointment, and Mike agreed to accompany me.

"Look, we've got a drug that can lead to the vaccine to cure AIDS," I remember telling her, "but we keep getting stalled by not having enough money to fund its development. Every breakdown has involved a lack of cash, so how can you help us get our financial issues together so that we can move on . . ."

In just a few sessions, Olivia helped us each determine what she called our individual "money personality," the style or approach a person uses in relating to wealth. We learned how, as a long-term couple, we'd become polarized in this respect, Mike being a "Hoarder/Avoider," and me being a "Spender/Amasser." These extremes were part of a struggle in our marriage that was sadly reflected in our business dealings regarding Peptide T.

With her tough guidance and wisdom, Olivia taught us to communicate with each other respectfully so that the money issues would solve themselves. I began to shift my way of being around the matter and had made much progress, but was still evolving and transforming this area of my life as we pursued further funding for Peptide T. The key, I learned, lay in forgiving and respecting all my selves and thus learning to forgive and respect the other people drawn into my life (especially Michael), who were, after all, mirrors of my own mind.

"Money is the root of all evil"—that's how we're used to hearing it, but quoted correctly from the Bible, the expression is, "the *love* of money is the root of all evil." The object itself is neutral, whereas *loving* it, not our fellow humans or God, is the source of much trouble. In a new paradigm, wealth can be a powerful force for good in the world, the summation of everything going on around us that either works or doesn't.

The fall on my sacrum had brought to my conscious attention exactly what it was that I needed to do at this time. For the next few months, I'd focus my efforts on the steps that would bring Peptide T into new clinical trials, raising the money to keep Mike and me afloat while we made it all happen. And of course, I'd continue healing and learning to fully forgive myself.

Forgiveness Is Divine

My talk at The Marsh was one of my more informal sessions, in which I allowed myself to step outside of the box more than usual. I arrived onstage with a cane but soon tossed it away, affirming that my foot was healed, but not letting on that my *tuckus* was killing me. I had to be careful not to fall off the stage, remembering how Ann-Margret had once plunged into her audience midway through a song-and-dance number in Vegas.

Jane was thrilled with my presentation and later called it "Candace Unplugged," providing an experience of the person behind the science, and a glimpse into my current thinking about life and my upcoming book. I had to admit that my delivery was definitely in an acoustical mode, but more intimate (if a bit disconnected) than my usual context as the serious scientist.

But what I hadn't mentioned were my thoughts on forgiveness—in particular, my theory on selves-forgiveness and how the subject relates to our many subpersonalities. So when my talk was over, and it was time for the Q & A, I tossed out the question: "What's the one thing you can do to instantly alter your consciousness and make yourself feel good?"

A man stood up in the audience and shouted, "Psychotherapy!"

"No," I told him. "It's *forgiveness*. When you forgive, you experience a deep level of emotion, one that's truly transformative. If there's no emotion, there's no real forgiveness. One of my favorite quotes is 'To err is human, to forgive is divine,' spoken by Alexander Pope a few hundred years ago. These words point to what I believe, which is that you can be born again—with or without religion—when you forgive others and yourself. And for some of us, that's a big job." I'd already shared my theory of subpersonalities with the audience, so when they laughed, I assumed that they understood just how complex it can be.

I thought of a Hollywood film I'd seen recently about how forgiveness can make it possible for a person to completely alter his or her personality, to literally become someone new. In an Oscar-winning performance, Jamie Foxx in *Ray* portrays the singer Ray Charles, who realizes that his little brother's death wasn't his fault and finally kicks his heroin habit. In a profoundly moving scene, Ray's little brother appears in a dream sequence and says to his older sibling, "It wasn't your fault!" (Interestingly, the singer's developmental blindness seems to have been precipitated by the early trauma of seeing his little brother drown in a wash bucket.)

The relationship of drug addiction and forgiveness as portrayed in the movie is an interesting one. Many recovering addicts have taken the path of religion on their way to becoming clean and sober. Do we need that type of faith to forgive? Perhaps—studies show that belief in a Higher Power is often the key for people to recover from drug and alcohol addictions. In the successful 12-step program for treating alcoholism, surrender to a Higher Power is often a crucial turning point.

In another film, *Good Will Hunting*, Robin Williams plays a psychiatrist who holds the tortured, tough-guy genius, played by Matt Damon, as he sobs at hearing his doctor repeat the magic words: "It's not your fault," referring to the young man's childhood abuse by his alcoholic father. The emotional release he undergoes frees him to pursue his goals and enjoy his life, something that wasn't going to happen without the profound moment of self-forgiveness.

Releasing blame requires a quantum shift in which the whole bodymind is altered, a true state change that affects the entire system. It isn't a small thing that's done by degrees, but a whole-body turnaround. Who you are when you forgive yourself and others is someone living in a new reality. You're free and experience true happiness. You can also be healthier, because physical inflammation in your body is diminished (it's no longer continuously triggered by resentment and rage).

If you experience a constant, suppressed state of anger in your bodymind over many years, holding grudges and not forgiving people for incidents that happened in your past, then you're most likely using energy to make antibodies, keeping yourself in a chronically inflamed state. As a result, you tax your immune system to overreact, aggravating autoimmune disorders such as lupus, multiple sclerosis, and rheumatoid arthritis.

Forgiveness is cleansing and revitalizing; it heals processes that contribute greatly to your health. Once you forgive someone, that shift penetrates all the way down to the cells of your immune system, becoming an instantaneous quantum change in your physiology. Somewhere along the line, as cells are being replenished, a decision is made to produce either more for the immune system or for the brain. If you're harboring resentment, that decision may be to make more of the kind of immune cells that stir up inflammation. If you're no longer blaming or carrying a grudge and don't need a fired-up immune response, the decision will go toward producing more brain cells and opening up the possibility of higher states of consciousness.

How to Forgive

My audience was intrigued to hear a scientist promoting forgiveness, and they wanted to know the fastest ways to forgive, if not through psychotherapy. I hadn't planned to be giving a sermon, but these people wanted some practical advice, so I reached inside myself for the resources that had helped me over the very trying past 15 years.

"First, I want to be clear that psychotherapy can help people forgive, but psychological processes can be long and drawn out, whereas other approaches can help people make this release a way of life," I said.

"I believe that the fastest way to forgive yourself and others is to study and embrace the teachings of the great masters and sages, such as Christ or Buddha, as found in the wisdom literature of the world. In this way, you learn gratitude and humility, ideas that pop up in every religion. They're important to practice for experiencing 'at-one-ment,' a state of consciousness that's deeply forgiving.

"Meditation and prayer support the release of old traumas, whether experienced alone or with a group. But like the transfer of vibration between two violins resonating in one room, forgiveness 'catches' more easily in places where like-minded people are gathered—such as a church; group-therapy session; or a spiritual gathering for worship, talks, or meditation.

"Positive affirmations spoken by yourself, or listened to on a CD or tape can help also. One of my personal favorites is: *I know that forgiving myself and others for errors of the past allows me to heal.* This statement helped me recover from grief and depression after the sudden death of my sister. It worked because of the deep emotional resonance I felt every time I heard or said those words. The important point is that emotional expression is transformative, whether it's religiously couched or not. You may have tears or rage before you forgive, but let yourself authentically express your emotions without judgment and you'll be on your way to feeling better . . . and feeling God."

Later, after the book signing (which I did standing up), Jane said to me, "Candace, that last Q & A was fabulous. People came to hear the science, but they got a hefty dose of good old-fashioned faith at the same time! I loved how the entire house fell into a hush as you talked of forgiveness. We all need to learn to forgive, and to hear someone who's also a scientist talk about it . . . it's so important. Thank you!"

I stopped myself from deflecting Jane's kind acknowledgement and actually took my own advice. "Thank *you*," I said, with surprising humility. "I'm very grateful to have had the opportunity to share what I know works, because that's all I can ever do."

Money Miracle

Back home in D.C., I nursed my still-painful injuries, using a wheelchair when I had to and staying horizontal if I could. In two weeks, Mike and I would be leaving for Italy to make a presentation to a group of Jungian psychotherapists at their annual meeting, and I wanted to be fully recovered. I was reclining in a lounge chair out on the back deck, soaking up the afternoon rays, when Mike called from inside the house.

"Horst is going to fund us," he said. "I just got off the phone with his foundation. We're good for at least another six months."

"That's fantastic!" I called back. But before I jumped up to share the triumph with him, I breathed deeply and closed my eyes. Birds were singing and crickets were buzzing in the stillness of our backyard. I smiled, letting go and allowing the warmth of gratitude to suffuse my entire physiology. Horst's support would allow us to move forward with our research and get it back on track, but we were still going to need more investors to help us bring about the large-scale trials that we planned for the near future.

A lot can happen in six months, I mused. I was beginning to experience, not just believe, that truly anything could happen in a world of infinite possibilities. I got up out of my lounge chair, planting both feet squarely on the ground, and rushed into the house to give Mike a big, warm, celebratory hug.

Chapter 7

Assisi: Dreaming,
Spirituality, and Synchronicity

Io amo Italia! I'd attended many scientific conferences in that stylish, fabulous country, and now Mike and I were getting ready to head off to Assisi, Italy, to speak on the mind-body connection at an annual meeting of Jungian psychotherapists. Our previous assistant had booked the plane reservations awhile ago, and we were hoping to find time to play and sightsee, something we sorely needed after our productive but harrowing trip to Minneapolis.

While en route back from Minneapolis, I'd bumped into a former colleague, a research psychologist still at the NIMH, and as we stood collecting our baggage, I mentioned my upcoming travel plans. He looked at me quizzically and asked: "With all due respect, why would a group of Jungian therapists invite *you* to their meeting? They don't do or follow any research, as far as I know." Shades of the lady professor! As if the business of research was the only pursuit allowable for a "real" scientist such as myself!

But the Jungians are less interested in pursuing research than in hearing the latest that science has to offer about dreams, synchronicity, and the collective unconscious—all the areas where I'm most comfortable wearing two hats, the scientist and the mystic. As therapists, they want to bring the leading edge into their practice, helping people heal trauma, transform key issues in their lives, and explore different states of consciousness. Presenting with Mike, who is definitely well grounded in causality—what Carl Jung called "the constant connection through effect"—I knew that the therapists would get the well-organized presentation about consciousness and healing they needed, and we'd have a great time.

On the Peptide-T frontier, things started to happen when we returned from Minneapolis. No longer preoccupied with a personal need for salary support, we could step up our petitions to the government for ownership of the long-stalled license to develop our drug and the search for investments to start the next round of clinical trials. My injuries had healed, our immediate financial woes were abated, and Mike and I were looking forward to a semi-vacation in Assisi, an ancient and timeless land of hills, olive groves, and terraced vineyards.

When I opened up the tour guide Mike had pulled out of the bookcase and left on my desk, the first thing I read was: "Assisi— the place where nature and mysticism meet." I knew that this was the city in central Italy where St. Francis had lived in the 12th century. He was the son of a wealthy merchant but had renounced all material possessions to preach a poor, simple lifestyle harking back to the Gospels. Not only was this holy man born in this region, known as Umbria, but so was St. Clare, the namesake of a branch of the Franciscan order for women called the Poor Clares. And to add to the bounty, St. Valentine, the patron saint of lovers and the heart, was also from the area. Assisi was starting to sound like my kind of place!

While I knew that the very idea would make my Jewish mother and grandmom Rose roll over in their graves, I'd acquired a strong, eclectic Christian identity. I enjoyed taking holy communion and participating in rituals with Michael at all kinds of churches near my home and in my travels.

Forever Jung

As a teenager, I'd been fascinated by Freud's interpretation of dreams, pointing to wish fulfillment and the repressed subconscious as the source of dreaming. But later I discovered that Carl Jung understood what Freud didn't, that dreams were doorways into another reality. It's in this altered state of consciousness, Jung believed, that we connect with our spiritual essence—our soul—which dwells in what he called the "collective unconscious."

To Jung, this concept explained many mystical phenomena, such as love at first sight, déjà vu, creative experiences shared by artists and musicians, and spiritual experiences of mystics of all religions. Dreams, Jung believed, allow us to tap in to our personal unconscious and then move closer and closer to our truer self, residing in the collective unconscious.

Jung is also known as the father of synchronicity, a term he coined to explain "the coincidence of events in space and time as meaning something more than mere chance." This occurs in dreams, for example, when a person dreams about the death of a loved one and awakens to find that the person did, in fact, die during the night. In waking states, you could pick up the phone to call a friend, only to find that your friend is already on the line, calling you. While a more materialistic observer might see these events as coincidence and attribute little meaning to them, Jung believed that they were indications of how we're touching each other and all of nature through the universal collective unconscious.

Quantum physics helps us understand synchronicity. In a quantum world, the boundaries of space and time are expanded, yielding infinite possibilities and opportunities. Jung himself collaborated with Wolfgang Pauli, a leading physicist of his day, in their joint attempt to integrate the principles of psychology. In their efforts, they came up with the term *indestructible energy,* which manifests in the nonquantum universe where causality rules, when synchronicity is happening. I believe that the fact that synchronicities occur much more often than is expected statistically points to the existence of God, the ultimate source of indestructible energy and information.

In the new-paradigm physiology, the human bodymind is a pulsing, electrical, informational phenomenon, more like a flickering flame than a solid machine. This nature allows us to share an emotional, resonant vibration from person to person, perhaps explaining how individuals are brought together in seeming coincidences that are actually synchronicities, attracted to each other for some healing purpose, or to receive guidance for what to do next.

Synchronicity has been a powerful theme in my life, guiding many of my scientific discoveries, as well as important turning points in my personal growth. Lately, I've been experiencing synchronistic occurrences many times in a day, and have gotten to a place where I'm anticipating "coincidences" to reveal directions that are meaningful to me. Such a practice of becoming aware of these phenomena, I find, links the mundane to the divine in my daily life, opening doorways into a future I'm more and more empowered to create. One day, I'm certain, through a scientific study of synchronicity, we will come close to the proof of God.

Creative Conflict

I was thinking about dreaming and synchronicity in preparation for my talk at Assisi when Nancy called me. We'd been working on our book bicoastally, with her in California and me in D.C., speaking during what we dubbed the "sacred hour," a specific time set aside for our daily communication. Lately, our conversations had focused on structure, voice, and other literary elements that go into organizing and writing a book.

At times, we'd fight like sisters as we went through this process. We often changed roles, as one or the other would take the left-brained approach, demanding that an outline be followed or more informational content be added. We took turns insisting that the best course was to just go with the flow, trust the process, and let rip with whatever was interesting at the time. Invariably, that point of view was opposed by a sterner voice of reason, so we went back and forth, whittling away to produce our creation.

In the call we had that morning, Nancy was holding forth for the straight-and-narrow approach, insisting that I present practical applications of my science in the form of advice, suggestions, and "how-tos." But I wasn't seeing it that way. For me, the book was about my answers to questions audiences had been asking me since my first book came out and I appeared in *What the Bleep . . . !?,* most of which included: "Please, Dr. Pert, just tell us how we can feel good!" My answer to that request would have to be an ever-evolving one, coming out of my own growth and journeys in consciousness, adventures that were still unfolding.

"No, no, no!" Nancy was reaching the limit of her frustration after listening to my fifth free-association riff in ten minutes. "I won't listen to any more rambling on about topics that don't fit into our outline! We're too far along to bring in all this new stuff!"

"Relax and just listen, okay?" I tried to calm her down. "The book is writing itself; it's evolving as we evolve, so it's always going to be a work in progress," I offered. "It's not a book about information and advice only, because that's too simplistic and boring. I don't have all the answers. I'm a scientist, not a guru, remember? This book is about my journey, and you're on it with me."

"Of course, I agree with you," Nancy said, relying on her best people skills and sounding more reconciled. "But I'm worried that we're not giving readers more practical, 'how-to' content. You can't just take them on Candace's Adventures in Consciousness-Land, popping up all over the place at a new conference in every chapter. You've got to stop, stand, and deliver. Address your readers and tell them—"

"—where I'm taking them," I interrupted, finishing Nancy's

sentence. "Which is down the rabbit hole—*with me!* The book is going to tell how my understanding of emotions and consciousness brings me ultimately to an understanding and embracing of spirituality. I've told you: I'm coming out of the closet. I'm going to talk about God, and I'm going to do it as a scientist. Remember, the title mentions *feeling good,* but also *feeling God.* I'm coming to a place where I no longer see them as separate."

There was silence on the other end of the phone. I continued, "They'll love it, and anyway, it's the truth. It's both magical and mystical, not simply practical. But for me to pontificate and give some formula for feeling good would be a cheap shot. I'm sharing my own experiences with them, which is all I have. I've got to be honest or I'm nothing. Please understand. . . ." I pleaded.

"Okay, but I just *don't* understand . . ." she trailed off, realizing that her best efforts at corralling some of my wilder excursions, doing her job as a conscientious editor and writer, weren't going to win the day.

"Trust me," I assured her. "In the end, it's going to be about how feeling good isn't just physical or emotional, but spiritual, which is where God—or whatever aspect of divinity you can relate to—comes in. Today, I'd like to talk about dreaming, as impractical as that sounds. I think dreams are the key to understanding how the scientific and the mystical come together, and—"

"Okay, so I'll stop fighting you and just listen," Nancy jumped in, now in my camp and seeing my point. "Go ahead, I want to hear what you have to say about how dreaming can help people feel good and feel God."

And I had a lot to say about the matter. I knew that I was on to something with this new topic, because synchronicities had started to happen more frequently in the past few days, a sign that I was entering a creative zone. Just that morning, I'd "accidentally" come across a book called *The Emerging Mind,* a collection of lectures on consciousness given at the Smithsonian Institute in 1999 and edited by Dr. Karen Shanor. The book (currently out of print, I noticed) had been left on our living-room coffee table by Michael, who'd ordered it with his dad, Robert, when visiting him in Florida. (My father-in-law, who's lived many years after diagnosis with a life-threatening cancer and multiple surgeries, attends morning mass daily and is a great example of the power of prayer and friendship.) I'd picked the book up and randomly opened it to a middle section where my eyes fell across the words *REM, lucid dreaming,* and *higher consciousness.*

"Our next adventure, of course!" I said out loud, standing in the center of my living room. Trusting synchronicity, our book was sure to get written by itself; all Nancy and I had to do was get out of our own way and follow the clues provided by the universe. And how perfect that the topic of dreaming fit in with my upcoming talk to the Jungian therapists in Assisi. I sat down on the sofa and spent the next two hours reading about dreams and organizing my thoughts to share with Nancy during our "sacred hour" phone call later that day.

Dreaming and Reality

I've always been fascinated by the blurring of the line between dreaming and reality. I get a "waffle-y" feeling just contemplating that I might be walking around inside a dream I'm having, dreaming I'm awake. You may have had a dream that seemed more concrete than reality, leading you to ponder the same possibility. In certain aboriginal cultures, people take their sleeping adventures as seriously as their waking consciousness, letting dream content inform and guide their daily lives. But in our society, treating a dream as reality is dangerous. Sanity, we believe, depends on keeping the two distinct!

Somewhere over the rainbow, where the dreams really do come true, is Dorothy's vision of Oz, which we all adore. "A dream is a wish your heart makes . . ." Walt Disney said it often to my generation of Mickey Mouse Club watchers, and his words still evoke the metaphysical aspect of dreams for me.

Does what happens in our dreams influence our waking reality? Can they heal the past, mending traumas that we may have experienced as children or adults? Can they help us develop states of higher consciousness? Can we solve problems, create new possibilities, and see new futures through dreaming? I believe that the answer to all these questions is yes, and there's plenty of good science to support it.

From my understanding of the bodymind as a network of energy and information, I view dreaming as a conversation between psyche and soma (mind and body). It's the nighttime dramatization of memories and emotions bubbling up from the cellular level on their way into consciousness. When we remember our dreams, we can process past trauma or experience what we aren't able to deal with in waking consciousness, integrating those events to make us more whole. Dreaming is also a by-product of cellular repair and replenishment.

I wrote in my first book about a pivotal dream I had that led to a deep and lasting healing of a rift with my early scientific mentor, Dr. Sol Snyder. The dream took place in an Oz-like world where Sol was the Wicked Witch of the West whom I splashed with water. I watched as this towering presence melted and then disappeared, no longer posing a threat to me. In my waking consciousness, I stopped seeing myself as a victim and was able to let go of my anger. My near-obsessive need to restore our broken relationship began to fade. I found myself forgiving Sol and getting on with the business of my life.

Dreams can solve problems and create new realities for the dreamer and for others. There are many cases of scientific discoveries that came from researchers' dreams, which provided solutions to particular problems, and thus gave a new future to humanity. One involves the 19th-century Russian chemist Dmitri Ivanovich Mendeleev, who had been trying for years to classify the fundamental elements according to their atomic weights. One night in 1869, Mendeleev had a dream in which he saw the table laid out with all known 63 elements in place. Upon waking up, he wrote down what he remembered, and amazingly, only one place needed correction later on. Thus, the periodic table of elements, a critical discovery of modern chemistry and a familiar page in any high-school science textbook, came into existence.

Recalling Dreams

I've kept a dream journal for years, recording what I can remember upon waking up every morning. Then I read over and examine the plots and metaphors as a way to understand myself better.

But many people can't remember their dreams, and some actually "poo-poo" the value of this information. A now-debunked theory of dreams saw them as nothing more than "garbage in, garbage out," a useless visual mosaic with no significance other than signs of indigestion from a heavy meal eaten before sleep. I take this view as a reflection of our materialistic culture, in which we don't take our inner life seriously, a taboo that not all cultures share.

You can cultivate a postdream memory by writing down even a snippet of what you remember as soon as you wake up. I kept a notebook and pen by my bedside for years and found that the more I wrote, the more I'd recall. Now I don't write down my dreams quite as often, but my recollections are still sharp. This technique of capturing what you can works because as you focus on any aspect of a dream, you draw the whole thing more completely into your waking consciousness. If you often record your memories in this manner, then each time you dream you'll remember more.

The Biology of Dreaming

When scientific researchers study dreaming, they find themselves in areas usually left to philosophy, religion, and metaphysics. Yet there's a lot of hard science done on the biology of the experience, and I'm familiar with data that points to the healing power of dreams, as well as how they can impact the waking reality that we normally experience.

Studies from the 1970s done in sleep laboratories showed how subjects' brain waves fluctuated as they went in and out of REM sleep. These letters are an acronym for "rapid eye movement," a physiological sign that a person is dreaming. We know that this plays a role in the reorganization and restoration of brain functions that involve problem-solving, memory consolidation, and creativity. These processes rely on the formation of neuronal networks, or groups of synaptic connections between neurons in the brain—what's been referred to as "neural nets," which provide the actual physical foundation for any given perceptual reality.

Coming from the bodymind continuity, I suspect that peptides play a role in how dreaming impacts reality and keeps us healthy. During REM, or dreaming sleep, a peptide called "vasointestinal peptide" (VIP) is released in the frontal cortex of the brain. I've done experiments in the lab with neurons from a developing brain, adding this substance to them in a petri dish, and watched as more neurons survived. There's a whole set of literature showing that VIP's purpose in the brain is to ensure that the organ's cells become stabilized and survive, not dying off too easily, as they would if VIP weren't present.

A recent study by a Spanish team of researchers showed that the secretion of this peptide actually increases REM sleep, and thus dreaming, while an "antagonist" (a receptor-blocking substance) is correlated to a decrease in REM and dreaming. It's very interesting to me that a peptide coming out of the frontal cortex, the area of higher decision making, planning, and intention, is nourishing brain cells at the same time it's increasing dreaming. Is VIP nourishing neurons that are active during a dream, thus stabilizing the neural networks being formed at the time of dreaming? If so, this could explain how dreams can literally become reality.

Studies done on sleeping infants may shed some light on the role of VIP stabilizing neuronal networks during dreaming, and thus "creating reality." Fifty percent of a newborn's sleep cycle is spent in REM sleep, compared to 25 percent of an adult's. Neural nets begin forming shortly before birth and continue at a high rate afterward, helping newborns learn how to coordinate visual input (such as the sight of a toy) with motor output (such as moving a toy to the mouth). No wonder newborns need huge amounts of REM sleep! They're dreaming and making important neuronal connections, which are being stabilized by VIP, allowing them to experience a new reality of functioning in their awake state. (Preemies show as much as 75 percent REM sleep, as they have even fewer connections established at birth and need to catch up by dreaming more.)

How important is dreaming sleep for adults? In one famous study, subjects were woken up only when they entered REM sleep. They were allowed to return to sleep, but only if they didn't enter REM; if they did, they were woken up once again. Within a few days of this pattern, the dream-deprived subjects started to hallucinate and became completely psychotic. Clearly, dreaming is necessary for our mental health, possibly due to the stabilizing and nourishing of new neural nets by VIP. Our dreams keep us sane!

And finally, there's a restorative aspect of these sleeping adventures that involves VIP. When we're sleeping, we're constantly recharging ourselves, and dreaming makes it possible, in my theory, to remain in slumber. During sleep, our brains are under construction, so dreaming may be a physiological function that allows us to get the rest we need and have our brains nourished. VIP works to stabilize and support the neurons as long as you're dreaming—so dream on for a healthier brain!

By practicing a few simple steps, you can recall your dreams, increase their frequency, and even use them to impact your waking experience.

1. **Keep a dream journal by your bed** to capture your dream stories and metaphors as soon after waking as possible.

2. **Intend to have healing or solution-oriented dreams,** providing some desired result. (This step will become even more important as you learn how to enter into a dream with full lucidity, which I'll discuss in the next section.)

3. **When you do capture a dream, inquire into its meaning for hidden messages,** knowing that this can be an interactive process involving different levels of consciousness.

Taking all these steps will contribute to the building of neural nets in your brain and help you make your dreams come true!

Lucid Dreaming

Nancy called me early the next morning, preempting our usual sacred hour and explaining that what she wanted to tell me couldn't wait.

"Did you go to LaBerge's lecture?" I asked before she could get another word out. I knew she was planning to attend a local talk by Stanford University dream researcher Dr. Stephen LaBerge the night before. The event was part of the same series where I'd be presenting later in the year when I visited Santa Barbara.

"I did," Nancy answered. "It was fascinating. LaBerge talked about something called 'lucid dreaming,' the kind where you're awake and fully aware that you're dreaming, but still in the experience. He talked about how you can heal past issues, get over phobias and fears, and even have moments of higher consciousness during lucidity." Nancy paused. "And guess what? Last night, I had a lucid dream!" she exclaimed.

"Really," I said, my interest piqued. "What was it about?"

"It was a recurring dream," she began, "one I've had many times, always involving some kind of heartbreak or loss, often a love affair gone bad. Basically, I get rejected, suffer terribly, and then become resigned that I'm unlovable and undeserving. It's my version of that low self-esteem subpersonality you deal with—I also struggle with my self- or *selves*-esteem."

I knew all too well what Nancy was talking about.

"I woke up early this morning," she continued, "with lingering emotions still present from the dream. But instead of jumping up, as is my usual habit, and forgetting about the whole unpleasant business, I chose to stay in bed. Lying there still half awake, half asleep, I posed a question to myself: *Is it* true *that I really don't deserve to be loved?*

"It's strange that I never thought to ask that question when I had this experience before! This time, I decided to go back into the dream and ask the 'leading man,' who was playing the part of the love interest, this very important question.

"Because I hadn't fully woken up, it was easy to slip back into the scenario with all its turbulent emotions and reconnect with the cast of characters. Addressing the love interest, a man from my past, I posed the question: *Am I not good enough, not worthy of being loved?*

"The dream man answered back. *No,* he said, as if speaking to me from a wise and authoritative place. *My decision to end the relationship had nothing to do with you or your self-worth. I had my own reasons for moving on, and they had nothing to do with you!*

"A flood of relief hit me as I heard those words, and I realized that for my entire adult life, I'd thought that something was wrong with me, that I was undeserving of love. But it simply wasn't so. Lucidity—being awake in my dream—helped me update the past with the present and shift something that had been impacting me and my happiness in many areas of my life." Nancy paused, obviously moved by her newfound sense of wholeness. Her dream experience had freed her from an old, false subpersonality of low self-esteem. . . . As usual, Nancy and I were on parallel paths in our personal growth.

Science, Spirituality, and Lucidity

Being awake in your dreams—this is surely where the metaphysical and the physical overlap, offering us a rich frontier in which to explore how consciousness creates reality. What Nancy told me on the phone was a fine example of the power of dreams to transform the dreamer and life itself.

Talking further to Nancy, I learned how LaBerge had studied lucid dreaming in his Stanford sleep laboratory and proved that something so subjective could be achieved and even measured. Subjects in his study agreed to use certain eye-movement patterns while dreaming—eyes moving back and forth four times, then two times, then four—to send a signal to researchers who'd be monitoring the movements. In a *Twilight Zone*-like conclusion to the study, the printouts from the monitoring devices showed that the eye-movement patterns had been sent exactly as agreed upon in the waking state, producing a kind of Morse code from dreamland and proving that the subjects were indeed conscious and intentional in their dreams!

LaBerge further studied how lucid dreaming could be used in healing, especially in psychotherapy. He got people with fears and phobias to enter dream states and simulate different behaviors, such as being calm at a cliff's edge where previously they'd been afraid. Making these changes in a dream state, it turned out, translated into changed behaviors in real life, as if the dream were a rehearsal for the waking event.

Other researchers have explored lucid dream states for understanding consciousness, among them Dr. Ernest Rossi, author of the classic book *Dreams and the Growth of Personality*. Rossi linked lucid dreaming with self-awareness, which he defined as the ability to reflect on yourself and your experience. He wrote that the more self-aware a person is, the easier it is for him or her to understand dream metaphors and also to dream lucidly. But when an individual is lacking in self-awareness, developmental blocks cause that person to reject the process. This is comforting if you're frightened by the possibility of waking up one night in the middle of your dream, a potentially disorienting experience. Don't worry—if you're not ready for it, it won't happen!

Exploring how lucidity in dreams relates to the spiritual aspect of consciousness, researcher Dr. Jayne Gackenbach studied meditators and found that the practice increases a person's ability to dream lucidly. These people generally have strong dream recall and a high percentage of lucid-dreaming experiences among them. In fact, some meditation traditions maintain that consciousness in sleep is a marker for the development of higher states of awareness.

Gackenbach's studies of an advanced group of long-term meditators practicing Transcendental Meditation (TM) showed that they could awaken in their dreams and manipulate the plot line to create whatever outcome they desired. They could change its course or, if it wasn't to their liking, back out of it.

She also found that there are higher states of dream consciousness than lucid dreams, ones that have parallels with spiritual or mystical experiences reported in philosophical systems of the East. Western psychologists call these "post-representational," because there's no object of attention in the dreamer's awareness. Instead, the person witnesses a pure or transcendental consciousness, a version of what Buddhists call the "void."

I know from my own experience, having practiced TM since the early '90s, that during meditation there are moments of transcendence or unity, a focused sense of total connection and communion with the universe—bliss! (This isn't to say that you can't experience such moments while you're out running, or even nursing your baby, but meditation makes them more available.) Such meditative states have been measured, showing on EEGs that they're identical to stages that we pass through when awakening from or going into a dream, so-called in-between states of consciousness.

In-between states have been studied by psychologists observing multiple personality disorders. My friend and colleague Frank Putnam observed an omniscient personality that transcended the others, acting like an "oversoul." In the nonpathological form of MPD that I believe we all experience, the same "oversoul" may exist as our higher self, our God or omniscient self, appearing when we aren't too tightly identified with one or more of our more mundane subpersonalities.

All three altered states of consciousness—the blissed-out meditator, the dreamer slipping between sleep and awakening, and the lucid dreamer "witnessing" transcendent consciousness—are scientifically measurable states that we could call the higher self, or simply "God."

And what about the altered state called synchronicity? As a long-term TM meditator, I know that meditation can alter states of consciousness. When I spoke with my friend and mentor Deepak Chopra, I mentioned that I'd been experiencing an increase of synchronistic events in my life. He laughed and said that he could tell I'd been meditating, because the more you do so, he declared, the more synchronistic awareness is available in nonmeditative states.

There are many kinds of meditation, but in the form called TM, a person learns to transcend ordinary reality and enter a state of transcendent consciousness. The state of synchronistic awareness is similar to this, which is why meditation increases the occurrence of synchronicity in a person's life. I wonder, too, if we studied these states of awareness, whether we might find the same EEG range of brain waves for both of them, indicating that, like TM mediators, people who experience synchronicity are living with a higher, transcendent consciousness, or experience of God.

Dreaming the Connection

Mike and I arrived at the Rome international airport sleep deprived (hence, dream deprived) and exhausted from the long transatlantic flight. We'd missed our connection in Paris and arrived in Rome at a different gate than expected, a mix-up that possibly explained why no driver was waiting to take us to Assisi as promised. We made the long walk through the terminal to the original gate but found no driver waiting there either. To make matters worse, the airline had lost our baggage, and our phone calls to the conference center went unanswered. In our exhausted state, we were beginning to think that we had dreamt the Assisi conference, and it didn't really exist at all.

This disorienting situation at the Rome airport was matching a recurring dream that I'd had much of my adult life. In it, I'm trying to get somewhere, and in the process become separated from my traveling companion, usually Mike. I anxiously rush to catch a plane, train, or cruise ship, but get lost and don't know where I'm going. I'm afraid that I won't make it on time, and then I miss the connection.

But in the waking reality of the Rome airport, I was experiencing just the opposite of the dream. Mike and I miraculously stayed connected and in communication smoothly during the ordeal, which wasn't our usual mode, given our exhaustion and the opportunity for bickering and meltdowns. I wondered, *Had my recurring nightmare over the years somehow healed this present reality?* Maybe I'd worked out my fears and insecurities in the old dream, where I'd replayed my anxiety about relationships, trust, and connection over and over again. Now, confronted by a stressful situation in real life, I no longer needed the drama and fear. It was over. The reality had been healed at the level of the dream.

LaBerge's research explains how such a transformation could be possible. To the brain, he says, dreaming and waking consciousness aren't all that different, since both depend on incoming perceptions. When awake, these come from sensory input, such as smell, touch, hearing, seeing, and taste. But while dreaming, we have no sensory input; we "perceive" from our memories. It's the same to the brain whether you experience something, or you imagine or dream it. Neural nets are formed by beliefs and visions, not by external data or sensory input alone. My recurring dream had very possibly caused new neural connections to become stabilized, handling my perceptual references so that my anxiety about real-life, stressful situations could be allayed.

In the end, we decided to take a $450 cab ride that wound us through the gorgeous countryside of central Italy and over the vineyard-covered hills I'd so longed to see. We found later that an error had been made in booking our flight, and the conference had started a day before we arrived. When we didn't show up then, our hosts figured that we weren't coming and went on with the event, which explained why we hadn't been met by a driver and why our frantic calls from the airport were never answered. Our luggage was found and delivered the next day to our hotel in Assisi.

I've said how airport adventures can be magical, touching on the timeless, nonlocal experience of quantum reality. The experience that Mike and I shared in Rome was more like a nightmare, but a transformative one that resulted in a breakthrough in how we communicate in our travels and when working together. We needed to have that in order to move more quickly through the final stages of bringing our new-paradigm child, Peptide T, into reality when we got back to Washington, D.C.

I knew that harmony in my relationship with Mike was a key to successfully accomplishing the goals of our research. We were two sides of the same coin, complementary in our personalities, a classic yin-and-yang profile. While I'm out gallivanting around to various consciousness events, he's home manning the lab and the phones, creatively carrying on our drug research when I can't. In thinking scientifically, I've always been the wilder speculator, while Mike sticks to the straight and narrow, grounding himself securely in the science before he proceeds. Sometimes our different modes of expression conflict; other times they provide a nourishing balance. But the key we've found to spanning the gap of our differences is communication, *staying connected.* In the quantum world, we already are. Relying on our bond, we experience love, which, after all, heals everything. It's what lets us feel good and feel God.

Emotions and the Bodymind

Carl Jung wrote in his book *Memories, Dreams, Reflections:* "Psyche and matter are contained in the same world and are in continuous contact with one another, and ultimately they rest on unrepresentable and transcendent factors. Therefore, it's possible, and even probable, that psyche and matter are two different aspects of one and the same thing."

Jung wrote those words more than 20 years before Michael and I started to think about a psychosomatic network in which the mind and body exchanged information to coordinate physiology for one bodymind. It was clear to me why we'd been invited to speak to the Jungians, in spite of my NIMH colleague who'd questioned the conference organizer's intent. They turned out to be a fascinating group, with shared interest in synchronicity, dreams, and consciousness, who were thrilled by Michael's clear presentation.

In the talk he gave to the assembled therapists, my husband laid the foundation and gave the basic science for many of our later theories about emotions and the bodymind. His talk was the perfect balance for a heady—yes, dreamy!—few days, bringing us all out of the clouds and back down to Earth, where our immune systems physically manifest health or disease. In his talk, Mike showed us how love and compassion are the true healers, the direct path to feeling good and feeling God. In his scientific, rational, and eloquent way, he demonstrated that they're one in the same! As you read his words for yourself, you'll see what I mean. . . .

Michael's Assisi Presentation

I was proud to introduce my husband to the group of therapists, and said, "Dr. Michael Ruff, whom I've been closely collaborating with since 1983, is an immunologist. He received his undergraduate degree in biophysics at Johns Hopkins University and his Ph.D. at the University of Florida. After doing his postdoctorate work at the University of Zurich, he came to the immunology department at the National Institutes of Health in Washington, D.C., where we met one afternoon at the campus bar." I paused as a titter went through the group, and then I sat down, leaving my audience to enjoy the moment as Mike took the podium to speak.

"Thank you," he began, looking handsome and suntanned after our morning spent together by the hotel pool, soaking up the warm Mediterranean rays. "It's my pleasure to address a group of therapists who treat both the mind and the spirit. I hope that my remarks will help you see that you have a much greater influence on your patients' health and well-being than you've ever imagined.

"As an immunologist, I'm interested in the true nature of illness, and more important, how we recover from illness and attain health. When I began my career at the NIH, I set out to answer this question: What are the root causes of illness and disease? Up to that point, I had been studying disease in a Petri dish, observing isolated immune cells as they interacted with microorganisms.

"But I was aware of emerging ideas that were pointing to a new role for the brain in the healing process, and I wanted to expand my understanding of how the mind functioned in causing or alleviating disease.

"Whenever I met people who experienced a spontaneous healing of some life-threatening disease, I was intrigued when they inevitably referred to a personal transformative event—a spiritual epiphany or some kind of psychic, mental shift—to which they gave credit for their recovery. *How did these events relate to the biology?* I wondered.

"I figured a good place to start would be with the opiate peptides found abundantly in the brain at first, and then later in the immune system. Working together, Candace and I found opiate receptors pretty straightforwardly in the immune system, our first indicator that mind and body were talking to each other.

"At the time, other scientists were doing experiments that revived much older Russian literature, showing that it was possible to condition the immune response. The old model showed how immune tissues and cells in the body simply responded to external stimuli. But with our discovery of brain peptides communicating with immune cells, we'd demonstrated an absolutely primal role for mental processes acting to condition the immune system.

"In looking closer at the opiate–immune system connection, it became clear to us very quickly that the bidirectional communication model was too simplistic. We soon recognized a network of information relay throughout the organism, involving many cells and tissues. It's this system that we've come to call the psychosomatic network of the bodymind.

"This psychosomatic communication network has many features, a few of which I'd like to touch on now.

"First, the system exists to send and receive emotionally encoded information. The endorphins are a good illustration, because they're the body's chemicals responsible for the ecstatic rush of feeling that comes from psychoactive drug use, such as heroin or morphine, both analogs of endorphin. There are other informational substances, such as steroid hormones like estrogen, which aren't peptides but function in the psychosomatic network.

"Another element of this informational network is that it accesses all components of the body—the systems, organs, tissues, and cells. The network is distributed and integrated, much like a computer system with its many sites plugged into a greater system and able to come online. There's no fixed hierarchy. The brain isn't in charge, nor is the immune system, nor any other system or organ. Instead, directional input moves around the network, accessing the system at different points, depending on what needs to be done at any given time or in any given situation.

"The psychosomatic network allows a very organic kind of prioritization to go on. You and I know that we can't do everything at once, so the psychosomatic network handles this unconsciously, sorting out what comes first and what comes second. For example, I can be conscious of sounds in the background while I'm talking to you, and at the same time focus on delivering my presentation. This is possible because the network of communicating molecules enables me to do one thing and then the other, prioritizing input in a way that allows me to function effectively.

"And finally, these shared molecules work to promote functions and behaviors that are consistent throughout the organism as it adapts to different environments. An example is the peptide angiotensin, which increases the sensation of thirst. On a biochemical level, when this substance communicates with the kidney, the organ concentrates urine, thus conserving water. At the same time, angiotensin receptors in the lungs cause less water-vapor secretion, also keeping fluid from leaving the body. You experience these activities as thirst and reach to open up a bottle of water, an integrated behavior.

"In the laboratory, when we inject angiotensin into a rat, the animal will become thirsty and seek water to drink, even if it's already sated. In this manner, the molecules of emotion traveling throughout the network unify body, mind, and behavior to gain a survival advantage.

"The psychosomatic network has proven its worth by what we scientists call 'evolutionary conservation.' There's a 600-million-year codevelopment of the immune, endocrine, and nervous systems common to all living creatures, from the humble unicellular yeast to the complex human being. The psychosomatic network, however simple it may be at some levels, has been conserved throughout the evolution of life, not lost or abandoned, as other, less important structures have been.

"As our research progressed, my understanding of disease

and immunology as operating in isolation, the body acted on by external stimuli or microorganisms, began to unravel. I could no longer accept the idea that recovery or wellness depends solely on eradicating microorganisms, which is the classical or institutional approach of modern medicine. It became clear to me that the causes of disease exist elsewhere throughout the pathways and nodal points making up the information superhighway that we call the bodymind.

"As a side note, I'm aware that this year's Nobel Prize for medicine was awarded to two Australian researchers who proved that stomach ulcers are caused by a bacterium—a discovery that seemed to refute the widespread belief that this condition is the result of emotional stress. I admire my colleagues for compiling meticulous proof that bacteria were involved, and the bottom line is that their discovery has led to treatments that work for people.

"Nevertheless, my colleagues' success does not necessarily discount that there are two components to disease: the agent that causes it (the microorganisms, bacterial or viral) and the way the body reacts to that agent. The research Candace and I have done suggests that a person's emotional state plays a major role in determining how well he or she is able to fight off infections.

"Louis Pasteur's last words on his deathbed were: 'It's not the microbe, but the environment,' pointing to a state or condition that surrounds the microbe as being part of what makes a person well or ill. This is a message that generations of immunologists have apparently missed.

"Using the new-paradigm physiology of a bodymind and psychosomatic network, we can understand how emotion and information can create a milieu or environment that closes down systems and interferes with healthy function, impeding wellness and causing disease. Memory, as we know, is stored or encoded in cells at the level of the receptor throughout the bodymind. When we experience a traumatic event, physical or psychological, an emotional component of that trauma exists in the body as well as the brain. For the most effective healing, then, it makes sense to engage the entire bodymind, not just the brain or the body.

"Candace has talked about the notion that the physical self is your subconscious mind. What she's saying is that at the level of the body, you are unaware of your mind. If you're not aware of memories and traumas stored in your bodymind, you can't do anything about them. So the first step in healing or recovery must involve awareness of where your past and injuries are stored, and then making an attempt to unravel them. This, of course, is where you therapists come in, helping people become aware of what they may not know of.

"I talked about how you can plug into the psychosomatic network at any nodal point along the axis for healing. We know that it's very powerful to use language, such as Drs. Hal and Sidra Stone's voice dialogue and healing affirmations from many sources, and to activate a wide range of mindful processes. Music and art are also effective modes of accessing the network for healing. Another way in is somatic, with the use of physical therapies such as chiropractic, massage, and other forms of bodywork.

"But back to my original questions: What are the optimal states of mind and emotion for recovery, for wellness, and for healing? A book published by the Institute of Noetic Sciences and now out of print presents a survey of the medical literature reporting the most frightening, extreme, and serious cases of diseases for which no hope had been given for recovery. Yet the people did recover, and in almost all cases, survivors tell about a personal transformative experience that preceded this. We could use the word *miraculous* to describe these people's experience, because there are no explanations for such events anywhere in the medical literature.

"While wrestling with this inquiry a few years back, I was at a conference in Munich, Germany, and received an invitation to join a small group of scientists meeting with His Holiness, the Dalai Lama of Tibet. His Holiness had come from India to address scientists on the subject of healing and transformation.

"When it came my turn to ask a question, I began by saying, 'I'm interested in what you think is the root cause of illness and disease.' The Dalai Lama responded: 'I don't know, really. I think you get a virus or you get a cold, and then you get sick.'

"I was surprised by his answer and wondered if the translator had gotten my question wrong. Certainly, this man hadn't attended the same medical school I had! I ventured further, hoping that by giving him a little more detail, I'd get a more interesting answer.

"'Excuse me,' I began, 'but with all due respect, that's not strictly true. We know from the experiments done by Drs. Ron Glaser and Jan Kiecolt-Glaser on medical students that when you drop a virus in students' nostrils before they take their exams, 75 percent will get ill. But if you drop the same virus in the same students *after* their exams, only 20 percent do.' The Dalai Lama was listening very closely, so I continued.

"'My point is that nobody gets sick the day before vacation, so there has to be something more than just the virus causing the illness. I was hoping that you could share some insight into what states of mind allow a person to recover from disease and regain their health and well-being.'

"The Dalai Lama pondered my words for a short period of time. Then he answered my question by telling us all a story.

"'This is the insight I can offer to you,' he began. 'I was traveling in India when I got very sick and was taken to a hospital. As I looked out from the window of the speeding ambulance, I saw the suffering, the poverty, and the starvation of so many people in the streets of the city. Eventually, my mind was no longer on my own discomfort, which was soon abated. By the time I got to the hospital, I no longer had the symptoms I'd started out with, and I no longer needed any treatment.'

"I thanked the Dalai Lama for his answer and later realized that he was saying that health and wellness demand relationship, some kind of human interaction. As people, we're no more individuals, no more autonomous agents, than the immune cells are on their own in the bodymind. To be healthy, well, and feel good, our biology insists that we be in relationship to others, and through our connections, we're able to bring health to our bodymind.

"I believe that this is what the Dalai Lama meant when he told us the story of how his compassion for people suffering had healed him. He was pointing to a path for us all, as individuals and collectively in our culture, the road to health and well-being. It's as simple as it sounds: Love, compassion, and relationship—these are the human emotions that can heal us and lead to recovery from disease."

The Jungians applauded as Mike took a bow and sat down. He had wowed them, and me. And I believe that he knew exactly what he was talking about.

Chapter 8

Santa Barbara: Energy Medicine, Coherence, and Connection

It was late October, and I was in the air again, this time flying an unexpected dogleg between Washington, D.C. and Santa Barbara, California. I'd missed my connection in Dallas and was headed for Los Angeles. From LA, I'd go on to Santa Barbara, where I was scheduled to present the next day at the Santa Barbara City College *Mind and Supermind: Expanding the Limits of Consciousness* lecture series. Mike stayed home this time, attending to business that involved the latest Peptide-T developments.

I'd accepted the gig partly because Santa Barbara is Nancy's hometown and by staying at her house, I could work with her more closely on the book. But I'd also lectured for *Mind and Supermind* before and knew the series to be on the leading edge, featuring such past presenters as Deepak Chopra, Jean Shinoda Bolen, Fred Alan Wolf, Fritjof Capra, and Richard Moss.

I knew all of these consciousness leaders personally, but had a unique connection to Richard Moss, whom I hadn't seen since he graduated from the same high school as Nancy and me back on Long Island, class of '64. Now, Nancy had informed me, Richard had settled his international offices in Ojai, a small town an hour outside of Santa Barbara.

While still in the air before landing in Dallas, I mulled over some topics to present in my lecture. Santa Barbara was a sophisticated West Coast center of consciousness and well-being, judging by the number of healers, massage therapists, and other new-paradigm practitioners living in the community. Adding to its burgeoning holistic population, the town boasted a university with three Nobel laureates in the sciences, more health-food stores and restaurants than I could count, and close proximity to a major city (Los Angeles). I must admit, I could easily see Mike and me escaping the suburbs of D.C. to settle in this hip paradise on the West Coast—after our work in Washington was done, of course.

For my talk in this community, I was clearly bringing coals to Newcastle, and I wanted to deliver the most exciting ones possible, maybe even some diamonds. The palette I was working from included my newly thought-out understanding of how energy heals, as well as my own personal transformative epiphanies and insights into the power of love and compassion. This last gem was coming straight from my recent personal evolution and related to advancements in Peptide T and other new drugs that Michael and I had been developing. Healing myself, I knew, was the key to all of our research moving forward.

Toward Wholeness

As the plane's engines droned on, I relaxed and thought back to my most recent talk, an invitational presentation for the annual Arthur P. Noyes Schizophrenia Conference in Philadelphia that I gave shortly after returning from Assisi. The theme of the two-day conference was *Toward Wholeness*, with an emphasis on expanding the view of schizophrenia research to include cross-disciplinary breakthroughs happening in neuroscience, gene mapping, and molecular biology. The Noyes Foundation encouraged the presentation of novel ideas on this sad and highly prevalent disease that claims 2.2 million sufferers in the U.S. and 51 million worldwide.

The night before my talk in Philadelphia, I dined with the

other presenters and was seated at a table between two of the world's most high-profile schizophrenics, Dr. John Nash, a Nobel laureate from Princeton; and Dr. Fred Frese, an author and faculty member in the psychiatry departments at two different Midwestern universities. Dr. Nash, of course, was the mathematician played by Russell Crowe in the movie *A Beautiful Mind.* He laughed when I couldn't help but make a joke about my disappointment that Russell himself was not going to be sitting next to me.

When I arrived to give my talk the next morning, I found out that the notorious Dr. AIDS Trials from the NIMH Peptide-T trial of the early '90s was attending the conference. This was the woman Michael and I had reviled these many years, blaming her for shelving important blood samples and ending their crucial study on a falsely sour note. Seeing her now, my many subpersonalities reared up wildly with a range of emotions, but I finally settled into a mode that was somewhat conciliatory. My inner selfhelper told me that a big dose of forgiveness for errors of the past could very possibly make a difference in the future for Peptide T's development.

Passing me in the lecture hall, Dr. AIDS Trials put on a friendly smile that I returned, and during the first break in the morning's proceedings, we found ourselves chatting at the coffee station. Prior to her involvement with the NIH trial, we'd known each other in another context, so our conversation picked up on happier times before the trial fiasco, touching on career moves and family news.

I struggled to keep a tight rein on my subpersonality that wanted to humiliate her and accuse her of burying our data and refusing to publish the evidence that our drug worked. Instead, I maintained a steady eyeball-to-eyeball connection, consciously choosing to accept her as a human being who'd done the best she could with the information she'd been given. I saw her as myself, inwardly acknowledging her persistence in doing a tough job, and made a spontaneous decision to completely let go of my anger and forgive her.

It worked! She knew from interoffice memos that Mike and I had been trying to secure the license for Peptide T from the NIH so that we could raise money to run more trials. I wasn't going to skip over what we were up to, and intending the best, I said, "You know, when we get the license for Peptide T, and the drug hits the market and goes big, the NIH will receive considerable financial benefits."

"Really," she said, surprised but obviously pleased. I could tell that she'd accepted my remark as good news, a win-win for everyone with no residual grudge on my part. Together, we were riding the same wave, and it felt good.

We smiled at each other and returned to our seats, a healing vibration now passing between us to cancel the former hostility. I felt a hundred pounds lighter, and when I was up at the podium delivering my talk, I included our one-time nemesis in my remarks, generously acknowledging her work in the AIDS arena and thanking her for the courage it took to do her job. In keeping with the conference's theme, I had moved *toward wholeness,* standing on a more solid foundation to go forward in my mission with Peptide T.

A New Theory of Schizophrenia

In my talk, I presented my theory of schizophrenia, one that's consistent with all the published literature and recent thinking about the disease. I'd first started thinking about a cure for it in the mid-'80s, and suspecting a viral etiology for the disease, I sought out a few immunologists at the NIH campus clubhouse. One of those immunologists, Dr. Michael Ruff, later became my husband.

Then in 1990, before I changed course to focus on HIV, my NIMH team, collaborating with the world's influenza experts, showed that antibodies made against a flu that caused psychotic symptoms in the population shortly after World War I also reacted with a protein found on cell surfaces in the brains of mammals.

This fit well with the idea that schizophrenia is a neuro-developmental disorder, occurring when a pregnant women contracts the flu in her second trimester, leading to a small but definite tendency for her baby to become schizophrenic approximately 20 years later. (The hallmark of this mental illness is that it strikes suddenly in a person's early 20s with auditory hallucinations and psychotic thinking.) There are enough other immune-system abnormalities associated with schizophrenia that it looks like a person afflicted with the disease is in an ongoing, hyperimmune (or autoimmune) state, which is primed by early exposure to the influenza, or as some data suggests, to other bugs as well.

I used to think that this late-adolescent onset was caused by a young person leaving home, going off to college, and becoming exposed to new germs. But the work of the brilliant, late Dr. Patricia Goldman-Rakic, who was tragically killed by a car some years ago, showed another, more cogent possibility. During a person's early 20s, new brain pathways are growing in the frontal cortex, the part of the brain where abnormal function is typical for schizophrenia.

This new work by Dr. Goldman-Rakic made it even more likely that some kind of autoimmune or allergic response occurred during fetal brain development, elicited by the mother's immune defense against a bug. And when the building blocks of the same brain protein were being assembled again in the early 20s, the same response occurred, this time in the developing frontal cortex of the young adult.

I learned from other presenters at the Noyes meeting that in her last paper before she died, Dr. Goldman-Rakic had shown the schizophrenic frontal cortex to contain more neurons and greatly reduced neuropil—axons and dendrites that form the brain's connecting neural networks. Her finding had been repeated by another scientist attending the meeting, and was completely consistent with my idea of schizophrenia as a neuroinflammatory disease. The mechanism, I proposed, was that activated, inflamed microglial cells were chewing up the networks, resulting in neuronal cell bodies with fewer connecting networks. Hence, the schizophrenic symptoms.

In the 20 or so years that I'd been thinking about schizophrenia—the "big enchilada" in the world of mental-health research—I'd come to the conclusion that something was off in the birth and migration process of new neurons originating in the body, resulting in an ongoing neuroinflammation. I'd learned in the AIDS arena about chemokines, a class of immunopeptides that are involved in inflammation and also in the regulation of neuronal numbers and migration in early brain development. Could these chemokines be responsible for the state of inflammation that underlies altered development in the brains of schizophrenics? The experiment to prove the theory was obvious, but no one had done it to date.

I leaned back in my seat and closed my eyes. In the good old days at the NIMH, it would have been easy to gather matched brain slices from both schizophrenic and control subjects, the necessary reagents, and the expertise to do the experiment. But those days were gone. There was no time now to get back on the trail of this disease and crack it, as I'd vowed to do before meeting Mike and the other immunologists, intuiting at the time that their knowledge and mine would lead to a useful understanding of the disease.

But I was pleased to have my theory of schizophrenia well received at the Philadelphia conference, and I knew that I would get back to finding a cure one day, probably in a lab funded by Peptide T's success. I could then do the experiments to see if activated microglial cells, the hallmark of brain inflammation, were to be found enriched in schizophrenic brain samples. I knew that the technology we'd used to invent Peptide T could lead us to other drugs that block the action of chemokines and other inflammatory peptides, providing a new therapeutic approach to schizophrenia.

Connecting Synchronicities

The Dallas airport was a nightmare. My flight leaving D.C. earlier that day had been delayed, causing me to miss my connection to Santa Barbara after running frantically to get to the departing gate on time. I tried to get the gate attendant to let me board the Santa Barbara–bound plane, which was still sitting on the tarmac, but he was firm and directed me to take the next flight out to Los Angeles. The only problem was that I'd be arriving in LA after midnight, with no connecting flight to Santa Barbara. Racing to the new gate, I didn't have time to call Nancy and let her know of my change in plans.

Most people don't realize that commercial airplane cabins are only pressurized for 5,000 feet, which is the altitude of Denver, the "mile-high" city. The Broncos football team benefits from this altitude because they train in a low-oxygen environment and then arrive to play at lower elevations with stronger lungs than their opponents. But for travelers, after spending six hours in flight with oxygen deprivation, there are no such benefits. Once on the ground, having to think on your feet and run for a connection can be exhausting. Missing my direct flight to Santa Barbara after so much running back and forth was making me fume.

But not for long. Once aboard the flight, I discovered that my seatmate was an executive for Walt Disney Studios and perhaps the perfect connection for my son Brandon, a senior at California Institute of the Arts, to secure an internship working on the soundtrack of an animated feature. We exchanged business cards, and I made a mental note to mention this synchronicity to Brandon, who'd be driving up to meet me for lunch in Santa Barbara on the day after my talk.

Another airport synchronicity occurred on the ground in LA, when one of the passengers on my flight, a woman who must have been in her 70s, approached me in the baggage-claim area. She, too, had been on the plane out of D.C. and missed her Dallas connection to Santa Barbara. I knew this because I'd been impressed by her stamina in keeping up with me during our hot (but fruitless) pursuit of the connection.

"I called my driver while we were still in Dallas," she told me, after getting my attention as we both searched for our baggage, which hadn't arrived. "He's here to pick us up and drive us to Santa Barbara." I accepted her offer instantly, and we got on the road, both sans luggage, which we were told would be delivered to our doorsteps the next day. On the drive up the coast, we enjoyed a de-stressing chat, and I was deposited at Nancy's house, just a few blocks down from my rescuer's hilltop home in the same neighborhood.

I marveled at how events were unfolding: a career lead for Brandon and now a door-to-door delivery service to Nancy's home in Santa Barbara. The law of attraction was operating smoothly in my life, and the right individuals were lining up to meet me. I said a silent prayer to the Great Arranger, thankful that I could trust the perfect alignment of people and events to bring me safely to my destination.

Energy Medicine Introduced

The next day I awoke early, still on East Coast time, my 8 A.M. being California's 5 A.M. Unable to sleep, I lay awake in the dark, trying to get comfortable on the futon that Nancy had set up for me in her office. I thought about what I'd share with people during my lecture that evening. I felt nervous but excited to present my new understanding of bioenergetic healing, a field that had been growing and was newly called "energy medicine."

The roots of this discipline go back 5,000 years, when Chinese medicine and the Indian system of Ayurveda set forth two of the most widely used and respected systems of the energetic or subtle body: the meridians of Chinese medicine and the chakras of Ayurveda. Both theories have at their foundation an understanding of the body and mind as a vibrational field extending and interacting with the universe. The role of the healer in both traditions is to monitor and clear energy pathways to keep the flow harmonious and tuned to the universe.

In the West, the Greeks and the Romans understood a primitive concept of bioelectromagnetism in describing the impact that the electric Torpedo Fish (or ray) had on human health. Up until the Renaissance, physicians were routinely employing these fish to shock patients as a form of electrotherapy, treating sleeping disorders, migraines, melancholy, and epilepsy.

Today, however, for a credentialed scientist—a pharmacologist like myself, no less—to grant credibility to energy medicine would be considered blasphemy. This rejection by my colleagues can be traced back most recently to the 19th century when, in the wake of the discovery of electricity, electromagnetic healing devices were touted to cure virtually every conceivable disease known to man. In 1894, over 10,000 U.S. physicians were regularly using electrotherapy in their practice.

That trend was derailed by the more modern pharmacological approach, and now the medical sciences emphasize drugs rather than electromagnetic healing in the training of physicians. While millions of people have benefited from the development of lifesaving drugs in the 20th century, an unfortunate side effect is that the electrical and energetic aspect of healing was tossed out as illegitimate, rendering it unworthy of funding for any kind of validating research.

Energy and Science

A favorite quote of mine is from Sir Arthur Eddington, whose observations of star positions during a total solar eclipse gave the first direct confirmation of Einstein's general theory of relativity in 1919. His words point to the ubiquitous nature of energy: "We have found a strange footprint on the shores of the unknown. We have devised profound theories to account for its origins. At last, we have succeeded in reconstructing the creature that made the footprint. And lo! It is our own."

This quote captures the uncomfortable relationship between science and energy phenomenon. Like a footprint on the shore, we can see the healing effects of energy therapies and even make up theories to explain why and how those treatments work, but we haven't been able to objectify the phenomenon for scientific study and thus prove its "reality." As we approach the ability to do that, I believe that we'll discover deeper keys to our own true nature.

When we talk about energy medicine, the modalities of Reiki, therapeutic touch, shiatsu, kinesiology, acupuncture, and energy-based chiropractic come to mind. In fact, energy is evident in every modality on the bodywork tree, from Swedish massage to craniosacral work and structural integration or Rolfing.

Alternative or complementary medicine, much of it based in energetic phenomena, has made great strides in the last decade. In 1998, David Eisenberg's landmark study reported in the *Journal of the American Medical Association* showed consumers spending up to $47 billion on health-care alternatives out of their own pockets. The fields of energy medicine and energy psychology have sprung up almost overnight, and although these therapies are still confined to a minority of allopathic practitioners in big cities or to integrative health-care centers associated with academic institutions, they're becoming more and more visible in the mainstream. We see a variety of energy-healing modalities showing up in hospital emergency rooms, hospice care, and some cancer-treatment programs in the form of distant healing (prayer), reflexology, guided imagery, meditation, massage, and biofeedback—all of which talk about sending, receiving, or moving energy in some way or manner.

Cyclist Lance Armstrong, the seven-time Tour de France winner, has had no problem making public the fact that his chiropractor/trainer Jeff Spencer uses energy therapies to treat his injuries. Relying on both the human hand and mechanical devices to electrically shield and ground him, Lance and the rest of the team are regularly treated to correct their injuries and restore vitality while training and racing. Anyone who's watched Lance pedal uphill can safely say that the man has got his energy moving.

Coming to Accept the "E word": Energy

My early-morning musings continued as the light began to dawn through the windows of Nancy's office. I recalled how back in 1996, as a speaker for a Midwest Wellness Conference in Wisconsin, I was reluctant to give my scientific blessings to the "E word." Naomi Judd, the well-known country singer and mind-body advocate, moderated a panel I was on and asked me to explain what scientists think about "subtle energy." I hesitated and then said I thought that the movement of energy in the body was possibly due to the flow of emotions going back and forth between the physical and the spiritual, existing on the physical level as peptides and receptors, but also in the spiritual realm as information. Chi, prana, and meridians—these phenomena could possibly be explained by the flow of information and emotions, but a scientific mechanism of action beyond that at that time eluded me.

A few years later, I was introduced to the work of Dr. James Oschman, the author of a revolutionary but scientifically sound text entitled *Energy Medicine: The Scientific Basis,* published in 2000. That book and his 2003 release, *Energy Medicine in Therapeutics and Human Performance,* have both been heralded as extremely important contributions to the field of energy medicine and psychology, as pioneered by psychologist David Gruder. Oschman's biological explanation of how energy medicine works has helped demystify the whole field of study.

I'd been hearing about Jim's work for a few years before I actually met the cellular biologist and physiologist with impeccable credentials who dared to associate with Rolfers, acupuncturists, and other bodyworkers in his search for the science underlying energy in the body. I'd experienced massage and many forms of energetic bodywork for years myself, but was unable to explain how they functioned to promote healing in the conventional biological paradigm. The experience of sensing power "move" is a common denominator in many of these techniques.

I was familiar with energy healing from receiving acupuncture in the '70s, and also from some early experiments that I did on myself and my family members. Once, when my youngest son, Brandon, was sick as a child, I used reflexology on his feet, pressing points along meridians shown on a chart to clear energy blockages in his body. Having no knowledge of the system I was using, Brandon accurately reported six places in his body where he felt "something move," each of them correlating with the points I was manipulating on the soles of his feet. From this experience, I became convinced that energy healing should be taken seriously and studied, not squelched or ignored simply because the reigning paradigm had no theories to explain it.

Connecting Energy to Emotion

I met Jim Oschman for the first time at an American Massage Therapy Association conference in South Carolina that I attended in the late '90s. He offered me a healing and proceeded to use a no-touching, hands-not-quite-on method to pull energy away from what he said was my stagnant liver. As he worked, I felt the appropriate movement before he even told me what he was doing. Like Brandon, I was blind to the anticipated outcome yet clearly experienced the effect, a kind of experiment that in scientific parlance is called a "blind study."

When Jim contacted me a few years later to invite me to write the Foreword to his book *Energy Medicine,* I was thrilled to support him and wrote:

I can now understand how different emotional states, by triggering the release of various peptides, can cause sudden, even quantum shifts, not only in consciousness but in behavior, memory, and even body posture. Perhaps this explains how the chiropractor's adjustments, manipulating the spine surrounded by peptidergic nerve bundles, AND hands-on healers, who claim to feel energetic differences and emit appropriate corrective energies, share common energetic mechanisms. Also, we may begin to have a new-paradigm vision of the human body as a dynamic, shape-shifting bundle of multiple personalities in the full sense of the term, not merely layered but capable of immediate, quantum transformations that are able to be stabilized in new healing states of mind and body.

Further, I'd talked frequently in my lectures about how the molecules of emotion are related to the electrical nature of the bodymind. When peptides bind to their receptors, an electrical charge is altered by ions flowing in and out of the cell, regulating nerve cells to fire or not. This activity gives rise to a field of electricity extending around animals and humans. Sharks rely on this fact to find food, having a tiny sensor above their lips that allows them to sense electronic fluctuations in the water as small as one-billionth of a volt. Every time our heart beats or our muscles move our arms, electricity flows. Both animals and humans are all emitting electrical signals.

But my scientist's mind still wasn't at ease with the idea of energy moving through the body and crossing over from person to person, directed and moved intentionally, to be utilized for healing—even though I'd experienced it myself! I didn't understand the mechanism, other than resonance, and that wasn't enough to explain the full phenomenon.

It wasn't until I met Jim again in 2005, when he presented for an American Polarity Therapy Institute conference, and heard him explain his latest update on the scientific basis of energy medicine, that I shifted my understanding. One month after I'd returned from Assisi, in September, I received an invitation to attend his lecture, which was being held at a location so close to my home in the D.C. suburbs that I could almost walk to it.

Talk about synchronicity! Here was the world's leading expert on the scientific basis of energy medicine, practically on my doorstep. I promptly responded and received two tickets to attend the conference with Mike, who was just as excited to hear Jim talk as I was.

It was the driest September on record for the area, but the night before the event, the rains finally hit, and they hit hard, somehow altering electronics in the hotel where the conference was being held, causing alarms to go off and attendees to be evacuated several times during the night. The next day, Michael and I sat in the room with a sleep-deprived but eager audience and listened to Jim's presentation. The hotel's sound and lighting systems went on and off, punctuating his delivery with all sorts of electrical high jinks—an appropriate display for the subject at hand!

As I listened, I understood Jim's complete vision for the first time: He was saying that the body is like a liquid crystal under tension, capable of vibrating at a number of different frequencies. The mechanism that allows for this is a physical structure, something he calls "the matrix," which explained spontaneous healing, hands-on energy healing, and the effectiveness of popular biomagnetic healing devices.

Now in Santa Barbara and anticipating my lecture, I was thrilled at the thought of presenting, for the first time since attending Jim's talk, my new understanding of energy, electricity, and emotions to an audience. I was excited and a bit nervous to be stepping out so boldly to share my own insights, but figured what better place to launch my new ideas than at *Mind and Supermind,* for the sophisticated audience I expected would attend that night.

A Blast from the Past

Typically, I spend the day before the evening of an event hunkered down with my slides, sweating over the details to get them just right, organizing my outfit, and fretting obsessively about being "the best." But on this day, my baggage with my lecture materials and clothes didn't arrive until the afternoon, so I had nothing to do, an unsettling feeling for an overachiever like myself. To make matters worse, I hadn't been able to get through to Michael, and even though Nancy was being a gracious hostess, I was feeling distraught, disconnected, and alone.

I decided to get a massage with Susan, a tenant of Nancy's who had an afternoon opening. Normally, I wouldn't consider doing this before a lecture, thinking that I'd be too relaxed afterward to be at the top of my game. But wanting to nourish myself and recover, to *feel good,* I booked a session for the afternoon. By 5 P.M., I figured, the massage would be over and I'd be dressed and ready to meet the organizers of the *Mind and Supermind* series (along with Nancy and her husband) at a nearby restaurant for a pre-lecture dinner.

Minutes before I stepped out the door to go to my appointment, Nancy said to me, "I've got a great surprise for you!" I was not in the mood for the unexpected, but that didn't stop her. "I just got off the phone with our old classmate Richard Moss, and he and his wife are driving in from Ojai to join us for dinner and your talk."

Our past!—here it was in yet another manifestation, and while I was slightly annoyed that Nancy had made these arrangements without my consent, I was also thrilled to reconnect with Richard, whom I hadn't seen since high school. Like Nancy, he'd come from the same roots as I had, a true baby boomer from the East Coast–establishment milieu. Even more, he'd been trained as a medical doctor and managed to cross over into the new paradigm of consciousness and energy healing. As I contemplated meeting up with him again, my heart warmed to the idea of all three of us having a reunion on this special evening.

Looking back, I remembered Richard Moss fondly as the cute teenage boy I'd had a crush on—or did he have a crush on me? When romance didn't work out, we became good friends, and he was a regular in the brainy crowd of high achievers that Nancy and I belonged to, known as the "advanced class." After finishing medical school, he went to San Francisco, where he finished his residency and then stayed on until a sudden, life-changing spiritual epiphany derailed his plans. Dropping out of medicine, he wrote a book—*The I That Is We*—and found himself surrounded by a near-cult following eager to explore healing and consciousness in the mid-'70s West Coast counterculture. Today he teaches seminars and workshops in the contemporary psychology of consciousness to groups around the world.

The massage was exactly what I needed. With my baggage still en route, an old boyfriend meeting us for dinner, Michael off God knows where, and 500 people soon to be sitting down, ready to hear me talk about the scientific explanation for energy healing—I really needed to just melt away for an hour. Susan, a petite woman who didn't hesitate to use every angle and appendage to get the job done, gave me one of the best massages I've ever had. While she did her magic, she played a soothing musical mix to create the perfect ambience. As I rested afterward, the lyrics that accompanied John Astin's gorgeous melody "Hold the World in Light" from his CD *Remembrance* resonated deeply in my bodymind:

Open your heart,
let it be filled with light.
Open your mind
let it be filled with light.
For there's a world
waiting to heal,
to feel your love.
So share your love,
Share it with all.
Can you hear the call?

Such a simple message, but in the "state of change" brought on by the massage, I heard the words of the song as direct marching orders from God. I got up from the table, freed from my worrying personality and with my heart wide open. I knew what to do. There was a world waiting to heal, and I'd be onstage in exactly two hours with an opportunity to do just that.

I arrived at the restaurant to find my dining companions already seated in a circle at our table. Meeting Richard Moss again was strange and wonderful, one of those rare opportunities in life to update the past and share the present. We embraced and were soon joking warmly about high-school adventures, the others enjoying our banter and play. Meeting Richard's wife was also a treat, having heard from Nancy that Ariel was a beautiful and accomplished partner for our friend.

Nonetheless, I noticed my old patterns of competition and overachievement rearing up as we sat around the table talking and eating. Recalling the near-cutthroat academic atmosphere we'd breathed back in high school, I mentioned that I'd graduated eighth from the top of our huge senior class. Neither Richard nor Nancy (or anyone else at the table) could recall their own graduation ranking, nor did they seem to care to!

As I relaxed and let myself enjoy the company, I realized that this pre-lecture hour was a most unusual one for me. Instead of preparing my talk obsessively up until the very last minute, I was letting myself be immersed in a resonating emotional field of warmth and support.

"You'll be great, Candy," Richard said, calling me by a childhood name that no one used anymore as I got up to leave for the hall. "Just come from your heart. . . . Inspire people; that's what they want, and it will be great." His words landed powerfully, echoing the lyrics of the song: *Open your heart. Feel your love, share your love.* I gave everyone a big hug and, glowing with the love and good wishes of my friends, walked out of the restaurant and across the street to the Lobero Theater, where people were beginning to line up for the evening's talk.

Showtime

It was a rainy night in Santa Barbara, and the line of attendees extended from the front entrance of the lecture hall around the block. Using a side door, I ducked backstage into a dressing room and took a few minutes to freshen up and give Mike a call. After a frustrating day of leaving messages, we finally connected. The contact with home and my husband's ongoing support resonated my already open heart and dissolved any remaining apprehension. Within minutes of talking to him, I was walking out onto the stage to deliver my presentation.

The house was full, not an empty seat in view, and I learned later that people had been turned away. Expectation was palpable in the air, generated in part by the full-page photo and article about my work that had run in the local paper the day before.

I felt unusually calm and connected to my audience in a strange new way. This was a wonderful and warm crowd for sure, but also my intention was different from other times. I was there to heal, teach, and share my love and light—to inspire. Not exactly what I was trained to do as a speaker for scientific symposia, where objectivity was the hallmark of success. But times, as well as myself, had changed, and I felt oddly like I was in my own living room back home. I glimpsed my high-school friends in the audience, Nancy and Richard sitting with their spouses, and I introduced them from the stage for a warm round of applause.

The initial slides came up, allowing me to give people a basic orientation to the molecules of emotion and the physiology of wellness. Very quickly after that, I introduced the topic of energy medicine and started to talk about the work of Dr. James Oschman.

"Oschman's work is important," I began, "because he's providing the gateway through which the energetic healing phenomenon—Reiki, acupuncture, hands-on healing, therapeutic touch, and a whole host of bodywork and massage modalities, as well as the new field of energy psychology—will move out of the realm of 'woo-woo' and into the scientific mainstream."

My audience shifted, coming into sharper focus and peaking in their attention. I had a feeling that they'd been waiting for what I was about to say.

"Jim talks about something he calls 'the matrix,'" I continued. "This is a physical structure in the body composed primarily of collagenous fibers, the kind that make up your connective tissue to hold your skeleton together. Think protein—a fine mesh or web extending throughout your body, coating every cell and connecting muscles, tendons, and bones to your brain. This highly malleable web actually reaches into each and every cell, which is a new understanding that flies in the face of the classical view of cells as empty little bags whose interior isn't hooked up to existing structures.

"The purpose of the matrix, Jim tells us, is to provide a high-speed system of communication, permitting information flow that unites the entire organism for spontaneous, seemingly miraculous healing and performance. Such information transfer includes but surpasses the speed of the peptide/receptor system that's the information network of bodywide communication that Dr. Ruff and I have posited. The matrix actually enhances this superhighway system and provides a mechanism through which previously unexplainable, bodywide communication can take place.

"You may have heard how nerve cells fire along an action potential, causing informational substances (neurotransmitters) to squirt out and jump across a synapse to reach other nerve cells. You may be surprised to know, however, that synaptic firing accounts for only about 2 percent of all information exchanged in the brain and body. The remaining 98 percent of data is carried out by informational substances binding to their cellular receptors, a very different process that uses a parasynaptic pathway. Most of that is distributed throughout the body, not only the brain.

"But my point is that neither of these systems—neuro-transmitters jumping across synapses or peptides binding to receptors—can explain the speed and distance of messages communicated spontaneously throughout the bodywide system. For that explanation, Jim had to look to another mechanism altogether, which is how he discovered the matrix.

"And he had some company in his quest. The Hungarian-born scientist Albert Szent-Györgyi, a Nobel laureate in biochemistry, wrote in 1937: 'Life is too rapid and subtle to be explained by slow-moving chemical reactions and nerve impulses. Something else is going on.' Szent-Györgyi arrived at this conclusion after watching his cat spring into the air when startled by a snake moving suddenly through the grass.

"The matrix is that *something else*," I explained, noticing that my audience had grown very quiet. *They're with me—good,* I said to myself, feeling stronger and more confident. The closer they listened, it seemed, the easier it was for me to speak. I felt as if I were channeling, effortlessly pouring forth the information that I wanted to give them, and they wanted to hear.

"The matrix is actually a semiconductor, a substance capable of supporting fast-paced, electrical activity," I went on. "In many ways, it's like a giant liquid crystal." I hesitated, momentarily paranoid that a colleague might overhear and dismiss my lecture as "New Agey." But I thought of Jim and his courage to stand by his out-of-the-box statements. "When we ignore energy," he'd said at the recent lecture I'd attended, "we miss 99 percent of reality." I kept on going.

"A final piece that explains the flow of energy and information throughout the bodymind is *tensegrity,* a term first coined by Buckminster Fuller, one of our greatest thinkers, who back in the '60s built domes and explored new realms of architecture. Tensegrity means 'tensional integrity,' a quality that makes it possible for a structure to yield increasingly without breaking or coming apart. Like Bucky's domes, tensegrity structures have the strength and durability of a rock-hard golf ball, yet they can flex and be fluid at the same time.

"Oschman postulates that our bodies are tensegrity structures, infinitely pliable and malleable, with bones, tendons, and joints held together by this matrix of connective tissue. It's tensegrity that makes it possible for the startled cat to jump straight up into the air, or the martial artist to perform maneuvers that don't seem humanly possible. It lets athletes win gold medals by performing superhuman feats and causes healing to happen spontaneously, all at once, without any observable time passing.

"It's really amazing. In the matrix, every cell and molecule in the body knows what every other cell and molecule is doing, so the whole organism can function in one cooperative, coordinated manner. When you touch or press the body, that pressure transduces an electrical charge through the matrix. It's called 'piso-electric forces,' a concept from physics 101.

"We understand the electrical nature of the molecules of emotion. We know that a charge is emitted every time a peptide binds to cellular receptors. Clusters of receptors embedded in the cell membrane pump ions in and out of the cell, creating an electronic flux that moves through the matrix like a wave, vibrating receptors where emotionally charged memory is stored.

"Today, most bodyworkers and energy therapists take as a fact the concept that trauma is absorbed and stored in the body and can be unblocked by correcting the energy flow. My theory of the psychosomatic network includes subconscious memories stored in the body, specifically in the receptors on every cell surface. You can see how closely all three—information, emotions, and electrical energy—are related and comprise what we experience as energy moving, a phenomenon often accompanied by a release of past trauma that is felt in the body—your subconscious mind."

The Power of Coherence

My audience was ready for the next level, and so was I, all of us riding a wave of information flow. "Now here's a leap for everyone, including me. I want you to consider that all of you in this lecture hall together form an enormous human matrix, a giant web of interconnected, individual matrices, vibrating one to the other through resonance. Pluck an A string on a guitar, and the A strings of all other guitars in the room vibrate in unison. Imagine the same direct resonance within this giant, universal matrix you're in.

"Consider that we're all part of a resonating network, connected not by rigid wires, but by a flow of pulsating energy passing through our vibrating molecules of emotion—receptors, peptides, and other informational substances—as they bind. Yours, mine, those of the person sitting next to you, and so on, creating one energetic, resonating field."

They need to feel this, I thought. *Maybe something experiential . . .*

"Okay," I announced abruptly, "we're going to church for a moment. I want you to reach out and hold the hand of the person next to you." A verbal cacophony broke out as people took my suggestion and greeted their neighbors. I waited a minute and then said, "There, you just perturbed the universal matrix, expanding it and causing receptors on cells to vibrate newly, sending a wave out through everyone, like ripples from a pebble dropped into a pond.

"Another physical law governing these phenomena is the law of entrainment. Occurring throughout nature, entrainment happens when systems or organisms—that's us—come into synchrony with each other, oscillating at the same rate, or harmonic, of frequency. An infant gazes into the eyes of his or her mother while suckling at the breast. We say that this pair bond is entrained, each following the same pattern of breath, sensation, and eye movement as the other.

"In a larger group, we can use the example of ticking clocks. Back in the old days when every clock had a pendulum, clockmakers noticed that clocks on the shop wall initially ticked at different times, only to fall into a synchronous pattern after a few days of being in the same room with each other. This is not weird or hocus-pocus; it's a law of physics in which vibratory frequencies in a closed system or room will reach the most stable, lowest energy state that, in this case, is a state of synchrony.

"The pendulums of the clocks become entrained, vibrating in

synchronous patterns with each other over time, which is true for any closed system, including the theater in which we're all congregated. The walls, the vibrations, the air swishing—all are waves, moving. A wave is created every time there's a charge. Pluck one tensegrity structure, and the whole vibrates, just as each body resonates with every other body in this room, all of us being entrained with each other.

"The patterns of our physical vibration, like those of the ticking clocks, come into synch together, a state we call 'coherence.' In this condition, everything is oscillating at the same frequency, and harmony—a single wave form—is achieved with no energy wasted. The quality is one of all systems being unified, flowing, flexible, and adaptable. *Oneness.*"

I paused. "This feels good, doesn't it?" A positive murmur came back in response, heads nodding, smiles on faces starting to appear. "I'm really going out on a limb here, because this stuff is not in any textbook of biological psychiatry. But I believe that coherence can explain how we attract the people in our lives who we may need to attract for our growth. Do you ever notice how often you bump into just the right person?

"Or better still, how you keep marrying the same person over and over again? Some of us stop at only two, but when the second husband is starting to complain about the same things the first one was upset about, you've got to stop and think: *Maybe it's me. Maybe there's a lesson for me to learn here.*" Laughter was flowing freely; people were feeling connected, happy.

"What I'm saying is that there are no accidents! And there are no mistakes. Each one of us is emitting an electrical pattern, and an energy exchange is going on all the time. Similar patterns or fields of energy find each other, gaining in strength and balancing, or in some cases canceling each other out.

"The idea is that what we put out, comes back. The vibrational pattern of your receptors seeks a coherent state, and so entrains with people around you who have similar resonance—all mediated, of course, by an emotional quality, your molecules of emotion. This makes for an effortless flow, the Tao of the Buddhists, the kind of life where you can let go and let God, trusting in scientific but mysterious organizing principles that can make this journey a magical adventure."

Connecting to the Earth

I had one more thing to say to about how pervasive, powerful, and potentially healing energy phenomena are:

"We're not only linked to each other in a giant, energetic crystal of interlocking matrices, but we're also all connected to our home, the earth. The planet itself vibrates at a frequency averaging around seven or eight Hz, called the Schumann Constant. This unique electromagnetic phenomenon is created by the sum of the lightning activity occurring at any one time around the globe. Electromagnetic pulses from lightning travel around the earth, bouncing back and forth between the ionosphere and the earth's surface.

"We know that this geomagnetic oscillation, produced at a much lower pitch than hearing range, penetrates the human body and overlaps with heart and brain electromagnetic oscillations, entraining our bodyminds in harmony with our planet. But modern lifestyles don't give us much opportunity to touch the soil. Our ancestors were more connected to the planet's vibratory oscillations, sleeping on the ground and digging in the fields, never leaving the surface, as we do, in high-flying machines! We've been existing for millions of years in resonance with the earth, having almost the same bodyminds as our ancestors of 30,000 years ago. But unlike them, our bare feet rarely touch the soil.

"To make matters worse, we're bombarded by so much electronic energy in our environments from TV, wireless computer networks, and microwaves that may impact us in a disruptive way. When you go to bed, even though the lights are completely turned off, the alternating current going through the walls of your house during the night creates a measurable field that might contribute to the daytime fatigue you experience. Knowing this bombardment is everywhere is enough to make me want to buy one of those crystal-necklace shields that claim to protect us— even though I'd be sure to keep it out of sight under my blouse until more definitive published studies are done on it!"

Looking out on my laughing audience, I saw a pattern of energy appearing like a lattice of connecting molecules arranged in a chemical configuration. A giant crystal emerged before my eyes, composed of electrons buzzing in constant motion, a brilliant, diamond-like structure. People were smiling, connected, touching, and vibrating, one matrix to another. They were ticking like clocks on the wall, pendulums all swinging to the same rhythm, all in total oneness and unity.

Despite the fact that I still had 15 more slides left to show, many illustrating how the laws of physics concerning resonance, coherence, and entrainment were relevant to biology, I knew that it was time to conclude my remarks. It seemed that a coherent field had engulfed us all and delivered the lecture for me. I had, in fact, truly come from my heart, an organ that has by far the strongest coherent, pulsing electrical field in the bodymind, measurable a good distance out into the audience.

But not everything can be explained by the laws of physics. I knew I'd been "on" that night and was grateful to God for giving the crowd what they needed through me. Later, someone mentioned that the lineup of folks outside in the rain before my lecture began looked in passing like pilgrims awaiting some momentous event, perhaps the opening of a great cathedral or church.

In closing, as I thanked my audience for their attention, I felt their thunderous applause in my chest and marveled at the mystery of it all.

Chapter 9

Santa Barbara Revisited:
Love, Play, and Entanglement

I awoke the next morning after my lecture, fully recovered from any lingering jet lag and refreshed from a good night's rest. Nancy had moved me out of her office to a spare room where I could organize myself and be ready for the day.

Santa Barbara! The rain from the night before had cleared, the air was balmy and mild, and I was looking forward to some serious beach time and seeing my son. Brandon, a classical pianist turned hip-hop musician and music technologist, would be driving up from school to arrive around noon. My plan was to take him out to lunch at a local beachside café.

Nancy, however, had some plans for me as well. Prior to my visit, she'd been getting anxious about the timeline of our book. With only a few months before the first draft was due to our publishers, she'd been scolding me about keeping my agreements, referring to the schedule we'd set out at the beginning of our project. Now, eating breakfast at the dining-room table in her Santa Barbara home and enjoying a panoramic view of islands floating on the surface of the blue Pacific, I listened to her concerns.

"We can't keep changing the outline with so little time left," she stressed. "And I can't write this book without knowing how it will end. . . . What happened to the structure we agreed on last March? It's changed a million times since then."

I tried to explain to her that what was happening to me in Santa Barbara was changing my life in a dramatic way. I was experiencing a new sense of relief at not having to think through each little idea and take responsibility for every last detail, which is my usual overachiever mode. Instead, I was learning to trust, and come from my heart. The book was writing itself, I promised her.

"Sure, it's writing itself," she said, "but it's not *publishing* itself, and that's the problem. We've got to get it together!" Being with Nancy could be so annoying sometimes.

Early that morning, in the wee hours before dawn, I'd awoken and gone roaming through Nancy and Richard's beautiful, pink hacienda high in the foothills overlooking the ocean and a scrumptious view of the city. Since my arrival, I'd noticed the titles of many books on their shelves that I wished I had time to read, and was grateful for the wisdom of my friends, both longtime leaders and participants in the consciousness movement.

In the half-light of dawn peeking through the living room's huge picture window, I stood before a towering case of books. Switching suddenly into my psychic, mystical persona, I closed my eyes and reached out to grab a volume off the shelf. With a certainty that was as strong as it was absurd, I opened the pages blindly and knew exactly where to read.

I flipped on the light and glanced down at the open book in my hands. My eyes fell on the word *workaholism,* which the author said involves "obsessive overachieving, beyond the need for creating." He went on to report the tendency "to over commit my energy to various worthy projects, which left me exhausted and isolated from my friends and family." The words bugged out on the page. It was so perfect. I read on: "Overwork can also be a way of burying fears, covering up emptiness, and avoiding anxieties about relationship issues."

The book, *Knights Without Armor* by Aaron Kipnis, Ph.D., was aimed at men, and written more than ten years ago. It occurred to me that in our current day, workaholism isn't just a problem for men, but also for women, teens, and horrendously enough, children, too, so many of whom are scheduled by their parents within an inch of their young lives. We all seek escapes from relationship issues: not feeling deserving, worthy, secure in our sense of belonging, or good enough. I'm certainly not alone.

Workaholism, I read, leads quite often to a numbness that includes the loss of emotional and even physical sensitivity. People come home from work, don't talk to their families, head to the refrigerator for a beer, and collapse in front of the boob tube. Ironically, this leads to an addiction to excitement. To counter their lack of feeling, people develop habits that provide stimulation and intensity, including unnecessarily stirring up conflicts in their relationships. Fighting over inconsequential things while avoiding addressing the issues that underlie the anxiety—old, buried issues for some of us, which have nothing to do with out current partners, who may merely be character roles in our ancient dramas.

I could see this reflected while staying with Nancy and Richard. Why was it so easy for me to see how they stirred up each other's dramas? Why do I have all the answers for healing *their* partnership, bringing it back to playful, childlike joyousness, but not my bond with my own husband? And why was I so resistant when Nancy, at least as wise and sensitive to interpersonal skills and psychological relationships as I am, shared her insights and held the mirror up to Michael and me?

Staying with Nancy, everything's on the table—we're each other's past. With her, I was in a laboratory of interpersonal growth and relationships. All the old records were available, right in front of my nose, and I didn't have to try to figure it all out. It's a deep and strange connection—lifelong friends circling around each other for more years than I care to remember. We're so much alike, and yet such opposites.

And while we'd both be considered successes in the eyes of most people, we shared a tendency to whiz right by the "here-and-now" goodness in our lives, relationships, families, and careers.

These were the issues we were dealing with, and we hoped to resolve them as we worked and played together, writing the book and growing as we went.

Family Bonding and the Endorphins

We drove with Brandon to a café at the beach, and since it was too early for lunch, the three of us took a walk on the sand. The October day was warm enough to wear a T-shirt and go barefoot, splashing in the waves that broke along the shore. Brandon and I hung back together as Nancy moved out to give us some space. It was an opportunity to bond, and we talked about school, his new girlfriend, and future plans. Our communication was easy, my expectations not dominating our interaction as they had in the past, and Brandon was free to share with me what was important to him.

Family, relationships, bonding, and loving—mother and child, husband and wife, friends and acquaintances—these are my prescriptions for feeling good, feeling God. Dean Ornish wrote about it in his book *Love and Survival,* and he presented a ton of data that the biggest, most important predictor of longevity isn't concerned with smoking, eating properly, or staying fit. Instead, according to the large-scale epidemiological studies that Ornish reports on, long life is correlated more closely with the number of social interactions a person has every single day.

Connection. Community. *Oneness.* These are the keys.

A sense of fellowship keeps us sane, which is why Mike and I no longer wait for the summer months to spend time on our magical island in the Chesapeake Bay, but make more frequent visits year-round. There, in the little microcosm of familiarity and low-stress lifestyles, we find ourselves volunteering for local efforts, attending block parties, and getting to know our neighbors. We understand that this kind of regular bonding and union with others on a daily basis is at least as good for us, if not better, than the vegetables we eat and the vitamin supplements we take daily.

Healing my relationship with my youngest son, restoring our mother/child bond, was part of my mission in coming to Santa Barbara. Brandon is my youngest, my baby, and I'd been reluctant to let go as he became more and more independent, first as a teen and now as a young adult. Part of my attachment came from my awareness that throughout his young life, he'd suffered from a lack of attention as Michael and I pursued our Peptide-T dramas, something I saw happening only in hindsight.

Academically, I'd compared him to myself and decided that he didn't measure up, not ever acknowledging that he was an artist in a family of scientists, and needed support for expressing his musical gifts.

As a scientist and a mother, I knew a lot about the biochemical basis of love and bonding from my work in the lab with endorphins. I'd studied them extensively as the chemicals of bliss, the body's own endogenous morphine, often associated with "runner's high." I'd mapped their existence throughout the bodymind and shown how these chemicals were major players in the psychosomatic network.

People often ask me about endorphins, since I was involved in their early discovery and am expected to be up on the latest research. The question is: "What do endorphins do?" I always have trouble answering this because, like the other molecules of emotion, they don't really *do* anything on their own, but are rather one component in a bigger process, playing a role in associated behaviors and emotions for both animals and humans. At one time in the '70s, the endorphins were expected to provide a panacea to heroin addiction, hopefully giving us a drug that would satisfy cravings without causing further addiction. But that hadn't worked out, because the laboratory versions all proved to be just as highly habit-forming as heroin, and the field had languished for lack of further developments.

Update on Endorphin Research

The latest and most comprehensive research I know of on the endorphins has been done by Jaak Panksepp, a scientist whose work has been published in the scientific literature, and whose *Textbook of Biological Psychiatry* has been well received. I've always had a lot of respect for him, so I was excited to attend his lecture, "Affective Neuroscience and the Social Brain," at the spring 2005 conference of the Bowen Center for the Study of the Family held nearby in Washington, D.C.

I recall how I raced across the Potomac River to the hotel where the conference was being held and slipped into the back row of the lecture hall just as Dr. Panksepp was beginning his talk. Thank God that he—not I, for a change!—had to find meaning in all the tiny, tediously proven factoids that he and other scientists had meticulously managed to collect, and then present them in an accessible and entertaining way. His job was to arrange and present the data to an overflowing roomful of family therapists gathered from all over the world, to give them something useful to take back with them to help their clients heal.

Bowen Family Therapy, as it's often called, is a very advanced form of psychotherapy. It's based on the idea that members of a family are so closely linked by invisible but powerful emotional forces that only one person needs to be regularly treated for the whole family to benefit. As that individual changes, the whole system then rearranges and corrects itself. Panksepp's research has shed much light on the strength of our human bonding, connecting it to endorphins and the opiate receptor, which is why he was speaking to this group.

Years before, Mike and I had sent Brandon into Bowen treatment, hoping to help his serious adolescent "acting out," not realizing that (as the Bowen therapists joke among themselves) it's usually the healthiest person in the family who gets sent in by the others! While my husband and I were having trouble dealing with our own issues, we alighted on Brandon's temporarily slipping grades as a distraction, sending him off for help when we were the ones who needed it.

Later, it became clear to me how interdependent the whole family is, how the most effective way to help your children or the family members you're concerned about is to begin solving *your own* personal issues, one by one. When you grow, the people around you do, too—once more, we're all connected.

Panksepp's work has shown that endorphins are the peptide not only for bliss, the "high" of the heroin addict, but also for bonding and attachment, scientific words for *love*. He studied maternal bonding in rats and chicks and noticed that when the babies were removed from their mothers, they made distress vocalizations, sounds of loss and grieving. When given a shot of morphine, or exogenous endorphin, these young animals ceased to grieve and instead became pacified, even blissful in their separated state.

But if given naltrexone, an antagonist drug that blocks opiate receptors, the babies were even more upset, showing that the endorphin was carrying the message of attachment and bonding. Naltrexone is the drug given to comatose, overdosed heroin addicts when they arrive at the emergency room, effectively bumping opiates from their cellular receptors and instantly awakening them, thus saving their lives.

Similar studies have been done with dogs, animals whose behavior is more familiar to us than rats. Tail wagging is shown to be associated with low endorphin levels, indicating an eagerness for social interaction, such as petting and touching. Give Fido some morphine, and the wagging stops; block the dog's receptors with naltrexone, and it increases.

So, should we worry about Fido becoming a junkie? Maybe! But that's another study. The point is that Panksepp showed endorphins are the balm, the antidote, the soother provided by nature to deal with the distress of separation, a condition we all suffer from in our alienating, modern world. His findings should give us pause to consider—is addiction to heroin caused by a profound sense of non-belonging, a painful disconnection from close relationships or even from community?

Does *feeling good*—slang used by heroin addicts to describe the act of shooting up—point to a more basic human need, such as the blissful bond of mother and child, or a close, loving adult relationship? Are people drawn to take the drug who lack either of these? If so, we have a new direction to look in for healing addiction closer to the source. Rather than focusing on a chemical cure, we could apply what we know about the healing power of *mind, emotions, and spirit*—not just the body alone—to help people feel their very real, but often unacknowledged, connection to each other, their community, and their planet.

Religious or spiritual mystics have reported experiences of blissful ecstasy when united with the divine through prayer, meditation, trance, and even dance. It makes sense that the 12-step program Alcoholics Anonymous, with its strong spiritual component of seeking help from a Higher Power, has been the single most effective method for recovery from addiction. Could that success perhaps be due to this connection between the experience of spiritual oneness and the body's own bliss juice, endorphin?

For his talk to the family therapists, Panksepp included some fascinating studies on laughter, joy, and depression in connection to endorphins. Guided by the concept of epistemics, which predicts that animal brain research can tell us about the internal experiences of humans, he discovered that laboratory rats were making high-pitched, supersonic chirping sounds, a behavior he called "rat laughter."

How did he know that the rats were laughing and not just making random noises? Easy—he and his research assistants tickled the animals, an action that elicited the supersonic chirping! Also, the amount of time the rodents spent chirping peaked as young adults and declined in age, which is a similar pattern for humans, who typically laugh less as they grow older.

It turned out that rat laughter was moderated by endorphins, which Panksepp proved by using naltrexone to block them from binding to their receptors. The chirping sounds were then stopped. Panksepp concluded that laughter is a psychological birthright of the human brain, the evolutionary antecedent of human joy, and perhaps the basis for a new approach to curing depression, if we can find ways to reliably augment it.

Panksepp's findings also shed light on how children learn through play. Tickling and touching, often a part of rough-and-tumble play, are normal activities that children engage in as they grow. During these activities, children are biochemically bonding, belonging, and connecting to each other—all a part of their healthy, natural development.

Children who don't laugh and play with other kids are vulnerable, Panksepp proposes, to attention-deficit/hyperactivity disorders (ADHD), pointing to well-documented findings that social isolation is associated with learning deficits. He questions our school culture's prohibition on rough-and-tumble play, and the related use of drugs like Ritalin to control children's classroom behavior. His findings suggest that these measures might be suppressive and detrimental to a child's development. The simple matter is that when laughter and play are curbed because they don't fit school agendas, endorphins stop flowing, children don't bond, and learning suffers.

Are We Having Fun Yet?

Play and laughter are vital to feeling good. Recreation isn't merely a frivolous addition to life or a hard-earned reward for work, two beliefs stemming from early Puritanical times. I believe that in a society driven by a strong work ethic, with so many individuals burdened with workaholism, people aren't getting enough endorphinergic surges throughout their bodymind on a daily basis.

For you to not be laughing and playing during some part

of every day is unnatural and goes against your fundamental biochemistry. I recommend that you consciously seek out opportunities to cut loose every day, scheduling them into your calendar, if necessary. Here are a few of my favorite ways to get those daily chuckles:

- Rent a stupid, funny movie and let yourself enjoy it.

- Dance for ten minutes to your favorite rock music.

- Play with small children and let them tickle you.

- Call someone up and tell a joke. Make sure the person knows why you're doing it, so he or she can call someone and do the same thing.

- Most of all, don't wait until you're depressed or in a low mood to do something playful. Be spontaneous! Include play every day as part of what you do naturally, like brushing your teeth or going to the gym to work out.

- Finally, don't worry about looking foolish. The only time you really look silly is when you're popping pills from a bottle while your natural pharmaceuticals are just waiting to be released from every cell of your bodymind!

Hardwired for Bliss

Dr. George Stefano, an innovative researcher whose Old Westbury, Long Island, laboratory I'd visited recently, reported that he could isolate biological morphine from animals. Not peptide endorphins, but *morphine*—the active ingredient of opium that's extracted from the poppy plant! In spite of much initial resistance from skeptical scientists, Stefano reported that he'd also found a primitive opiate receptor for this morphine: a tiny, truncated version existing in lobsters, mussels, and other primitive creatures. Most astounding was his discovery that we have the same enzymes in the human brain that are found in the poppy plant, providing a pathway for our bodies to make morphine using the same exact biochemical route as the botanical.

As I've said before, receptors for the bliss chemicals—morphine and endorphins—are located in the greatest abundance in the human frontal cortex, the most recently evolved and the highest command post of the brain. We have thus been hardwired to experience the pleasure of bliss, a bodymind state of unity and resonance with a loved one or the divine.

—·—

After lunch at the beachside café, we drove back to Nancy's house, and I said good-bye to Brandon. Before he drove away, I remembered to pull out the Disney executive's business card, acquired on my flight from Dallas to Los Angeles. "Call him soon," I said. "This could be your ticket. . . ." Trailing off, I caught myself and stopped. *He'll do it in his own time,* I thought, *in his own way.* I was letting go once again.

As he drove away, I was consoled that our bond had been strengthened by this meeting, and a new relationship was forming thanks to my own growth and increased self-esteem. Mother and son—we were a field, no longer isolated entities circling each other with one prying and the other defensive. I'd chosen to have a new respect for Brandon and his life and could let go, trusting that in spite of my empty nest, we'd always be connected.

Quantum Compassion

Back at the house, Nancy and I spent a few productive hours writing, and then decided to take a break. Before I arrived in Santa

Barbara, Nancy had asked me if she could book an hour of my time to be interviewed for a friend's film, the subject of which was the healing power of compassion. I didn't hesitate to accept her offer, knowing that this quality was indeed a key for healing and remembering the Dalai Lama's reply to Michael at the conference we'd attended in Munich, Germany.

The film shoot took place on the roof of the building where Nancy's friend Simon Fox had his offices for Adventures in Caring, an organization dedicated to bringing the quality of compassion into health-care settings. Fox's film, entitled *The Medicine of Compassion*, instructs health-care professionals in how to communicate to bring about healing and recovery, and he wanted me to say a few words on camera about the biological basis for this.

Arriving at the organization's downtown offices, we followed a long, winding staircase up to the rooftop, where the film crew was waiting to do the shoot. As they readied me for the camera, I took in the 360-degree view: streaks of low-lying fog, wide-open sky, and the city spreading out beneath us. Church bells were chiming from a nearby bell tower, the top of which I could see against a breathtaking backdrop of Shangri La–like mountains—the Santa Barbara foothills.

In a lively conversation while the camera rolled, we talked about how compassion can heal people who are ill. When a sick person senses the care of another human being, their physiology changes: blood flow increases, heartbeat slows, and breathing is enhanced, resulting in a healing state that we can readily see. Changes probably occur when the patient's cellular receptors resonate with the vibrating receptors of a healer, entraining both in a loving state that can initiate cellular processes to change physiology, behavior, emotion, and consciousness.

When receptors are vibrating, I explained, the tiny channels connecting the cell surface to its interior open and close, allowing ions to flow in and out of the cell. This ionic flux alters the set point that determines if a brain cell fires or not. The channels themselves have a quantal nature, meaning that they're either open or closed, never in between.

Hearing me talk, Simon suddenly got excited and interjected, "I just understood something about compassion! When our training teaches people how to communicate with patients in hospitals, we tell them that this caring doesn't take place in what the Greeks called 'chronos,' or normal, linear time. Instead, it occurs in 'kyros,' or nonlinear time." He paused to think. "When patients sense that doctors or nurses actually care about them and their suffering, then sudden quantum shifts occur. It's difficult to perceive, because this change is very subtle, but we can train people to notice that it's happening."

"I think I understand what you're saying," I responded. "Compassion is a quantum event, something that happens instantaneously."

"Yes," Simon continued. "My point is that it doesn't take any more time for medical professionals to be compassionate in their interactions than it does for them to be perfunctory and routine. What you're saying is that this caring is a deep, synchronizing vibration that, when resonant, produces a sudden shift to bring about a coherent, healing state that happens in almost no time at all!"

Coming down from the rooftop, I pondered Simon's insight about how one person resonating in coherence with another who is in pain or near death can heal. I recalled how the Dalai Lama told Michael about his own personal experience of the power of compassion, which transformed him physically and caused his symptoms to disappear.

Miracle healing—what was it, if not simply a natural, biological event for which a scientific explanation hadn't yet been proposed?

Inside the Labyrinth

Nancy and I left the shoot and headed for a downtown park, thinking we'd catch the last of the day's sunlight as we sat on a park bench and spent some time writing on her laptop. But Nancy took a sudden turn and parked the car in front of a nearby church, the same bell-chiming building I'd seen from the rooftop interview across the street.

"I want to show you my favorite meditation spot," she told me, jumping out of the car like an eager ten-year-old. We walked past some hedges and came upon a clearing with a beautiful labyrinth etched into the ground. Nancy briefly explained that the pattern is a spiritual tool for walking and meditation, modeled after the famous medieval structure inlaid into the stone floor of the Chartres Cathedral in France around A.D. 1200.

"Just get on the path and don't worry about doing it the right way. There is no right way!" she shouted as she entered the labyrinth. "Whatever you experience on the walk, let it be a reflection of what's going on for you in your life."

Eager for some play, I skipped along the twists and turns of the circular pathway, stepping out of bounds, not doing it perfectly, and rapidly arriving at the labyrinth's center. Standing in the vortex at the core of the maze, I was exhilarated with a profound feeling that somehow, everything was going to be okay—the book, the future of Peptide T, Brandon, and my relationship to Michael. *Don't worry about doing it right, just trust,* I told myself. The bells were chiming again in the church tower as I wound my way back through the lines to be deposited at the entrance where I'd begun my walk.

A Stroll in the Park

Arriving at the downtown city park, we strolled along a gravel path past foliage in full bloom, coming to a bridge over a koi pond where Nancy suddenly stopped. She'd seen two friends seated on a bench in the distance. "It will only take a moment," she said. "We have to stop and say hello."

"No," I said, returning all too quickly to my rebellious personality. "Come on, you wanted to work for the hour, and this is a distraction." It was my turn to be the taskmaster. "We don't have time to talk to your friends." But before I could do anything else to change our course, we were standing in front of them. *Trust* . . . the message echoed once again.

Nancy introduced me to Justin, who gasped so loudly when he recognized my name that I had to joke and tell him I wasn't *the* Candace Pert, but only Nancy's friend with the same name as the scientist in *What the Bleep . . . !?*

"No, no . . . I can't believe it," the astounded man went on, acting as if he'd seen a ghost. "We were just talking about you at the very instant you approached," he said, still stunned, but starting to smile. His companion also looked shocked and delighted, as if I'd materialized out of thin air in the middle of their conversation about me—which I had!

"What were you saying?" I asked, sensing a synchronicity about to unfold.

"I was telling my friend that I didn't like the way the film fails to give God an important place," he said, "as if quantum physics explains it all. And if we hadn't been turned away from your lecture last night, I would have asked you right then and there if you believed in God yourself."

I burst out laughing and jumped for joy. What were the odds of meeting two people who were at that exact moment discussing the same question that had been rolling around in my own subconscious bodymind?

"Let me answer you right now!" I exclaimed. "First, I want you to know that as a scientist, I believe in God with all my heart. I see God everywhere in the matrix that unites us all. Our meeting here today, the sheer synchronicity of you talking about me and then me showing up, is due to the vibration of our molecules organizing at the highest levels to achieve coherence and harmony. This is the demonstration of what I know as *God.*"

I was giving them the lecture they'd missed, and so I continued.

"In fact, the kind of synchronicity we're experiencing here today, I believe, is the raw data for what one day will be the scientific proof of God." I paused for a breath. "Such 'chance' encounters are clues that something is going on, giving us hints much like the shadows of moons did before early astronomers saw the heavenly bodies themselves. Eventually, the invention of the telescope enabled astronomers to prove their theories. We scientists simply don't have a theory or a formula to explain what we're seeing, but we will. Someday people will be looking back, having a good laugh and saying, *Remember when most scientists didn't believe in God?*"

Justin thanked me generously, letting me know that he was overjoyed to come across a scientist who not only believed in God but wanted to explain the divine scientifically and wasn't afraid to talk about the possibility. We chatted a bit more, and then Nancy's friends had to go.

We took their seats on the bench and popped open the laptop. I was getting excited and said to Nancy, "Remember the consciousness panel in Santa Monica that I was on with some of the talking-head physicists from *What the Bleep . . . !?*"

"You mean the one where you were late, because we were having lunch and talking about writing the book?" she asked.

"Yes," I said. "They were all talking about some heady stuff, but at the end, all I could say was, 'You're forgetting the God piece.' Fred Alan Wolfe asked in jest, 'Do you mean the *cod*piece?' He was referring to the leather pouch that men wore in medieval times to cover their privates. Wolfe likes to be profane, always the merry jokester. 'No, I mean the *God* piece,' I repeated, emphasizing the word because none of the experts had used it, as if the idea didn't have a place in the new quantum science. Later, after the panel was over, people from the audience came up and thanked me for being the only one who'd mentioned God."

Nancy nodded. "I guess that's why we're writing the book," she said, and she began typing away on her laptop to capture the moment.

Are Emotions Addicting?

Back at the house, we relaxed with a light supper and then popped in the DVD of *What the Bleep . . . !?* Nancy wanted me to watch the movie with her so that she could quiz me on some of the content.

Since my appearance in the film, I'd often encountered people who thought that I wrote the cartoon sequence in which colorful animated cells and peptides act out a host of human emotions, such as anger, lust, and self-pity. People love the raucous wedding-party scene, where these cartoon characters run amok, displaying behaviors only visible to the wedding photographer. It's a wonderfully artistic and hilarious segment, but I didn't write any part of the movie, which took a bit of artistic license with my theory by showing each peptide as a specific emotion. In reality, a peptide is more like a chord than a single note, changing vibrations not at one pitch but several, giving a more complex richness of tone than a single note.

"So, are we addicted to our emotions?" Nancy asked. "That seems to be the message of the film. But what do *you* say?"

"The truth is," I replied, "we aren't addicted to our emotions—but rather, each of us is hooked on our own personal sequence of strong feelings that occur during reenactment."

I explained to Nancy that this is the compulsive, subconscious re-creation in adult life of a core trauma we experienced in childhood—pure, classical psychoanalytic theory. An example is the case of a woman whose father abandoned the family when she was a child, leaving her crying and shrieking. Her addiction to reenactment has her end every one of her adult relationships with men by screaming at her departing lover.

I knew from my own blonde-in-the-bed episode that we crave returning to the place of our most intense core emotional traumas over and over again, replaying them in current settings as we try to find solutions. Unconsciously, we re-create old emotional scenes, searching for a new answer obsessively and automatically, like a computer scanning its hard drive from beginning to end. Reenactment is a very machinelike process, a throwback to a preverbal survival mode mediated by our primitive or reptilian brain.

Post-traumatic stress disorder (PTSD) is an extreme example of this behavior. Traumatized military personnel returning from war have very real flashbacks, reexperiencing every detail of the terror of bombs bursting over their heads. Core emotional traumas from childhood are experienced the same way, only less literally than for veterans. Instead, we civilians play out the original traumas with new players, casting friends, lovers, and bosses in the original roles, hoping subconsciously to resolve the incident and have it go some other way.

"In *What the Bleep . . . !?*" I continued, hoping that Nancy would have the patience to let me weave my thoughts together, "another animated sequence shows how neural nets are formed as a result of brain cells firing. A neural net is a very complicated pathway, meandering and convoluted—kind of like the pattern we walked today, a similarity that may explain why the labyrinth has been such a powerful meditation tool over centuries of human use. The more you repeat a particular neural pathway, the more it becomes fixed—which is how spoken affirmations work to create reality, by the way.

"*Nerve cells that fire together, wire together*—this is a catchy phrase I've heard many times and is a clever way to describe how connections are formed when neurons fire repeatedly over time in the same patterns," I continued. "But it's a mistake to think that neural nets are only located in the brain. They involve your spinal cord, heart, and any number of organs hooked up by autonomic ganglia—all part of the psychosomatic network. Because this web is so vast, stuck emotions can be located anywhere, coloring your filtered perceptions with memories of old traumas. Remember, your memory isn't just in your brain, but lives subconsciously in your body, stored and accessed by the molecules of emotion.

"What the film didn't show is this: Reliving a core emotional trauma is a whole bodymind event, not just one occurring when nerve cells fire in repeated patterns. Remember, less than 2 percent of biochemical information is flowing at the neuronal synapse, so the formation of neural nets can't possibly explain all of our experience. We can't deny that the mind and body are one, united by cellular receptors strewn throughout the matrix and vibrating to create waves of emotion and information. The body doesn't exist only to carry the head around."

A Pain in the Neck

The DVD was still playing when the doorbell rang. It was Joe Migliore, an eclectic-energy chiropractor who'd approached me after my lecture and offered to treat me with his own special brand of "multidimensional bodywork," which he'd evolved from observing many chiropractic mentors, including Donald Epstein. Following my instincts, I'd invited Joe, who'd recently moved to the West Coast from Long Island, to drop by on my last evening in Santa Barbara and give me a treatment.

He set up his table and was soon focusing on adjusting my neck, where I told him I'd had some recent pain.

"This is a tough one," Joe said softly, applying a light touch to a tight area in my neck.

Curious, I asked him, "Do you think it's from carrying my bags through the airport?" I was recalling my recent misadventure at the Dallas terminal.

"No, it's older than that," he answered. "I'd say this knot in your neck comes from something that happened about three and a half years ago."

Once again, I marveled at a healer's ability to sense how long ago an injury or perturbation in the field had been in place. It was almost like reading the rings of a tree trunk and being able to tell by the demarcations just what had happened in the environment and when.

I thought back to the date Joe suggested and almost immediately recalled a traumatic incident—Michael and I were rushing to an important and stressful meeting with a new lawyer to regain control of our stagnating invention. In the car, Mike suddenly blurted out that he'd bought a plane ticket to Europe and was leaving me behind to visit old friends at the end of the summer. Distraught, I literally collapsed in grief, sobbing, oblivious to any sensations from my body—only focused on my fear of impending loss. That moment had kicked off the summer we almost split up, and Joe was finding the residue of the trauma I hadn't yet resolved.

As he worked, my inner vision of the rift with my husband became clearer. An image arose of Mike's face, his eyes looking tenderly into mine. The words formed on his lips: *I love you so much.* I became one big vibrating symphony, and all my stories of the past melted away. I knew in that moment that Mike loved me and always had—and that my own insecurities had driven a wedge between us. I'd been addicted to reenacting my childhood trauma of the blonde in the bed! Driven by the low self-esteem and sense of undeserving originating from the early experience of my abandoned three-year-old self, I'd almost destroyed my marriage.

The pain in my neck abruptly resolved, and Joe lifted his hands away from the area where the block had been. I could now be responsible for my reenacted dramas, the victim no longer; I could forgive myself and my husband. It was as if a spell had been broken, providing a happy ending to the scary fairy tale I'd been living in for many years.

"There," Joe said, as I burst into the laughter of relief. "I think you just got your release." And he was right . . . I definitely had.

Entanglement and Departure

Four in the morning came hard and fast. It was still dark when I threw my bags into the trunk of Nancy and Richard's car, and all three of us piled in for the drive down the coast to the airport where I'd catch my plane to go home. As we pulled out of the driveway, I saw the city lights twinkling below and said a silent good-bye to the city I'd come to know and love.

Richard drove while Nancy and I sipped hot drinks and watched the slow dawn spread over the Pacific Ocean. How gorgeous it was, this stretch of coastal beaches with the sun just starting to illuminate the nearly still ocean! I mused silently about whether the smooth texture of the water's surface could be an optical illusion caused by the low angle of the sun. Passing through Malibu, we could see the early-morning stirring of people and cars, as Richard pointed out the many celebrity homes, and the clubs and restaurants where movie stars played.

"I've been meaning to follow up on something," I said to him, knowing that he'd read widely on quantum theory and synchronicity. "How do you think quantum entanglement explains synchronicity?" Nancy and I both listened carefully, as Richard took his chance to hold forth. "Quantum entanglement is a theory in physics, now proven experimentally," he began. "The idea is that when you separate matter into two coupled particles, regardless of how far apart those particles may travel, whatever you do to one, the other will instantly respond the same way. This is because everything in the universe is entangled, meaning that there's no real distance between one thing and another, a condition known as nonlocality."

"And synchronicity?" I prodded. "How does that fit in?"

"When you apply nonlocality, or entanglement theory, to the human mind, it can explain synchronicity, as well as telepathy, clairvoyance, precognition, and distant healing. It started with the big bang, the moment at the beginning of time when our universe was created from a cosmic explosion. Everything was entangled until being flung out from the cosmic womb into creation. Somehow, nonlocality has persisted, and when we focus attention on events, people, or ideas not yet manifest—as happens in synchronicity—it's not a far leap to see how seemingly unconnected elements are affected."

Nancy was seeing something for herself out of what Richard was saying. "Oh, I get it," she joined in. "That's how we manifest what we want in the world!" She continued, "What Gandhi said now makes sense: 'Be the change you want to see in the world.' He knew that *me* changing affects the rest of reality. Everything is entangled, so as I shift, everything else does, too. In other words, every thought counts—consciousness matters!"

Our cosmic conversation had the effect of a time warp, depositing us sooner than expected at the curbside of the tiny Long Beach terminal, where my plane waited close by for what turned out to be an effortless departure. Thanking my friends and hugging them good-bye, I quickly found myself on the plane, rejoicing in the unexpected bonanza of three empty seats across, allowing me to spread out my work and later lie down to take a nap.

In the sky, I mused about the stark contrast between this departing journey and the exhausting, missed connections of my arrival a week earlier. This time, I was carried along on a very different current than the one I'd ridden in on. It was as if the two opposite wave functions of my arriving and departing flights completely cancelled each other out, leaving me with the experience of time as seamless and whole. I'd experienced some profound changes during my visit to Santa Barbara, yet somehow I felt as if I'd never left home.

Chapter 10

Monterey: Imagination, Empowerment, and Manifestation

"I request—no, I *insist*—that you meet me in Monterey at the annual Academy for Guided Imagery conference in a week," I said to Nancy over the phone from my office at Georgetown. I'd been home from Santa Barbara for a few weeks and had already begun to repack my bags for a return trip to California. "It's an important event, and maybe it will help us write the final chapter of the book."

I waited while Nancy thought about my offer. She'd been on a roll since I departed Santa Barbara, and our book was almost in its final draft. It took discipline, a muscle she'd built, and I admired her stamina, even though I often pulled her from her task with my impulsive hunches.

Finally she replied. "At this point, I really think my hours are better spent writing, not traveling," she said. "From what you've told me, it doesn't sound like you're going to have much time to spend with me working on the book, anyway."

"Don't worry—it's going to work out perfectly," I interrupted, feeling only a twinge of concern, since I'd promised the conference organizer, an old friend, that I'd be available to participants over the entire four days of the conference. But my intuition was telling me that big changes were afoot, both in my own personal journey and in the evolution of Peptide T, two major threads that were increasingly coming together in my life. I wanted Nancy to be there to capture and even catalyze it all. In a weird way, I was now living my life for the book, hoping that the Monterey experience would bring me the happy ending that I needed for both.

I tried again, this time letting go of my bossy approach (which never seemed to work with Nancy, anyway) and suggested, "You could drive up in the afternoon, stay over in a bed-and-breakfast, catch a few workshops, and meet some of the presenters and participants."

I continued, pleading, "At least come for the Saturday session to hear Dave Bresler's talk. He's the organizer of the meeting and also one of the earliest pioneers in the academic mind-body movement. He works with people, not rats, and is going to talk about how mental imagery can be used to heal, and also create, new futures. You know, the practical application of the research I've been talking about, the stuff you want more of in the book."

Nancy thought for a moment. "Okay, I'll come," she said. "But only if you agree to do more work on Chapter 4, and then give me your edits when I get there so that I can type them in." She paused. "I could use a change of scenery, get out, and have some fun. . . ."

"Of course I'll do that," I said. I'd already been working on the last draft of the chapter that Nancy was talking about, adding in more information from a recent scientific meeting. I was, in fact, planning to spend the five-hour plane ride poring over a final edit.

"I'll get a place nearby in Pacific Grove," Nancy said, referring to the small community adjacent to Monterey where the conference was to be held. "You should bring warm clothes—Monterey isn't Southern California!"

So it was set. Nancy would come for the last two days of the conference, skipping the opening-day workshop that Mike and I were putting on, since she'd already attended an earlier version at the Noetic Institute conference in D.C. This time, I wanted her to focus less on what I had to offer and more on capturing the state of the art in mind-body applications by professionals who were on the front line in their practices. As for me, I intended to take full advantage of the convergence of top people in this field to create the future of Peptide T with the help of the powerful techniques and processes that I knew would be available at the conference.

Hello, Dalai

In the weeks between my return from Santa Barbara and my departure for the Monterey meeting, I'd attended the 35th annual Society for Neuroscience meeting held at the convention center in downtown Washington, D.C.

Thirty-five years ago, just before starting graduate school at Johns Hopkins Medical School, I'd attended the society's very first meeting, also held in Washington. The year was 1970, and Agu and I drove down to attend each day from our apartment on an Army base north of Baltimore. How excited we were then to join about 200 other scientists who weren't content to consider the brain as an unapproachable "black box," but were coming from disciplines such as psychology, biology, and neurophysiology to crack the brain's secrets. Over the years, the society had prospered, and now, in 2005, the annual meeting would draw more than 30,000 neuroscientists from all over the world.

At the invitation of the society's president, guest speaker Tenzin Gyatso, the 14th Dalai Lama of Tibet, was presenting a talk billed as "The Science and Clinical Applications of Meditation." Advancements in brain-imaging technology had led to an interest in finding *consciousness* in the brain, a word that most neuroscientists still didn't use in their work.

The Dalai Lama, who called science "the slayer of religion," had lent his expertise in meditation to several studies of consciousness. I must say, I never thought I'd see 20,000 neuroscientists in three overflowing conference rooms enthusiastically attending a religious leader's talk. Several friends of mine who felt that science and religion should be kept in their separate arenas stayed pointedly away.

In his talk, the Dalai Lama had something to say about emotions: "If you want a happy life, you must . . ." and he swiped his arm in a broad gesture to indicate the words *get rid of,* "negative emotions, like hatred, anger, and jealousy." And then he joked, "If neuroscientists can find the locations in the brain of these things . . . and can take them out, I will be the first to have the operation!" bringing down the house in laughter.

In the end, the spiritual leader's message was very simple: "All want happy life, and why do we study neurobio-mechanisms? But to find happy life." He recommended meditation and compassion, citing compelling evidence from recent studies that showed focused attention and positive emotions—such as compassion, empathy, and love—can impact the physical structure and wiring of the brain.

While I was thrilled to hear the Dalai Lama saying that *consciousness matters* in such a setting, I was especially inspired to reconnect with my original tribe, the neuroscientists attending the meeting. This was my family, which I'd parted from long ago in order to pursue my HIV research, attending meetings only infrequently over the years. These people were my real roots—my "hood!"—and I felt even more at home with them than with the Dalai Lama, who represented for me the new directions I'd been traveling in my journey. A full circle was closing again, more like a spiral of growth and evolution. So many elements in my career, my personal growth, and the science I'd done and was still doing came together at this meeting, giving me a new level of integration and wholeness in my life.

I couldn't help but think that in the old NIMH days, my lab would have had as many as a dozen presentations over the weeklong conference, at least eight posters and three or four talks presented with slides in darkened rooms. But at this meeting, I was just a stroller, dropping in to see the presentations of other neuroscientists, people who'd spent the year working in their lab to gather data so that they could present their findings to their colleagues at this annual event. I'd have to wait for the 37th annual Winter Conference on Brain Research, held next year in Steamboat Springs, Colorado, for Michael and me to present our latest findings about Peptide T.

As I walked down the rows and rows of poster presentations, I was (as usual) moved by the dedication and nobility of these scientists. There were over a thousand displays, each with research summarized in intricate detail tacked up on the wall and attended by one of the researchers who'd worked on the team.

These representatives—real scientists!—were eager to share their work and answer questions from the 5,000 scientists clogging the aisles on the enormous floor, passing by during each three-hour slot before another group replaced them. Morning and afternoon, the rotation went on, while simultaneously, other experts addressed audiences in ballrooms and breakout sessions, creating a veritable ten-ring circus of exciting scientific performance and interaction.

I strolled the poster aisle related to my own work and reflected. I saw exhibits showing research on neurogenesis, immune-cell-to-brain migration, and the importance of neuro-inflammation in disease. Here was evidence that science was filling in the details, validating the psychosomatic network and mind-body unity—the fundamentals of the new-paradigm physiology. Yes, the approach was still a reductionist one, but the millions of little factoids being discovered and documented by neuroscientists today are leading to a bigger picture that will eventually translate into cures for many human diseases and conditions.

I thought of Galileo, who'd first seen the shadows of Jupiter's moons moving across the planet with his new telescope. From this discovery and the movement of sunspots, he could be sure that despite his era's dogmatic belief in a static universe, "it moves, nonetheless." I thought about how astronomers in later years came to accept Galileo's findings, filling in the details and bringing his discovery into full manifestation over time. Now, five centuries later, I could see that same pattern repeating, this time as the mind-body revolution ushered in new avenues for healing body, mind, and soul.

Adventure by the Sea

Soon after the plane dropped Mike and me at the tiny Monterey Airport, we were in our rental car hurtling down a winding chute of a road that delivered us steep and fast into the tiny community of Pacific Grove.

Pacific Grove, the home of the Asilomar Conference Center, was strictly storybook: deer grazing in the forests and meadows, woodpeckers and squirrels gathered in the pine trees, pounding surf on white-sand beaches, seals basking on the rocks, and otters swimming in the coves. Our destination was situated at the very tip of the Monterey Peninsula, which we reached by passing quaint bungalows on tiny streets, each with chimneys giving off wisps of smoke to fill the crisp November air with the scent of burning pine.

Asilomar, meaning "refuge by the sea," was the name given to the sprawling 100-acre conference grounds built over a century ago as a summer camp for YMCA leadership training. Now owned by the state of California, the buildings are preserved in the original, stunningly designed architecture. This includes a central social hall with giant fireplace, a glass-walled dining hall tucked in a wooded corner, and over 300 guest rooms clustered in rustic lodges—all without telephones or TVs. The atmosphere was so wholesome and close to nature that it made me want to roast marshmallows and sing campfire songs! But best of all, the place couldn't have been further in ambiance from the top-down, hierarchical bureaucracy that Mike and I had been battling back on the East Coast, and we were very grateful for the temporary reprieve.

The past few weeks, we'd been trying to contact the NIH's Office of Transfer Technology (OTT), making calls and sending e-mails to our congresspeople. We wanted to bring some political influence to bear in our efforts to regain the license for Peptide T through the OTT. A further complication was that our former investor had been interested in developing Peptide T to treat psoriasis instead of AIDS, and the government had split the license to allow this alternative direction. Mike and I knew that to continue such a plan was a recipe for disaster, leading very possibly to the abandonment of our creation as an AIDS drug. We were unwilling to go that route without a fight, knowing that it was effective for AIDS—we had the proof! Yet all our heated, demanding phone calls were getting us nowhere.

Just before leaving for Monterey, under miraculous circumstances that occurred during a weekend stay on our magical little island in the Chesapeake Bay, we manifested a brilliant strategic planner, a man who had years of experience with Congress and the Washington bureaucracy. Like us, he desired an end to the global AIDS pandemic and got involved and began discussions with our former Dutch investor and the government.

We were hopeful and pleased that progress was being made, proud of ourselves that at last we were standing up to the interlopers who wanted to use Peptide T for purposes other than what was intended. The pain in my neck was gone, and Michael and I were aligned and in action, kicking ass together like we hadn't done in years.

Yet the closer we came to success, the more I saw my old self-sabotaging patterns vying for a takeover. My low-self-esteem persona, the abandoned child, would suddenly emerge to draw attention and fix blame in an attempt to re-create and remedy my original trauma from childhood, the blonde-in-the-bed episode. Then, the rebellious teenager would sometimes kick in, spewing harsh criticism when things didn't go my way, making it difficult for my accomplished self to plug ahead with creative solutions.

But something had definitely shifted. I was now more keenly aware than ever of the emotional re-enactment patterns of my multiple selves, and if I couldn't stop their expression, I could at least observe the psychodramas as they unfolded, an important first step. A more integrated state of consciousness was beginning to surface that I recognized as the observer self—the *inner self helper,* the soul perspective, the "I" from my many years of meditation.

In this new state of consciousness, I had no need to defend and blame, no compulsion to criticize or push Michael's buttons in a battle to be right, or yell at bureaucrats to force my way. Slowly but surely, the hurt and traumatized little girl who'd been grabbing for the wheel on the bus of my life was losing her grip, taking a backseat and giving over to a wiser, more mature driver.

All Shook Up

Leaving Washington for Monterey, an airport incident allowed me to catch a self-sabotaging personality in the act. Minutes before the flight was ready for boarding, I asked Mike to dash to a nearby concession stand to buy me a chocolate milkshake that I suddenly and uncharacteristically craved, to take on the plane. I don't quite remember what happened, but the next thing I knew, we'd boarded the plane, and I was wondering what had become of the milkshake.

Mike was carrying my large valise down the aisle, asking me if I wanted it stashed overhead or under my seat, when I suddenly recalled with horror where my drink was. I grabbed the bag that my husband was juggling, sat down, and found that the milkshake inside had spilled all over the contents, soaking my carefully gathered papers and the draft of Chapter 4 that I'd planned to rewrite on the plane!

I was crushed and instantly lashed out at Mike, complaining that the spill was his fault, because he'd been warned to keep the valise upright! His jaw dropped in disbelief, and he started to defend himself as the two of us quickly headed down that old road again.

But this time, my tantrum was short-lived. *Who stowed the milkshake away in the valise? Who demanded that Mike buy it in the first place?* I asked myself. My angry, demanding child-self was caught and stopped like a deer in the headlights, and this time by me!

Looking back, I can chuckle about how successfully I sabotaged my plan to edit the manuscript Nancy had given me. There was absolutely no way now to clean it up and do the work. *What's done is done,* I said to myself, thankful that my higher observing self wasn't interested in any berating. Time for some *selves-*understanding and *selves-*forgiveness! I apologized to Mike for my ridiculous attempt at making him responsible for my own error. Then, exhaling deeply, I picked up a copy of *People* and read it from cover to cover as we continued on our flight.

After we arrived in Monterey, unpacked, and settled into our lodge, I noticed a message had been left on my cell phone. Joe Migliore, the eclectic chiropractor who'd done the breakthrough session at Nancy's house in Santa Barbara, was passing through the area on his way north. I called him back and we made a plan to meet at Asilomar the day after our workshop. I wanted Mike to experience Joe's "multidimensional bodywork," and maybe even get a double session in, so the two of us could become more energetically aligned.

Emotional Myths Dispelled

The conference theme was *The Power of Suggestion,* aimed at physicians, psychologists, social workers, nurses, psychotherapists, drug-and-alcohol counselors, and other health-care profession-als. Participants here were looking for effective ways to bring imagery techniques (such as hypnotism, guided visualization, and suggestion) into their practices with clients.

My three-and-a-half-hour workshop was the kickoff event of the conference, an exploration of new-paradigm physiology with an experiential section that utilized the music and words of my CD. Michael would share the podium with me, providing the "straight" science to balance my more speculative excursions.

The science of the mind-body connection is important to explain and validate the role of mental processes in healing, which is why people were interested in hearing from me and Mike. In the days before the conference as I prepared to give my workshop, I'd asked myself what I could say that would help these doctors, nurses, and therapists in their practices. I wanted to bring a deeper understanding of the emotions as key transformative agents, fundamental to the effects brought about by guided imagery, hypnosis, and any of the suggestive therapies.

I decided to dispel a few myths that I'd encountered in both conventional- and alternative-healing communities about the nature of our emotional expression, and perhaps offer a more biologically compatible understanding for emotional health and well-being.

First and foremost, I wanted to tell people that there are no "bad" emotions. There are only ones that are stuck, meaning those that aren't freely expressed, usually the result of suppression and denial. On a biochemical level as well, information molecules get blocked at the level of cellular receptors, impeding the free flow of important functions throughout the psychosomatic network of the bodymind.

There's a lot of confusion about the expression of emotions. They can be dark (such as rage, grief, and fear), but these feelings aren't *bad*. It's a misunderstanding to think that we must get rid of our dark emotions, banish them, and avoid their uncomfortable effects. They're harmful, ironically, when we resist their natural expression. Once acknowledged, we can begin to examine our shadow side, and even integrate it so that it doesn't ambush us, as disowned parts of the self tend to do. When we don't admit to or accept responsibility for these less comfortable emotions, they can be more dangerous.

I believe that all feelings are good, as natural parts of our physiology. On a biochemical level, our molecules of emotion—ligands such as the neuropeptides and their receptors—are smoothly coordinating all functions of the organism through an interactive, distributed network of information exchange. Letting them do their job of moving around ensures healthy functioning and makes us whole. Blocking the process by suppressing or denying a particular feeling can lead to the loss of integrity, both biologically and psychologically. We've had it the wrong way: It's emotion that changes *us;* we don't need to fix what we feel.

At my workshop, I began by defining emotion as "the flow of information perceived to be essential for the survival of any particular state of consciousness making the observation." I believe that emotions freely flowing and expressed can trigger altered states of consciousness, revealing subpersonalities that may have been abandoned because they were too painful to keep in our conscious awareness. Once emotional information is available, it can help us acknowledge our natural multiplicity, opening the way to heal and restore emotional integrity.

How can we interact with our emotions to get them free and flowing? The answer is through various emotionally focused methods: psychotherapy, massage, bodywork, spoken affirmations, music, art, dance, meditation, guided imagery, and forms of energy medicine that often combine several of these modalities. Forgiveness will loosen up even the numbest and most walled-off emotional states, freeing up old "axes" long buried in the body, which is your subconscious.

Although I believe that the expression of authentic emotion is healing, it's not always necessary to surrender to that release—to beat pillows, cry, rage, and tremble in fear—in order to heal. Integration of old, stuck patterns can occur through more subtle interventions, such as observing or creating art. Writing about film (my favorite art form), Robert McCracken, the author of *Directors' Choice: The Greatest Film Scenes of All Time and Why,* proved that the most moving, highly regarded art requires emotion mixed in with craft. And of course, meditation is a quiet way to let suppressed and buried feelings bubble up to the surface for conscious integration.

Finally, this work takes trust and courage, but most of all, it takes willingness. There are no "quick fixes," no shortcuts to the work of transforming ourselves and our lives. With a skilled facilitator who understands that all emotions are healthy and lead to integration, the job is easier. Most important, the feelings are a bridge between the inner world of consciousness and the outer world of manifestation, and must be felt and experienced if any kind of real and lasting result is going to come about.

A Bold Stand

After our workshop, Mike and I stayed around to talk with the participants, but soon retired so that we could rest and recover from jet lag. Walking in the dusky light, we saw deer grazing peacefully on the grounds, taking notice of our human presence but remaining unperturbed by it. The tranquil setting of pines and surf, the absence of electronic media, and the cozy fire in our lodge all contributed to a soothing night's rest.

The next day, after attending the Friday-morning workshops and social events, Mike and I met up with Joe as planned. Nancy would be arriving that evening, so when Joe offered to play tour guide and show us the surrounding scenery, we jumped at the chance.

The three of us took off on a whirlwind tour of the Monterey Peninsula, including the 17-Mile Drive, famous for its incredible ocean vistas and multimillion-dollar homes. We stopped frequently for photo ops with friendly sea mammals on nearby rocks and ended up for lunch at an Indian restaurant in Monterey.

As we feasted on a buffet of exotic dishes, the conversation turned to Peptide T. I'd given Joe a business prospectus to read back in Santa Barbara after he told me that his treatments often helped people manifest their visions. Now he was asking us questions, and Mike and I were attempting to answer him between bites of samosas and paneer. But the two of us soon lapsed into correcting each other on minor points, becoming sidetracked in our bickering.

"Wait a minute," Joe interjected, halting our rant. He was excited but bewildered. "I'm lost. I thought you had a drug that could effectively treat AIDS? You haven't even mentioned that—in fact, you glossed right over it!"

We fell silent. Joe was a savvy marketer and had a financially successful healing business. Maybe he had something to teach us. We nodded, encouraging him to continue.

"I think that I can help you with your presentation," he offered. "You need a bold and precise statement of what you're doing with Peptide T." This is called an 'elevator talk,' and the idea is to convey exactly what you're up to in the amount of time it takes to go from the ground floor to the level you're getting out at, as if that's all the time you have to say everything.

Joe's coaching pointed to what had been missing in our presentation of Peptide T, which was a powerful articulation of the state of our invention in a way that others could easily understand. Over the years, we'd lost our edge, getting bogged down in many twists and turns, and making more enemies when we could have been forming alliances. We'd become demoralized, believing that we didn't garner respect from our colleagues, and frustrated at trying to get the story out.

"A good elevator talk puts your intention out in the real world where things can happen," Joe continued. "Once you take that stand, the results you want will organize around your vision—doors will open. But first, you have to know how to put your dream out there."

Over the next hour, with Joe's help, Mike and I honed our Peptide-T elevator talk. Once we'd articulated the main points of our work, we put our full attention on practicing and rehearsing the words until we could deliver them flawlessly. It was as simple as *a, b, c:*

a. After 20 years of research, we've developed an effective treatment for HIV/AIDS that's nontoxic, cost effective, and useful in the developing world. The substance is called "Peptide T," and once developed as a drug and vaccine, it will end the global pandemic of AIDS as we know it.

b. RAPID, the company we've founded, is about to receive the worldwide exclusive rights to develop Peptide T for AIDS from the US government.

c. We're now offering an investment opportunity to people who wish to make a difference by helping us bring this treatment into the world.

On the drive back to Asilomar, Mike and I rehearsed our elevator talk, taking turns as we worked to get it just right. Having a scripted statement ready for use anywhere and with anyone bolstered our confidence and focused our joint energies—our *in*tention and *a*ttention—into laserlike intensity. And since everyone and everything are quantumly entangled, who knows what impact our newly focused light beam might have on other particles in our universe—future investors included?

Resonating Selves

Back at our lodge, Mike and I got the double bodywork session I'd hoped for, while a fire crackled on the stone hearth. We lay facedown and side by side on twin tables as Joe worked on us, helping us relax and hopefully setting up a resonance between us. As long-term partners with so much passion about our mission on the planet, we could easily become polarized at times, while at other points we stayed steadily on the same wavelength.

The Drs. Stone, the husband and wife psychologist team who developed the voice-dialogue process mentioned earlier, brilliantly teach how couples bond, then separate and rejoin energetically over the years (sometimes going through the entire cycle within an hour!). One subpersonality reacts with another: the dutiful son with the loving, attentive mother; the rebellious teenager with the controlling parent; the perfect, pleasing daughter with the loving, attentive father; and the exacting taskmaster or mistress with the pleaser—these are just a few of the possible combinations. In long-term relationships, the Stones had observed, couples often switch over the duration of their partnership from the primary, positive bonding pattern that attracted them in the first place to a negative one, resulting in friction and conflict.

As Mike and I lay there, thoughts of the changing relationships between our equally complex multiple selves popped up. I relaxed and sighed deeply, knowing with every cell in my body that our love was profound and eternal, and that our mission would succeed. I heard Mike's echoing sigh as he relaxed, and I knew that our days of playing out unconscious psychodramas in the exhausting and nonproductive pattern we'd developed over the years of our relationship were now numbered.

Power and Self-Esteem

The next morning, I headed out to catch the end of breakfast with the intent to share our newly crafted elevator talk at the first reasonable opportunity. Mike was still sleeping, and Nancy had left a message that she'd be writing in her room for the morning. As I set out for the day, I trusted that we'd all hook up at Dr. Bresler's afternoon workshop.

Scanning the last of the breakfast crowd at the dining hall, I looked for a familiar face and spotted Dr. Emmett Miller, whose workshop on "The Heart of Hypnosis" I'd missed the day before. I joined him at his table.

I knew Emmett to be a highly respected, early pioneer in the mind-body movement, a medical doctor who integrated physiology with transformation. In his early practice, he discovered that when patients were guided to create certain mental images, they could enter a healing state of consciousness and profoundly influence the course of their illness. From that finding, he developed a method using words and imagination to remove barriers to success so that people could access their inner potential for deep healing and peak performance.

"Good morning, Candace," he said brightly as I sat down. "I missed you yesterday. What have you been up to?" *Talk about a leading question*, I thought . . . and launched immediately into our Peptide-T elevator talk.

Like most of my friends and colleagues in the mind-body-consciousness movement, Emmett knew me only as the endorphin/emotions theorist, and he listened very carefully as I explained the promise of Peptide T, laying it out for him: *a, b, c*. I was pleased at how seriously he took me, obviously engaged in what I was up to. I knew that he'd have some helpful ideas, and indeed, he didn't skip a beat in responding.

"I'd like to do a session with you," he said with commitment. "I think I can help you eliminate your script of *I don't deserve*, awaken your self-esteem, and expand your power to get Peptide T on the market."

Power *and* self-esteem—now that was a combination that definitely got my attention. It was exactly what I needed. "I'm interested," I responded. "Let's do it right now!"

"First, tell me more about what's been happening," he replied, and I described how it had all started 20 years ago, when Mike and I hiked to the top of the Haleakala Crater on the island of Maui; how three days later, exhausted but exhilarated, I spoke at a symposium on neuro-AIDS and was moved to tears by seeing the suffering inflicted by the disease. I recounted how during my talk, I was shocked when a Higher Power spoke through me, encouraging my scientific solution to block the HIV virus from entering the cell, resulting in the invention of an effective, nontoxic, receptor-entry-inhibitor drug for AIDS—Peptide T.

I also told Emmett about the disappointment and frustration that followed our discovery, as we battled with the government to get the drug developed; and how painful it had been to stand by and watch our "child" of the new paradigm lose credibility over the years through a series of wrong experiments and misleading conclusions. I confessed how the demise of our company had impacted my relationship with Michael, driving us to blame each other as chances for success passed us by; and that until very recently, we'd become resigned and had almost given up, avoiding dealing with the bureaucratic hassles, the sudden reversals of our investors, our own darkest demons, and multiple personality machinations. I told him of my grief and guilt over Wynne's death, and of the many breakthroughs I'd had in forgiving myself and others. We talked until we were the only ones left in the dining hall, except for the waiters clearing the tables. Finally, the noise of clattering dishes and trays became too distracting for us to go on.

"Let's go down to the beach, and we'll continue," Emmett suggested.

I giggled at the prospect of a dream come true: a guided-imagery session with this pioneer, happening on the beach—the special, relaxing place that I usually chose for my own personal meditations.

Outside, we followed the wooden walkway that led away from the conference grounds toward the ocean, taking us over gentle dunes to a sheltered cove. The day was overcast, with low-lying clouds on the horizon, but we were uplifted by the sight of whitecaps dotting the blue-green water and waves breaking on black, jutting rocks. As we sat down on a driftwood log, Emmett took out a handheld tape recorder.

"I'll send you the recording that I'll make, and you'll play it every night before you fall asleep," he said. He then asked me to close my eyes and began to speak in a resonant, melodic voice that blended with the sounds of the crashing surf and the birds crying overhead.

"You are in touch with an awareness of yourself as deeply connected, feeling your oneness with others and with God," he began. *Wow!—a medical doctor who invokes God,* I remember thinking. And then my brain relaxed, letting my bodymind reverberate with his words, taking them in deeply. *Trust. Breathe. Feel.*

He continued: "What is it that you need to let go of in order to experience that deeper aspect of yourself?" His question hung in the air. I hadn't a clue.

"Is it your perfectionist personality, insisting that no one can do anything the right way, except you?" He was definitely on to something. "Is it belief in a world made of separate, conflicting parts, a Newtonian world, in which force conquers all?" I let go even more . . . his voice was soft, forgiving.

"As a child, people blamed you for something you didn't do, and now you allow yourself to be right and make others wrong. That's how you felt powerful in the past, but that was power based in fear. You can now let go of that power from fear . . . let go of it now." I cringed inwardly as I recalled how I'd blamed Michael so often, refusing to see my own part and making it all about him.

"Go now to a place of compassion within yourself, a place where you can allow your sadness to enter in," Emmett's voice intoned. "Float all the way back to the top of Haleakala, as if on a magic carpet. Feel the air, see the silhouettes of the raised hills. Feel the expansiveness and see a shimmering rainbow spanning the sky. Be present to this vastness, and in the center of the huge space, feel your deep and profound sadness. See the women and children, people everywhere dying, and notice the feeling that arises from your very center."

I allowed a wave of sadness to sweep over me, letting go of the struggle to restrain myself, to push it back and down. I felt light and free as I surrendered deeper to the sound of his voice.

"Let the power that exists within you to save these suffering people arise. Sense the source of that power, a spirit that moves through all things, that gives birth, gives life, gives vision, love, and mercy. Be in touch with that source; be one with that strength, and bring it together with your sadness.

"The strength, the sadness, and the power . . . let them interact, and resisting none of it, allow yourself to experience the joy of your true nature. Stay in touch with the spiritual source of all these feelings, the source of that inner voice that spoke the cure that day in front of all those people on the island of Maui.

"You are filled with joy, yet you're able to feel the depths of despair, admitting all of your emotions in the huge, vast space within you. Experience the gratitude you have toward the source of all, and give yourself permission to express that gratitude, to honor it, to respect it. You bring not just a cure for saving a few lives, but tens and hundreds of millions of lives. Enter that state of consciousness that comes with this awareness. Organize your thoughts, your feelings, and your actions to be directed toward this state of consciousness that connects you to all.

"Now, see yourself as a person who is worthy, clear, and focused . . . who understands that she speaks for everyone. People around you are empowered out of who you are being. You are part of a team, moving forward for the benefit of all. See yourself as the person you'd like to be, the symbol of what you believe in at the deepest level. Commit yourself to learn the lessons you need to learn to become the person you truly are, and let go of the need to feel separate; allow yourself to trust. Know there's nothing you have to defend against. Step into that image and become that person . . . because she is you."

I felt myself open and expand, bigger than I'd ever experienced myself being before. I felt the presence of everyone in my life—Michael, our investors, the NIH bureaucrats, my sons and daughter, the many healers who'd contributed to me, and the people who came to hear my lectures over the years. I felt the grief of all the people dying of AIDS in Africa, India, and around the globe. I was no different—not better or worse—than any of them. And yet at the same time, I was totally myself, infinitely empowered and connected to the source.

Emmett continued, evoking powerful images for me to step into, shifting how I related to myself and others, opening me up to endless possibilities. Time didn't exist as I hung on his words.

Soon he began to wind down. "As you look into the future from that place of infinite power, that place of compassion at the top of the mountain, feel the balance, love, and empathy. Surrounded by that endless majesty of space, see the future and be unattached to the past, pirouetting on this moment, one with all that is. This is the place from which to act, and your first act is always one of choice. Be in touch with your desire to choose wisely. Trust yourself that you choose for all.

"Take a deep breath in, and as you breathe out, gently release into the space around you. Return to the sound of the ocean here on the beach, the waves crashing and the birds singing. And when you are ready, you can open your eyes."

I walked back to Asilomar feeling like a new person. But before I left the beach, I thanked Emmett for facilitating what I told him had been a deeply transforming experience. "The future looks different," I said, barely able to articulate my gratitude. "You took me past my fear and into my heart. I'm back in touch with my original purpose, and I'm very grateful to you."

He replied, "I didn't do anything but suggest a new way to see yourself. You did the rest, and the gratitude that you feel right now will strengthen as you play the tape nightly." Which is exactly what I did in the coming months, when I needed to be inspired, to restore my wholeness and purpose, and keep myself on track.

I waved as we parted ways and spent the next hour meandering through the dunes, letting the wooden walkway take me where it would. There was plenty of time before meeting for the next workshop, and I was enjoying being by myself, my *whole* self, which I was now more in touch with thanks to Emmett.

Imagining the Future

Returning from the beach around noon, I found Nancy and Michael at the dining hall and joined them for lunch. My husband—quiet, calm, and thoughtful, as usual—had come from a late-morning talk, while Nancy seemed tense.

"I want you to spend some time with me on the book," she said frostily. "How can I draft the final chapter without some input?" Since she'd arrived at Asilomar, I hadn't given her or the book a minute of my time, and Chapter 4 was still an uncorrected, sodden, chocolate-covered mess.

"Absolutely," I reassured her. "We can get together later, but you have to understand, I'm living the final chapter, and it's happening right here at Asilomar. We can't write it until it's over, and there's still more to come—for both of us." I could tell that Nancy thought I was putting her off, but I wasn't. "Let's take it easy tonight, and then when we're both fresh tomorrow morning, we can spend a few hours together before my flight leaves."

"I have a better idea," Nancy countered. "I'll give you another copy of the chapter you were going to edit on the plane." Since she'd arrived, my friend had been tugging her rolling computer briefcase with her everywhere, a visible and annoying reminder of the work we still had to do. She pulled out a sheaf of paper and handed it to me. "If you edit this tonight, we can talk about it tomorrow and then outline the book's final chapter together."

I smiled, despite my urge to throttle her, then chuckled at the thought of how Nancy had just held up a mirror to my own behavior. I saw how the grating, goal-directed, hard-driving personality that I often assumed with Michael and others in order to get things done could create resistance and have just the opposite effect. One of my favorite affirmations popped into my head: *I know that liberating myself from harsh criticisms and unrealistic demands upon myself and others will give me greater energy and focus.*

"I'll do my best," I said, and the three of us walked over to the Asilomar chapel, where Dr. Dave Bresler was presenting his workshop: "Positive Planning: An Antidote to Worry." I had a hunch that hearing about the leading-edge applications of guided imagery and hypnosis would help me more fully integrate my experience on the beach, and might even help me with Nancy when we went to work later on.

Dave, a founder of the Academy for Guided Imagery and a pioneer in applying mind-body concepts in clinical practice, comes from a solid scientific background in neurochemistry, and comparative and physiological psychology. I knew him when he was the whiz-kid grad student studying along with Agu at Bryn Mawr College, Vanessa's and my alma mater. His innovative joint thesis, which spanned the departments of biology and psychology, had been dubbed "The Superfish," since he'd transplanted extra cortex into fish brains to create smart creatures who learned more like rats. We'd remained friends over the years.

In his opening remarks, Dave explained how the term *guided imagery* referred to a wide variety of mind-body techniques, including visualization, direct suggestion using images, metaphor, storytelling, fantasy exploration, game playing, dream interpretation, and active imagination. These techniques allow elements of the unconscious to appear as images that can communicate with the conscious mind.

Numerous studies that he cited showed that visuals affect almost all major physiological control systems in the body, including respiration, heart rate, blood pressure, metabolic rates in cells, sexual function, stress-hormone levels, and immune response. Researchers who use guided imagery and suggestion in pain management, Dave's specialty, report benefits in treating headaches, arthritis, burns, postsurgical discomfort, pediatric pain, and a variety of chronic problems.

Tracing the use of imagery back to ancient ritual and ceremony in all major religions and belief systems, he pointed to this technique as the oldest and most ubiquitous form of therapy, a way of exploring the subconscious mind. In more modern times, hypnotism (which relies on evoking images during concentrated states of attention) was one of the first psychotherapy tools, used first by Dr. Frederick Anton Mesmer in the early 19th century, and later by Sigmund Freud.

Today, hypnosis in the therapeutic setting is understood as a state of focused, concentrated attention in which there's an increased openness to suggestion. That definition certainly fit my experience on the beach with Emmett, during which I'd focused my attention on his voice and opened myself to the visuals he suggested.

Dave went on to explain that we all use imagery every day when we engage in the two most common forms of worry: either regretting the past or fearing the future. Both of these rely on our imagination to evoke scenarios that are played over and over again in our minds. He suggested that we can use that same ability in a more positive way—for example, by imagining a tropical vacation we want to take, or a room we want to redecorate—a process that he referred to as "positive planning."

Here were attention and intention, the twin manifesting keys that Deepak Chopra had taught me, surfacing once again! The idea is that the more you bring your *at*tention, or conscious awareness, to something you intend to manifest, the more likely that *in*tention will become real in the world. William James, the psychologist who wrote and practiced a full century ago, called this process "attentional reality," and noted that when we withdraw our focus from a possibility, it fades and becomes less real. Deepak taught that by applying this principle, we tap in to the field of infinite possibilities to spontaneously bring about a desired future, a way of life he called "synchrodestiny."

As I listened to Dave, I was intrigued to learn about a hypnotherapy concept called the "affect bridge" that explained how guided imagery could access an emotional trauma from the past and link recollection to present-time awareness. The key was to get a person in touch emotionally with a prior event, freeing the memory from the subconscious and allowing it to rise to awareness, where it could become updated with current knowledge. As I've often said, emotions are the link between consciousness and the material realm, between mind and matter. This emotional affect bridge then, was a therapeutic application of this idea.

In the same way, this technique allows us to access past states of positive emotion such as courage, confidence, and peace—not just trauma—and bring those beneficial states into the present. This was exactly what Emmett had done with me on the beach, taking me back to a time when I was deeply moved and inspired by my mission to find cures for disease, and integrating that feeling state with my current awareness. Being present to the full range of past emotion was the key—memory alone wouldn't suffice. By letting myself be deeply moved, I'd allowed the past positive emotion to transform my current reality.

Dave talked about trauma, defining it as "an experience of extreme stress that may have long-lasting psychological effects." We've all experienced this, he pointed out, not just those who've been victims of molestation, rape, physical abuse, or torture. His intention wasn't to diminish the severity of those experiences, but to include shame, humiliation, and embarrassment, which often have serious—but less well acknowledged—effects.

Dave mentioned the Talmud, a collection of ancient Jewish laws and sacred traditions, which says that to humiliate is to murder, because it destroys self-esteem, robbing a person of their very essence as a human being. In a semihumorous aside, Dave called for the abolition of junior high school, a place where most of us have experienced being bullied, ostracized, and made fun of. In this expanded concept of trauma, those who deny having had any such significant event in their youth have room to explore childhood experiences for new awareness and integration.

A Closing Harmony

Dave brought his remarks to a close by requesting a volunteer from the audience to work with him at the front of the room to demonstrate some of the principles he'd presented. A woman named Beth, who'd been sitting next to me, jumped at the chance. Her issue, she explained when Dave asked her, was that she'd been unable to sing in front of people, freezing up whenever she had an opportunity to perform. She'd written several songs and trained her voice, but had almost abandoned her aspiration to become a singer when she couldn't conquer her fear.

We all watched as Dave took Beth back to a time when her father had admonished her for making "noise" when she attempted to sing as a child. Dave worked with her, letting her release the emotions of shame and fear as she updated the past with her current knowledge. Then he suggested that she give us all a sample of her newly integrated self-expression, and she did, belting out a tune that shook the rafters of the tiny chapel and left us all deeply moved.

When Beth sat down, she whispered into my ear, "I wrote that song a year ago and dedicated it to you, Dr. Pert, because you've been my hero for a number of years." I was floored, and asked her what she meant. "You never gave up," she said, "even when it looked like your dreams weren't going to manifest. I'm never giving up either, and I wanted to thank you by writing that song." I received her compliment and didn't cringe—the bigger, more expanded me now able to accept acknowledgment and be glad about how I'd contributed to others' lives.

At last, everyone was ready for the conference's closing ceremony. In keeping with the campfire mood of the past four days and the feeling of camaraderie the sessions had inspired, Emmett came up front to play guitar and sing a few heartfelt songs. Moved by the music, I joined several others in singing backup onstage, and found myself enjoying this new role. I didn't need to be a diva, nor did I need to shirk the spotlight, which were two conflicting expressions of subpersonalities that had caused me so much past angst. I sang in harmony with the whole group, experiencing myself as part of a team—echoing Emmett's suggestion of working with others and being supported in turn.

I especially threw myself into the refrain of the final song, a poker-themed country tune that everyone seemed to know. The lyrics were about knowing when to hold your cards and when to let it all go. I heard the words as pointing to a wiser way for Michael and me to conduct business back in D.C., a new direction of wisdom for our efforts in furthering Peptide T. Very soon, we'd be "sitting at the table" back home and dealing with the government officials. Only now I was empowered in knowing we had our ace in the hole, the final card: a treatment that would save millions. It wasn't about raising the money anymore, but about being a player who abides by the rules of the game, conducting myself as an adult businesswoman and not an angry, demanding child. I could stop worrying and trying to force the action. *All I need to do,* I thought, *is play my cards from the top of the mountain while staying connected to my inner source—the source of all power—and I know that the funds will be there.*

Back at our lodge for the evening, I read the clean chapter that Nancy had printed for me, making a few edits to correct the science, adding a few paragraphs here and deleting some there. On the whole, I liked how she'd taken my words and expressed my ideas, and I intended to acknowledge the hard work she'd done when I saw her in the morning.

With a busy morning and a 1 P.M. flight the next day, I carefully packed my bags and laid out my clothes before going to sleep. As I organized and folded my things, I hummed the tune from the closing ceremony's songfest—there'd be time for everything once the negotiations were finished. As far as I was concerned, the "deal"—my restored faith in my mission—was done.

Book Breakthrough

I arrived at Nancy's place early, as promised, and found her sitting comfortably in front of the fireplace with her laptop open, typing away.

She jumped up when I came into the room. "I've had a breakthrough about writing the book," she said excitedly. "You know how I've been acting lately, trying to control everything, keeping both our noses to the grindstone, and working so hard?" I nodded.

"Well, I see now that I've been coming from worry and anxiety—fear that we wouldn't get the book done. Attending Dave's workshop yesterday, I realized how much time I've been wasting by worrying."

"Good!" was all I could get out before she raced on.

"You know, I've got a pain-in-the-neck subpersonality, too. You're not the only one with self-sabotaging behaviors. I call it my 'suffering-at-work' self, the one who frets and stresses, slaving away and having no fun." We both chuckled, and Nancy continued. "Writing this book has forced me to confront that aspect of myself—do some real soul searching. And this morning I woke up knowing that the book would get done in the perfect time. I've been cooking along, drafting this last chapter since 6 A.M., and it's going great!"

I got excited, too. "Yes! I told you the book was going to write itself! You've stopped doubting it, which is a great breakthrough!" I thought back to how I'd had my doubts at times, but lately had been more certain that this book was pulling us along in our lives, sitting out there in our future and beckoning us to move forward.

"That's how it works," I said. "First comes our intention, and then the universe organizes around it. And as that happens, the book gets written. But we have to live it in order to write it, which is the real magic—don't you think?"

Nancy nodded. "And I have to give it to you, Candace. You were right about my coming to Monterey—it was the perfect thing to do. I only need a little more input from you to finish drafting this last chapter. What was it that you were trying to tell me at lunch about your session with Emmett Miller? And of course, we still need an ending."

"Great" I said enthusiastically. "Get out the tape recorder and let's get started."

We talked, wrote, edited, and wrote some more, until it was time to leave for the airport. Nancy followed Mike and me to the rental-car agency, and then staked out a table in the tiny terminal's restaurant so that we could all have lunch before the plane took off.

Synchrodestiny at High Noon

After checking our bags with only a half hour before flight time, Mike and I were glad to discover that Nancy had ordered for us as we slipped into the restaurant booth just a few minutes before noon. While my friend and I had had a productive morning, we were still discussing how to the end the book as the food was served. Mike listened and offered a couple of wise suggestions—when he could slip in a word or two! We were all in the zone, resonating together and on the verge of an ending to bring our opus to completion.

I was just wondering, *What should the final paragraphs be about?* as I saw Nancy glance up and over my shoulder, trying to make out someone coming toward our booth. Then, both she and Mike blurted softly in unison: "Isn't that Deepak?"

I turned around and saw Deepak Chopra walking toward our booth on his way out of the restaurant, accompanied by his wife, Rita.

"Candace!" he spoke my name as I spoke his, both in mutual surprise and full synchronistic delight. We embraced warmly, then made effusive, genuine, and speedy greetings and introductions all around.

"This is my friend Nancy. She's helping me with my new book, and we were just thinking about how to put an end on it. What are you doing here in Monterey?" I asked, amazed that our paths were crossing at this exact moment. He mentioned a meeting that he'd been attending for a new spa he was opening in New York City and invited me to visit when it opened and be his guest.

But I didn't get any more of the details. I was too blown away that Deepak had magically arrived at our table at the very moment that the end of my second book was being written, a stunning synchronicity and symmetry, like bookends to a past and nascent reality. He'd not only been my first mentor in learning that consciousness creates reality, but he'd generously graced my first book with a Foreword presenting my scientific work, which had helped me get it published. For him to appear as I was wrapping the current book, breaking through on Peptide T, and coming into my power as a manifestor, was—well, it was pretty damn astounding.

It turned out that we were boarding different flights in just ten minutes, and although we really had no time to talk, it was hard to break away. Strangely, the clock slowed as I experienced a peaceful silence and became aware of Deepak's chic red glasses setting off his dark, sparkling eyes. "What's the new book about?" he asked, smiling at Nancy and me.

"I think it's about God," I said simply.

"I wish you the best with it," he said.

Before I could say another word, Deepak turned to follow his wife, who was picking up a take-out order at the cash register (it wasn't a milkshake, I hoped!). As they left, we all connected one last time to wave good-bye.

Sitting back down, Nancy and I turned and looked at each other, her expression matching mine in wonder and glee at the magical synchronicity that had just taken place—in an airport, of course, where the usual time-and-space limitations of the linear world had fallen away.

Mike looked at his watch and jumped up from the table. "Boy, was that weird," he said, shaking his head. "It's time to get back to Washington." Together, we bolted from the restaurant, running to catch our plane with Nancy following us in hot pursuit to send us off.

"I'll call you as soon as I've got the ending for the book," I yelled to her from the boarding area over the glass wall that divided us.

As Mike and I rushed through the gate to board the plane, I glanced back over my shoulder to see my friend's expression of hope mixed with mild confusion. *Trust. Breathe. Let go,* I thought. *God is in control.*

Epilogue

I learned to ski at the Winter Conference on Brain Research when I was 30 years old. Because I was so afraid, it took me four days of fruitless lessons to progress beyond "Checkerboard," the beginners' slope. The fear of the other students was contagious as they hunched over, leaned uphill, and fell because they were trying too hard not to. On the evening before my final lesson, I determined not to give up and ventured out alone after the chairlift had closed.

I sidestepped to the top of what I now realize was only a tiny hill, peaceful in the deepening twilight. I proudly stood up tall on my skis, took a deep breath, and astounded myself by gliding smoothly all the way to the bottom, stopping myself with a triumphant turn and loving every minute of it.

The next morning, I finally passed the test that allowed me onto the actual mountain and excitedly took the ride to the top with the rest of my class. But once again, fear with its bad-skier posture gripped me as I struggled and thought about the dangers. Suddenly, the handsome blond instructor moved out ahead of me, turned around, and skied backwards, all the while encouraging me with outreached arms and a joyous smile.

God, he's skiing backwards—it must be an easy trail, I thought, tensely awaiting his further cues.

"Look up at the sky," he commanded.

I did and suddenly noticed the white mountain peaks jabbing the stunning blue Colorado sky. I thought exultantly about how I'd never seen anything so gorgeous, and the views must be why people enjoy this sport so much.

My God, I'm skiing! I suddenly realized, and I began to laugh with my instructor as we floated down the mountain together, two happy people on a divinely beautiful day.

Back home in the D.C. burbs, I mused that learning to ski is about overcoming fear. While I was pondering the true nature of this emotion, I was simultaneously worrying about making my publisher's deadline for completing this Epilogue. The manuscript had been submitted on time, but this final piece wasn't yet finished. Could I bring the whole project to a close and at the same time help Michael with the intricate business maneuvers around Peptide T, all of it heating up at the same time? Book and life were now colliding!

Just the night before, I'd been thinking about how fear, the basic animal survival emotion, was the underlying cause of us humans *not* feeling good. Always planning, and forgetting to be in the present moment, a tendency I have, is a habit rooted in fear. Dread of dying is at the bottom of it, and yet in my work and travels, I'd often met people living with AIDS and cancer who have been the most alive, happy, and *fearless* people I'd ever seen.

The root of fear, I concluded, is more about being alone, feeling unconnected to others, and not realizing that we're all one. As my long-term massage therapist Adam Helfer poetically put it: "If you're connected to the divine, you'll always feel fine!" Adam had also told me he thought the best universal advice to "feel good" is to remain in the present moment as much as possible.

The Promise of Perfection

My musings were interrupted by Mike calling on the phone from his upstairs office. We'd both been working at home for the last two months since making the decision to leave our positions at Georgetown (and all academic distractions) behind. We were really clicking together, aligned in our business decisions and focused fully on manifesting our dream to deliver Peptide T after 20 long years.

In a smart move, we were now working closely with Michael Colopy, a career foreign-policy analyst and political-communications practitioner, who has been a lifelong supporter of U.S. assistance to the most desperate cases of poverty and disease around the world. We'd met him through his engaging wife Steffi (elected head of the faculty of the German School Washington in Potomac, Maryland) at a dinner party on our magical little island in the Chesapeake Bay. Fully aligned with our vision to cure AIDS, he was providing the pivotal final push to break the legal logjam around the license to our invention that was preventing the start of new clinical trials.

I picked up the jangling phone and heard Mike say, "It's time to get going if we're going to bike to the Mall and be back in time for our afternoon conference call."

I excitedly recalled that this was the day the National Mall cherry trees that surrounded the tidal basin and the Jefferson Memorial in downtown D.C. were predicted to be at the very peak of perfection. Mike and I had planned an outing by bicycle to view the famous pink blossoms on what had propitiously turned out to be a gorgeous, warm, and sunny early-spring day.

Michael lifted the two bikes onto the back of our truck, and we headed off. We rolled past the suburban houses with their white-flowering Bradford pear trees and budding yellow forsythia. Soon crossing a bridge on the Beltway, I had a clear view of the C & O Canal running along the Potomac River.

The canal, which has 74 locks to handle the changing elevation along its 185-mile course, was conceived by George Washington and funders to carry goods on barges pulled by mules between Ohio and the Chesapeake Bay. The ambitious engineering feat, begun before railroads were imaginable, took decades to build and was closed by flooding in 1924. Our starting point, "the towpath," where the mules had once labored, was a fabulous biking and hiking trail that had been preserved by Supreme Court Justice William O. Douglas, himself an avid hiker and naturalist.

Wasting no time, Mike parked the truck at a boathouse on the river and efficiently unloaded the two bikes. We set off on the towpath, feeling the perfection of the plan: the balance of work, nature, exercise, and play. As we rolled along, we chatted happily about our plans for the afternoon conference call, feeling perfectly aligned with each other and the decision we'd made the day before.

At four o'clock, we'd be talking to the California company we'd chosen to partner with, experts in intranasal drug delivery. In the meantime, we raced our bikes along the Potomac, passing the Kennedy Center and the Watergate Hotel, going over the Memorial Bridge, past the Lincoln Memorial and on to the National Mall.

At the exact moment I saw the cherry blossoms, exquisite but a few days short of full bloom, my cell phone rang. I dismounted and answered, while Michael biked the last few hundred yards to check out a Mennonite choir singing hymns and passing out booklets entitled *4 Ways to Know God*.

It was Jessica, one of my editors at Hay House, returning my call. "Exactly how much time do I have left to finish the book's Epilogue?" I asked her nervously. When she gave me the date—months sooner than I'd expected-—I gulped down my fear, trying to hide it. For weeks I'd been stuck in my attempt to bring the book to a close in a satisfying way. I felt that I had an enormous responsibility, having channeled this invention of Peptide T, and couldn't leave the book hanging without some resolution.

"Of course you want to resolve your Peptide T struggle," she empathized, sensing that I was feeling anxious. "But don't worry, the reader doesn't need to know every single business detail. Just share your vision."

Nancy had been pleading with me as well, urging me to just write the Epilogue already. "Peptide T doesn't have to be tied up in a bow," she'd said.

I thanked Jessica, hung up, and thought about how my enormous desire to finally break through on Peptide T, to attain my vision of the business success so essential for getting the drug out to the world, was driving the completion of the book. And vice versa, the push to finish the book had been propelling our actions in the business and science arena all along, urging me to bring matters to some kind of completion in my life.

I caught up with Mike, who'd moved on from the Mennonites by that point. We parked our bikes and strolled among the cherry trees, examining them closely and taking pictures like tourists, not the proud locals we were. Some branches exposed to the sun had pale, fully opened flowers on them, but most had tiny, darker pink buds interspersed with the blooms. Full-blossom perfection was now being predicted for the next day, a National Park Service guide informed us.

But Mike and I admired the buds mixed with the more mature, open flowers, agreeing that they were the most beautiful we'd ever seen. We didn't regret for a moment that we'd arrived a day early, accepting the perfection of the moment we were in. The cherry trees perfectly reflected our partnership and marriage, which was not yet at the fullness of its maturity, but newly focused in a powerful alignment of vision and purpose. No longer the isolated, struggling rebels, pitted against each other and the forces greater than ourselves, we got back on our bikes and enjoyed the rest of our ride.

Success in Toronto

I Can Do It!—a powerful affirmation—is the title of the conferences put on by my publisher, Hay House, in Toronto (and other locations around North America). I was giving a workshop, this time billed as "Everything You Need to Know to Feel Go(o)d." The weekend featured a lineup of star power from the consciousness world, including authors and presenters such as my friend Joan Borysenko, life coach Cheryl Richardson, psychiatrist Eve Wood, popular psychic Sylvia Browne, and of course, the inspirational guru Wayne Dyer. No wonder Hay House had four books on the *New York Times* bestseller list in the last year, reflecting the success of the movement that I was now proud to be a part of.

Alone in my hotel room, I'd dressed for the speakers' dinner in a peach-colored, antique-silk Chinese jacket I'd bought for myself, a costume piece elaborately beaded with sparkling gems to depict a scene of graceful cranes. I'd purchased it from a vendor at the IONS conference the previous July, its reflections grabbing my eye after my final presentation. I finally felt good enough to wear it for the first time and had even had my nails done in matching peach and rhinestones! I hurried into the elevator and down to the restaurant for the evening's event.

I was thrilled to see the owner and founder of Hay House, Louise Hay herself. Dressed elegantly but casually in a bright-red Chinese-silk dress, her platinum blond hair lavishly swept up, and her diamond earrings matching more gemstones on her long, elegant fingers, Louise was instantly inspiring. She was clearly the queen of the dinner party, a woman at the pinnacle of her success. Coming over to welcome me, she had the energy of a woman decades younger. I thanked her profusely for her generous support, which had helped me get my book published.

At dinner, psychics abounded unabashedly, and I was relieved to find that they no longer made me uncomfortable, thinking that the word "supernatural" was simply used for natural things that we still lacked the science to understand.

One of the psychics, who didn't know me from Adam, gave me a spontaneous reading. "Your struggle is over," she said. "The final resolution has already happened in the spiritual realm and is now filtering down to the very molecules of your body."

Peace, finally, I realized. I envisioned a life no longer fraught by personal and professional struggles, a world free of disease and suffering.

As the evening progressed, I realized that even close up, Louise was stunning and regal. All my fears about growing old and reaching "the big 6-0" in two months flew out the window. When I told her that I'd be turning 60, she laughed and called me a "baby," assuring me that I still had plenty of time to accomplish all I wanted to do.

Our entire table laughed uproariously when she wisely explained how we spend our first couple of decades wishing we were older, and then, when we *are* older, we lie about our age or hide it to pretend we're younger. Finally, she told us that she'd reached a stage in her life where she was proud to be her age and even enjoyed bragging about it, planning to celebrate her 80th birthday with a major bash to be held in a few months.

To my eyes, Louise was a role model of a successful businesswoman who was living her vision. She told me how she'd self-published her first book back in the '80s, the best-selling *You Can Heal Your Life,* eventually starting her own publishing company so that her work could be distributed and published exactly as she'd written it, without the "big boys"—men who ran the powerful media conglomerates—changing one word.

I resonated with her feelings, but also silently thanked God for our successful recent connections to corporations with the big money essential to make a drug rapidly available all over the globe. Louise went on to compliment me on my sparkly peach jacket, insisting that I wear it for my workshop the following day, then hopped briefly to another table.

When she returned, I learned that she'd been on the AIDS frontier long before I became involved. When the condition was first recognized and the sufferers scorned—before there was any medical hope for the infected men—she formed a support group dubbed the "Hayride" that went around Santa Monica giving comfort and affirmations to people gathered in living rooms. Within three years, she was attracting 600 to 700 participants every week to an auditorium in West Hollywood Park. Soon, her drawing power was so great that AIDS organizations sought her out and planned their fund-raising schedules around her.

As Louise talked about her early mission, I felt her huge heart and incredible dedication to those living with AIDS. Suddenly, I understood why she was so excited about my book—she really cared about finding a cure more than understanding the science of how affirmations work!

When I finally left the party, Louise hugged me good-bye, then called after me: "Remember Candace, it's about *them*—the people with AIDS!" I was rejuvenated by the evening, filled with vim and vigor and the love of completing my projects. *I can do it. I am successful. Mike and I are a highly successful couple, and we deserve our success,* I affirmed.

On the way back to my room, I passed a fabulous formal celebratory banquet of Chinese-Canadian citizens. A beautiful Chinese woman in the hall complimented me on my jacket and told me that the crane symbolized strength, longevity, and health.

Just add peace, I thought, *and I've found my vision.*

The next morning, I gave my workshop to an enthusiastic group. I talked about living this Epilogue with them while wearing what Louise had insisted I don: my peach-colored energy jacket with cranes proudly displaying their sparkling promise for my future. Divine!

The AIDS Vaccine and the Promise of the Future

I'd been back in Washington for two days when Michael and I decided to attend the fifth-anniversary-celebration symposium of the founding of the Vaccine Research Center in Bethesda, Maryland, which was taking place the next day. Everyone knew that the only way to eradicate AIDS from the face of the earth was with an effective vaccine, which had been proving to be much more difficult to create than anticipated since, among other reasons, the viral envelope kept mutating so rapidly.

On the night before the event, Mike and I stayed up late, addressing the announcements for Brandon's graduation from Cal Arts, which was only a few weeks away. Now operating efficiently at a new level of mutual respect, trust, and teamwork, we were determined not to let our Peptide-T business, which was coming to a head, interfere with supporting our son at this big moment in his life. Earlier in the evening we'd picked up envelopes from the printer and assembled a collage of old photos of Brandon to be printed and picked up the next day.

The next morning before the symposium, we rushed to the printer's and put the collages and announcements into the stamped, addressed envelopes right there. We weren't sure there would be time to mail everything and still catch Tony's opening talk. "Tony" is Dr. Anthony Fauci who heads up the National Institute of Allergy and Infectious Disease (NIAID), which has become the government's focus for funding and hope for a cure for AIDS, due in no small part to Tony's political skills and fund-raising genius. I'd known Tony since we'd shared an award for top federal servants under 40 in 1978.

Mike and I were rushing to the event, hoping to schmooze with my old acquaintance, knowing that a lot was at stake. We truly wanted to help with the NIH vaccine effort and had been in frequent contact with Tony's scientists and administrators in order to redirect attention to the Peptide-T part of the viral envelope, which had been ignored for incorrect theoretical reasons.

Things worked out perfectly, as they always do. As we returned to our car with the big box of announcements ready to be mailed, Mike saw a post-office truck whose driver, heading directly to the mail-distribution center, gladly took them!

Then as Mike raced into the auditorium four steps in front of me, he practically collided with Tony, who was stepping out briefly before his talk. "Good to see you, Mike!" the director greeted him and smiled genuinely at us. Our behind-the-scenes lobbying to bring Peptide T's positive NIH clinical results to his attention in an unaggressive way was obviously working.

Tony kicked off the symposium with a slide showing himself briefing then-President Clinton and Vice President Al Gore on the importance of the CCR5 receptor, joking that Al later claimed to have invented it. The packed audience of scientists and federal staff laughed heartily. Everyone there knew that Tony's meeting with Clinton in the Oval Office had led to the billions required to jump-start AIDS-vaccine research in test tubes, rabbits, monkeys, and people all over the world.

An effective vaccine, I believe, isn't far away. Michael and I made an antibody to Peptide T that neutralizes all types of HIV from all over the world. The NIH had repeated these experiments and asked for more antibodies for additional testing. Funny how it all works out perfectly.

Amen

Two days later, Sylvia, our long-term, once-a-week housekeeper, interrupted my train of thought as I rushed into the kitchen to prepare a nutritious breakfast shake for Mike, who was already upstairs on the phone in his office. The license was being settled at last, and the paperwork for our new joint company, RAPID Therapeutics, was under way.

"Miss Candace," Sylvia began, "I feel horrible, so stressed out. What can I do to feel good?"

"God is the answer," I mumbled, still groggy from the all-nighter I'd just pulled working on the Epilogue. I was startled by the synchronicity of her question and embarrassed by my answer, since I knew that she already talked to God every day, always including Mike, me, and our project in her prayers.

Saying something to herself in Spanish, Sylvia suddenly turned toward me, beaming, and said, "You give me a very big lesson this morning."

I faced her intently to learn what she meant. "And what lesson is that?" I asked, honestly dying to know.

"Trust in God."

I thanked her sincerely, then chuckled as I looked around at my vast collection of antiaging supplements and shelves full of health books.

And then I breathed a sigh of relief. . . . At that moment, I knew that the Epilogue and this book were complete.

APPENDIX

Endnotes

Chapter One

1. See my book *Molecules of Emotion: Why You Feel the Way You Feel* by Candace B. Pert, Ph.D. Scribner, 1997.

2. See the DVD *What the Bleep Do We Know!?* presented by Captured Light Industries.

3. See abstract by M. Ruff et al: "Sustained, 6 month antiviral benefits in HIV patients receiving peptide T: Flushing of cellular reservoirs and reduction of plasma viral load." Presented at the Winter Conference for Brain Research, January, 2006. Posted on **www.tinm.org**.

4. See Website for The Institute for New Medicine: **www.TINM.org**.

5. For listing of New Thought churches, such as Religious Science, Home of Truth, and Divine Science, see **www.findthechurch.org**.

Chapter Two

1. See paper published by C. B. Pert and M. R. Ruff et al: "Neuropeptides and their receptors: A psychosomatic network." *Journal of Immunology,* vol. 135 (2), 820s-826s, 1985.

2. See paper published by C. B. Pert, H. E. Dreher, and M. R. Ruff: "The psychosomatic network: foundations of mind-body medicine." *Alternative Therapies in Health and Medicine,* (4), 30-41 (88 refs), 1998.

3. See M. Polianova, C. B. Pert, F. W. Ruscetti, and M. R. Ruff: "Peptide T (DAPTA) chemokine receptor-5 (CCR5) is a receptor for the HIV entry inhibitor peptide T (DAPTA)." *Antiviral Res.* Aug; 67(2):83-92, 2005. Readers of my earlier book, *Molecules of Emotion,* may recall reference to chemokine receptors in the Epilogue, and note how long it took to be able to do the scientific experiments and get the paper published that conclusively proved what we'd suspected in 1997.

4. For S. Krippner et al's publication of studies of J. Z. Knight/Ramtha, see "The Ramtha Phenomenon: Psychological, Phenomenological, and Geomagnetic Data." *Journal of the American Society for Psychical Research*, vol. 92, No. 1, January 1998.

Chapter Three

1. Drs. Hal and Sidra Stone's materials (books, tapes, CDs) are available through their Website: **http://delos-inc.com**.

2. See Eric R. Kandel, *In Search of Memory: The Emergence of a New Science of Mind.* W. W. Norton, 2006.

3. See report published by A. Pert, C. Pert, and M. Mishkin: "Opiate receptor gradients in monkey cerebral cortex: Correspondence with sensory processing hierarchies," *Science Magazine,* 1981.

4. See Dr. Eva Mezey: "Transplanted bone marrow generates new neurons in human brains," *Proceedings of National Academy of Science,* February 4, 2003.

5. Donald Overton, Ph.D., McGill University. Professor of Psychology, Director, Social Neuroscience Laboratory.

6. See the Swedish study by A. Reckner-Olsson et al: "Comorbidity and lifestyle, reproductive factors, and environmental exposures

associated with rheumatoid arthritis." *Annals of the Rheumatic Diseases,* 60:934-939 (October) 2001.

7. The primary scientific studies that discuss the stem-cell origins of small-cell lung cancer and the ability of emotional neuropeptides to direct tumor cell metastases are: M. R. Ruff and C. B. Pert: "Origin of small cell lung cancer." *Science,* 229: 679-680, 1985; and M. R. Ruff, E. Schiffmann, V. Terranova, and C. B. Pert: "Neuropeptides are chemoattractants for human macrophages and tumor cells: a mechanism for metastasis." *Clinical Immunology Immunopathology,* 37, 387-396, 1985.

8. See David Healy, M.D., *The Anti-depressant Era.* Harvard University Press, 1997. This historical and neurochemical analysis leads to a clear look at what antidepressants reveal about both the workings of the brain and the sociology of drug marketing.

Chapter Four

1. See Cori Brackett's DVD, *Sweet Misery: A Poisoned World,* produced by Sound and Fury Productions, 2001.

2. See the Harvard study by M. C. Jenson et al: "Magnetic Resonance Imaging of the Lumbar Spine in People with Back Pain," *The New England Journal of Medicine,* July 14, 1994.

3. See Dr. John E. Sarno, *Healing Back Pain: The Mind-Body Connection,* Warner Books, 1991.

4. From talks presented by Drs. Nemeroff and Jeremy Coplan, "The neurobiology of early life trauma: Role in the pathophysiology of mood and anxiety disorders." 2005, Washington, D.C.: Society for Neuroscience.

5. See Dr. Cynthia Kenyon's UCSF study paper: "A *C. elegans* mutant that lives twice as long as wild type." *Nature,* December 2, 1993.

6. See paper by E. B. Rimm et al: "Diet, Lifestyle and Longevity—The Next Steps?" *Journal of the American Medical Association,* September 2004.

7. See Anne Louise Gittleman MS, CNS, *The Fat Flush Plan,* McGraw-Hill, 2002.

8. See Laurel Mellin MA, RD, *The 3-Day Solution Plan,* Ballantine Books, 2005.

9. Both Richard Wurtman, M.D., and Judith Wurtman, Ph.D., are scientists at the Massachusetts Institute of Technology (MIT) who first linked food with mood when they found that the sugar and starch in carbohydrate foods boosted a powerful brain chemical called serotonin. Soon, they linked serotonin and other neurotransmitters to our every mood, emotion, or craving. For instance, they noted that eating carbohydrate-rich foods (breads, cereals, pasta, fruits, and starchy vegetables such as potatoes, winter squash, or corn) elevated serotonin levels, helping you feel more relaxed and calm; high-protein foods (nonfat dairy products such as cottage cheese, yogurt, or milk; or beans, peas, nuts, and soy products such as tofu or soy milk) had the opposite effect: They released other substances that let you think and react more quickly, or feel more alert and energetic. See Judith J. Wurtman, Ph.D., *Managing Your Mind and Mood Through Food,* Perennial, 1998.

10. How food affects our mood and who we are is a huge topic, but readers should be aware that the accumulation of chemicals in our bodies over the years and the failure of today's processed and chemically grown food to supply us with needed minerals and nutrients both play a significant role. Thus, aspartame and trans fats are but two examples of unappreciated chemical toxins in our food. Also, most over-the-counter vitamins contain chemical additives that, while *generally regarded as safe* (GRAS), an FDA term, may paradoxically promote aging and inflammation when accumulated over many years.

11. See Dr. Nancy Lonsdorf, *A Woman's Best Medicine for Menopause: Your Personal Guide to Radiant Good Health Using Maharishi Ayurveda,* Contemporary Books, 2002

Chapter Five

1. See Lynn McTaggart, *The Field: The Quest for the Secret Force of the Universe,* Harper Perennial, 2002.

2. Maxwell's Demon is a character in an 1867 thought experiment by the Scottish physicist James Clerk Maxwell, meant to raise questions about the second law of thermodynamics. This law forbids (among other things) two bodies of equal temperature, brought in contact with each other and isolated from the rest of the universe, from evolving to a state in which one of the two has a significantly higher temperature than the other. The second law is also expressed as the assertion that entropy never decreases.

3. Belleruth Naparstek's CD *Grief* is available online at **www.healthjourneys.com.**

4. See my CD, *Psychosomatic Wellness: Healing Your Bodymind* available online at **www.CandacePert.com.**

5. See Joseph J. Sweere, D.C., *Golden Rules for Vibrant Health in Body, Mind and Spirit: A Holistic Approach to Health and Wellness,* Health Publications, 2004.

6. For a fascinating essay on how dance can fit with quantum mechanics, see the selection by Marcia Plevin in *Authentic Movement: Moving the Body, Moving the Self, Being Moved,* a collection of essays edited by Patrizia Pallaro, Jessica Kingsley Publications, 2006

7.   Dr. Joe Migliore, DC, coined the term *Network Classic.*

8.   Karl H. Pribram, *Brain and Perception: Holonomy and Structure in Figural Processing.* Lawrence Erlbaum Associates, 1991.

Chapter Six

1.   For the NIMH study see "Heseltine, et.al. 1998. Randomized double-blind placebo-controlled trial of Peptide T for HIV-associated cognitive impairment." *Archives of Neurology* 55:41-51.

2.   In the San Francisco trial effort (2000), we were tremendously helped by Mark Bowers, Dr. Gifford Leoung, and other members of St. Francis Hospital HIVCare, who listened to our scientific and clinical presentations and agreed to help us design and execute the next clinical study, this time to look specifically at HIV viral and immune endpoints, exactly what had been lacking in the earlier NIH trial. The results were published in our paper, Polianova et al, "Antiviral and immunological benefits in HIV patients receiving intranasal peptide T, (DAPTA)." *Peptides* 24, 2003. Posted on **www.tinm.org**.

3.   See Dr. Richard C. Schwartz, *Internal Family Systems Therapy.* The Guilford Press, 1995.

4.   See Olivia Mellan, *Money Harmony: Resolving Money Conflicts In Your Life and Relationships,* Walker and Company, 1994, and her latest book, *The Advisor's Guide to Money Psychology* (Second Edition), Investment Advisors Press, 2004. Olivia, whose practice is now focused on training and consulting, can be reached through her website: **www.moneyharmony.com**.

5.   See Horst Rechelbacher with Victor J. Zurbel and Ellen Daly, *Alivelihood: The Art of Sustainable Success.* HMR Publishing, 2006. Order online from **www.hmrpublishing.com**. Also, see Horst's Website for information and opportunities regarding Intelligent Nutrients: **www.intelligentnutrients.com**.

Chapter Seven

1. See Dr. Karen Shanor, editor, *The Emerging Mind: New Research into the Meaning of Consciousness*, based on the Smithsonian Institute Lecture Series, 1998.

2. See research done at the Instituto de Fisiologia Celular, Universidad Nacional Autonoma de Mexico by A. Jimenez-Anguiano et al: "Brain distribution of vasoactive intestinal peptide receptors following REM sleep deprivation," *Brain Research*, July 22, 1996.

3. See Dr. Stephen LaBerge, *Lucid Dreaming: A Concise Guide to Awakening in Your Dreams and in Your Life,* Sounds True, 2004.

4. See Ernest Rossi, Dreams and the Growth of Personality (Second Edition), Brunner/Mazel, 1985.

5. See Dr. Jayne Gackenbach, *Control Your Dreams: How Lucid Dreaming Can Help You Uncover Your Hidden Desires, Confront Your Hidden Fears, and Explore the Frontiers of Human Consciousness*, HarperCollins, 1989.

6. See Carl Jung, *Memories, Dreams, Reflections,* Random House, 1961.

Chapter Eight

1. David Eisenberg, M.D., noted in his landmark 1993 article that an estimated 60 million Americans tried at least one of several alternative medical therapies, and more than 70 percent of them never told their physicians that they had or were doing so. See D. M. Eisenberg et al, "Unconventional medicine in the United States: Prevalence, costs, and patterns of use." *New England Journal of Medicine,* 1993; and D. Eisenberg, "Advising patients who seek alternative medical therapies." *Annals of Internal Medicine,* 1997.

2.   See Dr. Richard Moss, *The I That is We*. Celestial Arts Publishing, 1981. For seminars, additional books, and tapes, see his Website: **www.richardmoss.com.**

3.   A government-financed study that compared drugs used to treat schizophrenia found that newer drugs offer few if any benefits over older medicines that are less expensive. The new drugs account for $10 billion in annual sales and 90 percent of the national market for antipsychotics. See J. Lieberman et al, "Effectiveness of antipsychotic drugs in patients with chronic schizophrenia." *The New England Journal of Medicine,* September 22, 2005.

4.   John Astin's CDs are available online from **www.integrativearts. com.** For more about Suzanne's dance and massage work in Santa Barbara, see her Website: **www.dancingfromtheheart.org.**

5.   Sir Arthur Eddington's quote is from *Space, Time, and Gravitation,* published in 1920 and now out of print.

6.   See Mae-Wan Ho, *The Rainbow and the Worm* (2nd Edition), World Scientific Publishing Company, 1998, for her discussions of quantum machines, rapid intercommunication, and liquid crystalline di-pole structures within cells.

7.   See James Oschman, *Energy Medicine: The Scientific Basis*, Churchill Livingstone, 2000, and Jim's Website: **http://www.energyresearch. bizland.com/** for more details on how energy fields affect our body structure. See also **http://news.independent.co.uk/environment/ article362557.ece** regarding the invisible electronic smog created by the electricity that powers our civilization.

Chapter Nine

1.   See Aaron R. Kipnis, *Knights Without Armor: A Practical Guide for Men in Quest of Masculine Soul.* Tarcher, 1991.

2.   See Jaak Panksepp and Jeff Burgdorf: "Laughing rats and the

evolutionary antecedents of human joy?" *Physiology & Behavior,* 2003; and Panksepp's *Textbook of Biological Psychiatry,* Wiley-Liss Inc., 2004.

3. George Stefano, director of the Neuroscience Research Institute at the State University of New York at Old Westbury. See, e.g., his paper, "Morphine Synthesis in Animal Ganglia" in Neuroendocrinology Letters, Vol. 25, No. 5, 2004.

4. See Simon Fox's Website for more information on Adventures in Caring: **www.adventuresincaring.org**.

5. See Dean Ornish, *Love and Survival: 8 Pathways to Intimacy and Health,* Harper, 1999.

Chapter Ten

1. The first book approaching mind-body medicine from the scientific end is edited by James S. Gordon, M.D.; Dennis Jaffe, Ph.D.; and David Bresler, Ph.D., entitled *Mind, Body and Health: Toward and Integral Medicine,* published in 1984 and still very interesting. For more information about the Academy of Guided Imagery, see **www. academyforguidedimagery.com**.

2. Dr. Joe Migliore, DC, can be reached through his Website: **www. magicalbodywork.com**.

3. For Robert D. McCracken's definition of art as craft plus emotion, see *Directors' Choice: The Greatest Film Scenes of All Time and Why.* Marion Street Publishing Co., (Las Vegas), 1999.

4. See Dr. Emmett Miller, *Deep Healing: The Essence of Mind/Body Medicine.* Hay House, 1997. Visit Dr. Miller's Website for listings of his superb audiotapes: **www.drmiller.com**.

5. See Deepak Chopra, *The Spontaneous Fulfillment of Desire: Harnessing the Infinite Power of Coincidence,* Harmony Books, 2003.

Some Organizations That Sponsored
Presentations by Candace Pert

The following organizations have sponsored at least one keynote presentation by Candace B. Pert between 1989 and 2005. This list excludes academic presentations of scientific work at universities and scientific meetings (for example, the Society for Neuroscience, American College of Neuropsychopharmacology, and the like).

Academy for Guided Imagery: www.academyforguidedimagery.com
AIDS, Medicine & Miracles: www.csd.net/~amm/
Alberta Heritage Foundation for Medical Research: www.ahfmr.ab.ca
American Massage Therapy Association: www.amtamassage.org
American Polarity Therapy Association: www.polaritytherapy.org
American Society of Clinical Hypnosis: www.asch.net
Arthur P. Noyes Research Foundation: www.noyesfoundation.net
Assisi Conferences and Seminars: www.assisiconferences.com
Bastyr University: www.bastyr.edu
Bioneers: www.bioneers.org
Body Therapy Institute: www.massage.net
Bowen Center for the Study of the Family: www.thebowencenter.org
Cancer Resource Center of Mendocino County: www.crcmendocino.org
Center for Spirituality and Psychotherapy: www.psychospiritualtherapy.org
The Chopra Center (Deepak Chopra): www.chopra.com
The Continuum Center: www.continuumcenter.net
Defeat Autism Now!: www.danconference.com
Gawler Foundation: www.gawler.asn.au
Gustavus Adolphus College, Nobel Conference XXVIII:
    www.gustavus.edu/events/nobelconference/archive/
Hay House: www.hayhouse.com
Himalayan Institute: www.himalayaninstitute.org
Indralaya, Orcas Island Foundation: www.rockisland.com/~oif/
Institute for Attitudinal Studies: www.alternative-medicine.net
Institute for Functional Medicine: www.functionalmedicine.org
Institute of Noetic Sciences: www.ions.org

The International Center for the Study of Psychiatry and Psychology
www.ICSPP.org
International Council for Scientific and Technical Information: www.icsti.org
International Society for the Study of Subtle Energies and Energy Medicine:
www.issseem.org
John Templeton Foundation: www.templeton.org
Kaiser Permanente: www.kp.org
Laureate Research Center: www.laureate.com
Life University: www.life.edu
The Message Company's International Conference on Science and
Consciousness: www.bizspirit.com
Midwest Brain & Learning Institute at Hope College:
www.hope.edu/brain/
Music for Healing and Transition Program: www.mhtp.org
NAMI Oklahoma: http://ok.nami.org
The Naropa Institute: www.naropa.edu
National Association of Nurse Massage Therapists: www.nanmt.org
National Cancer Institute: www.cancer.gov
National Institute for the Clinical Application of Behavioral Medicine:
www.nicabm.com
National Wellness Institute: www.nationalwellness.org
Nurse Healers—Professional Associates International:
www.therapeutic-touch.org
Omega Institute for Holistic Studies: www.eomega.org
The Ontario Cancer Treatment and Research Foundation:
www.cancercare.on.ca
Pfizer Journal: www.thepfizerjournal.com
Santa Barbara Community College's Mind and Supermind Lecture Series:
http://ce.sbcc.edu
Schumacher College: www.schumachercollege.org.uk
Theosophical Society in America:
www.theosophical.org/centers/indralaya/index.html
UCLA Collaborative Centers for Integrative Medicine:
www.uclamindbody.org
Unitarian Universalist Womenspirit: www.uuwomenspirit.org
University of Minnesota School of Health Sciences: www.umn.edu
Utah College of Massage Therapy: www.ucmt.com
Western Michigan University's College of Health and Human Services:
www.wmich.edu/hhs/

Suggested Reading

Detoxification and Healing: The Key to Optimal Health, by Sidney MacDonald Baker, M.D. Keats Publishing, Inc.; New Canaan, CT, 1997

Fast Food Nation: The Dark Side of the All-American Meal, by Eric Schlosser, Harper Perennial, 2002

Feeling the Soul in the Age of the Brain: Why Medication Isn't Enough, by Elio Frattaroli, M.D., Penguin Books, 2001

Healing Through the Dark Emotions: The Wisdom of Grief, Fear and Despair, by Miriam Greenspan, Shambhala, Boston/London, 2003

I Had It All the Time: When Self-Improvement Gives Way to Ecstasy, by Alan Cohen, Alan Cohen Publications, 1994: **www.alancohen.com**

Internal Cleansing: Rid Your Body of Toxins to Naturally and Effectively Fight Heart Disease, Chronic Pain, Fatigue, PMS and Menopause Symptoms, and More, by Linda Berry, D.C., C.C.N., Three Rivers Press, 2001

The Invisible Disease: The Dangers of Environmental Illnesses Caused by Electromagnetic Fields and Chemical Emissions, by Gunni Nordström, O Books, 2004

Invisible Heroes: Survivors of Trauma and How They Heal, by Belleruth Naparstek, Bantam Dell, 2005

Living Downstream: A Scientist's Personal Investigation of Cancer and the Environment, by Sandra Steingraber, Vintage Paperback, 1998

Love Poems from God: Twelve Sacred Voices from the East and West, by Daniel Ladinsky, Penguin Compass, 2002

Making the Brain/Body Connection, by Sharon Promislow. Enhanced Learning and Integration Inc. 1238 Seymour Street, Vancouver, BC, Canada. V6B 6J3: **www.enhancedlearning.com**

The New American Spirituality: A Seeker's Guide, by Elizabeth Lesser, Random House, 1999

The Omnivore's Dilemma: A Natural History of Four Meals, by Michael Pollan, Penguin Press, 2006

Seeds of Deception: Exposing Industry and Government Lies about the Safety of the Genetically Engineered Foods You Are Eating, by Jeffrey M. Smith, Yes Books, Fairfield Iowa, 2003

The Seven Spiritual Laws of Success: A Practical Guide to the Fulfillment of Your Dreams, by Deepak Chopra, Amber-Allen Publishing and New World Library, 1994

Sources of Healing: A Physician Reveals the Therapeutic Power of Sound, Voice, and Music, by Mitchell L. Gaynor, M.D., Random House, 1999

The Spirit and Science of Holistic Health: More than Broccoli, Jogging, and Bottled Water . . . More than Yoga, Herbs, and Meditation, by Jon Robison and Karen Carrier, Author House, 2004

A Substance Called Food: How to Understand, Control and Recover from Addictive Eating, by Gloria Arenson, McGraw-Hill, 1989

When the Body Says No: The Cost of Hidden Stress, by Gabor Mate, M.D., Alfred A. Knopf, Canada, 2005

Why God Won't Go Away: Brain Science and the Biology of Belief, by Andrew Newberg, M.D.; Eugene d'Aquili, M.D., Ph.D.; and Vince Rause, Ballantine Books, 2001

You Can Heal Your Life, by Louise Hay, Hay House; 10th Anniversary edition, 1994

Discussion Questions for Book Clubs

1. Dr. Pert talks about "personal integrity," the experience of "walking your talk," both professionally and personally. Her discomfort in meeting the lady professor on the plane shows how difficult it is to embrace a notion as far-out as "creating your reality" and still maintain professional respect. In what ways do you experience your personal integrity being "stretched" beyond your comfort zone in your own life? Have you changed and grown in areas where the status quo tends to pull you back or make you uncomfortable? How do you deal with these challenges?

2. The notion of spirituality is introduced as distinct from religion. The divine is evoked as our potential human experience, linking us together as one and at the same time, being scientifically sound. Discuss you own experience of spirituality as distinct from religion.

3. Dr. Pert's tale of the discovery of her invention, Peptide T, embodies elements of both spirituality and the feminine face of science. What qualities does she bring to the scientific inquiry and discovery that are specifically feminine? How does her struggle to bring the drug to market reflect the more masculine elements so dominant in science and medicine today?

4. As the two friends, Candace and Nancy, strike the deal to work together, they take on more than simply writing a book, also setting out to heal themselves and the world. Fame and fortune aren't enough; for them, self-healing, purpose, and contribution are the motivating factors, all elements in a game worth playing. Courage, caring, excitement, and sharing—how do these elements play out through the book to shape their creative efforts? Think of times in your life when you've taken on playing a big game and the stakes were high—what was it, and what was on the line for you?

5. Dr. Pert talks about the challenge of being a woman who's made a major scientific discovery. Do you think there's a level playing field for women in the sciences, especially medicine, today? If not, why do you think this is?

6. The body *is* the subconscious mind, a reservoir holding memory and emotion below our conscious awareness. What implications does this have for health, healing, weight loss, depression, and so on?

7. Dr. Pert claims that emotions aren't only in the brain, but also in the body, something that bodyworkers and psychic healers have long intuited. How does her claim open a pathway for nontraditional wellness modalities to gain credibility in the mainstream? How could the notion of a body-centered mental and emotional health be a threat to conventional medicine?

8. How does Dr. Pert explain that emotions span the material and the immaterial realm of human experience? Do you agree that feelings are the link between the human and the divine? What emotional experiences have you had— healing, inspirational, or even cathartic—that have brought you closer to spirituality, to God?

9. If your brain is continually growing and regenerating, as the newest scientific advances tell us, how might you expand your current life? What would you do differently, knowing that thinking new thoughts would actually shape your physical brain?

10. What's the connection between memory, learning, and emotion? What does their interdependence mean for how we raise children, provide education, and train people for professions?

11. Dr. Pert says that emotions act similarly to drugs, and that they can be just as powerful in altering our behavior. Have you had any experiences that support this idea? When in the grip of a powerful feeling, have you felt as if you were "taken over," out of control, until it had passed? Is it possible that we should take our emotional states as seriously as the conditions produced by certain drugs?

12. Why do you think that modern medicine doesn't seriously investigate and address three of the areas so important to Dr. Pert: chemical toxicity, emotional stress, and food and nutrition? How do you experience these three areas in relation to your own health?

13. Do you think that identifying your core emotional trauma helps you let go of negative emotional patterns, or do you believe that people doing trauma work are simply wallowing in the past? What's the difference? Do you think that "wallowing" is a mental activity, while doing the emotional work involves a whole-body approach? If you've identified a core trauma, how has it helped you heal?

14. Does God have a place in quantum physics? How do you see the divine as "alive and well" in today's new science,

even though very few scientists (especially those featured in the film *What the Bleep...!?*) are willing to talk about a deity?

15. Can you entertain the idea that having multiple subpersonalities is a normal state? Are you able to identify any of yours that may have been disowned and need forgiveness and integration? Does your spouse or significant other remark that you're different from the person he or she fell in love with and/or married? What subpersonalities are you aware of that could use a dose of selves-esteem and forgiveness? What difference would that healing make in your relationships, career, level of abundance, and success?

16. How do you see your relationship to money? Can you trace your attitudes back to an earlier time? Why do you think there's such a sharp separation between finances and spirituality in our culture? Who do you know who's both wealthy and good?

17. Have you ever had a lucid dream? If so, did it have any connection to your waking reality? What kinds of dreams— lucid or not—have you had that translated in some way to what was going on in your waking life at the time?

18. The Dalai Lama pointed out the necessity of community in staying healthy. Does love increase your overall well-being? Talk about a time when your health was affected by the state of your emotions, either for the better or worse.

19. Receptors for endorphins, the body's internal bliss chemicals, are found abundantly in the frontal cortex—the part of the brain associated with higher thinking, choice, and creativity (planning for the future). It's also the structure in the brain that makes us human as compared to apes. Do you think that as we evolve, we become happier? If so, why?

20. A common theme in the book is how we appear to make progress in a linear world, yet are actually moving in a spiral, arriving back where we started, only on a higher level (the labyrinth). How does this view open us up for synchronicity and diminish the stress associated with the linear process of achievement? Can you see patterns in your own life where you thought you were "going somewhere," but in reality never left home? Discuss what you learned from those experiences.

21. What are some of the "missions" you've had that have been forgotten or derailed in the twists and turns of your journey? Share a time when you were deeply connected to a vision, a purpose for your life. What was it, and what do you intend to do to restore that sense you once had?

Acknowledgments

First and foremost, I want to thank Nancy Marriott, who forced me to write this book against my will (only kidding), and helped me deliver the kind of quality literary work that only two closely collaborating English majors could. I value her brilliance, professionalism, and friendship.

A close second, I acknowledge our husbands, Michael Ruff and Richard Marriott, without whose support this project would never have seen the light of day. Always on the front line, they lived this book with us, read our drafts, and solved our numerous technical difficulties. To them goes full credit for keeping Nancy and me loved and fed. No woman is an island—even feminists like ourselves—but if we were, these are the two guys we'd take with us!

I am very thankful to Leanne Ekstrom for her unwavering administrative and spiritual support of the book and Peptide T. Her fresh ideas and ability to work with all my changing subpersonalities has been essential to the success of both.

Next, and equally crucial to our book manifesting in reality, are the folks at Hay House: Louise Hay, founder, early consciousness pioneer, current grande dame, and shining inspiration to us all; editors Jill Kramer, Jessica Vermooten, and Shannon Littrell for their kindly, thorough, and constructive editorial feedback at every turn; and all of the other great human beings on the Hay House staff whose efforts have gone into producing this book, including President Reid Tracy; Stacey Smith; Shelley Anderson; and Christy Salinas, whose simple cover design inspired me. Of course, I want to especially thank my friend and agent Kirk Schroder, Esq., who made it possible for me to work with Hay House in the first place.

I would like to acknowledge a number of leading-edge health professionals who have helped me in my healing journey in recent years, and who do not appear in the book. These include Drs. Dan Monti, Linda Hegstrand, Deb Stokes, Asha Clinton, Kate Berman, Joanne Towne, Mitch Stargrove, and Bill Pettit; also, Larry and Arlene Green and J. P. Panek. The boundary between friend and health-care provider for me has tended to evaporate. I am extremely grateful for the care offered to me by these and other friends who have helped me through difficult times.

Finally, I want to thank my children, Evan, Vanessa, and Brandon Pert. Being your mother is really my greatest accomplishment and underlies all I do.

About the Author

―――――――――

Dr. Candace Pert is an internationally recognized psycho-pharmacologist who is a former Research Professor at Georgetown University School of Medicine and Section Chief at the National Institute of Mental Health. She received her undergraduate degree in biology from Bryn Mawr College and her Ph.D. in pharmacology from Johns Hopkins School of Medicine. She has published more than 250 scientific articles and lectured worldwide on pharmacology, neuroanatomy, and her own leading-edge research on emotions and the bodymind connection.

Dr. Pert's recent appearance in the film *What the Bleep Do We Know!?* and her 1997 best-selling book, *Molecules of Emotion: The Science Behind Bodymind Medicine,* have popularized her groundbreaking theories on consciousness, neurpopeptides, and reality. She's currently developing Peptide T, a therapeutic for treatment of HIV, and has recently released a new CD package, *Psychosomatic Wellness: Healing Your Bodymind,* which includes meditations, affirmations, music, and an illustrated booklet.

Website: **www.candacepert.com**

Notes

Notes

We hope you enjoyed this Hay House book.
If you'd like to receive a free catalog featuring additional
Hay House books and products, or if you'd like information about the
Hay Foundation, please contact:

Hay House, Inc.
P.O. Box 5100
Carlsbad, CA 92018-5100

(760) 431-7695 or (800) 654-5126
(760) 431-6948 (fax) or (800) 650-5115 (fax)
www.hayhouse.com® • www.hayfoundation.org

Published and distributed in Australia by: Hay House Australia Pty. Ltd., 18/36 Ralph St., Alexandria NSW 2015 • *Phone:* 612-9669-4299 • *Fax:* 612-9669-4144 www.hayhouse.com.au

Published and distributed in the United Kingdom by: Hay House UK, Ltd., 292B Kensal Rd., London W10 5BE • *Phone:* 44-20-8962-1230 *Fax:* 44-20-8962-1239 • www.hayhouse.co.uk

Published and distributed in the Republic of South Africa by: Hay House SA (Pty), Ltd., P.O. Box 990, Witkoppen 2068 • *Phone/Fax:* 27-11-706-6612 orders@psdprom.co.za

Published in India by: Hay House Publications (India) Pvt. Ltd. www.hayhouseindia.co.in

Distributed in India by: Media Star, 7 Vaswani Mansion, 120 Dinshaw Vachha Rd., Churchgate, Mumbai 400020 • *Phone:* 91 (22) 22815538-39-40 *Fax:* 91 (22) 22839619 • booksdivision@mediastar.co.in

Distributed in Canada by: Raincoast, 9050 Shaughnessy St., Vancouver, B.C. V6P 6E5 • *Phone:* (604) 323-7100 • *Fax:* (604) 323-2600 • www.raincoast.com

---

Tune in to **HayHouseRadio.com**® for the best
in inspirational talk radio featuring top Hay House authors!
And, sign up via the Hay House USA Website to receive the Hay House online
newsletter and stay informed about what's going on with your favorite authors.
You'll receive bimonthly announcements about: Discounts and Offers,
Special Events, Product Highlights, Free Excerpts, Giveaways, and more!
www.hayhouse.com®